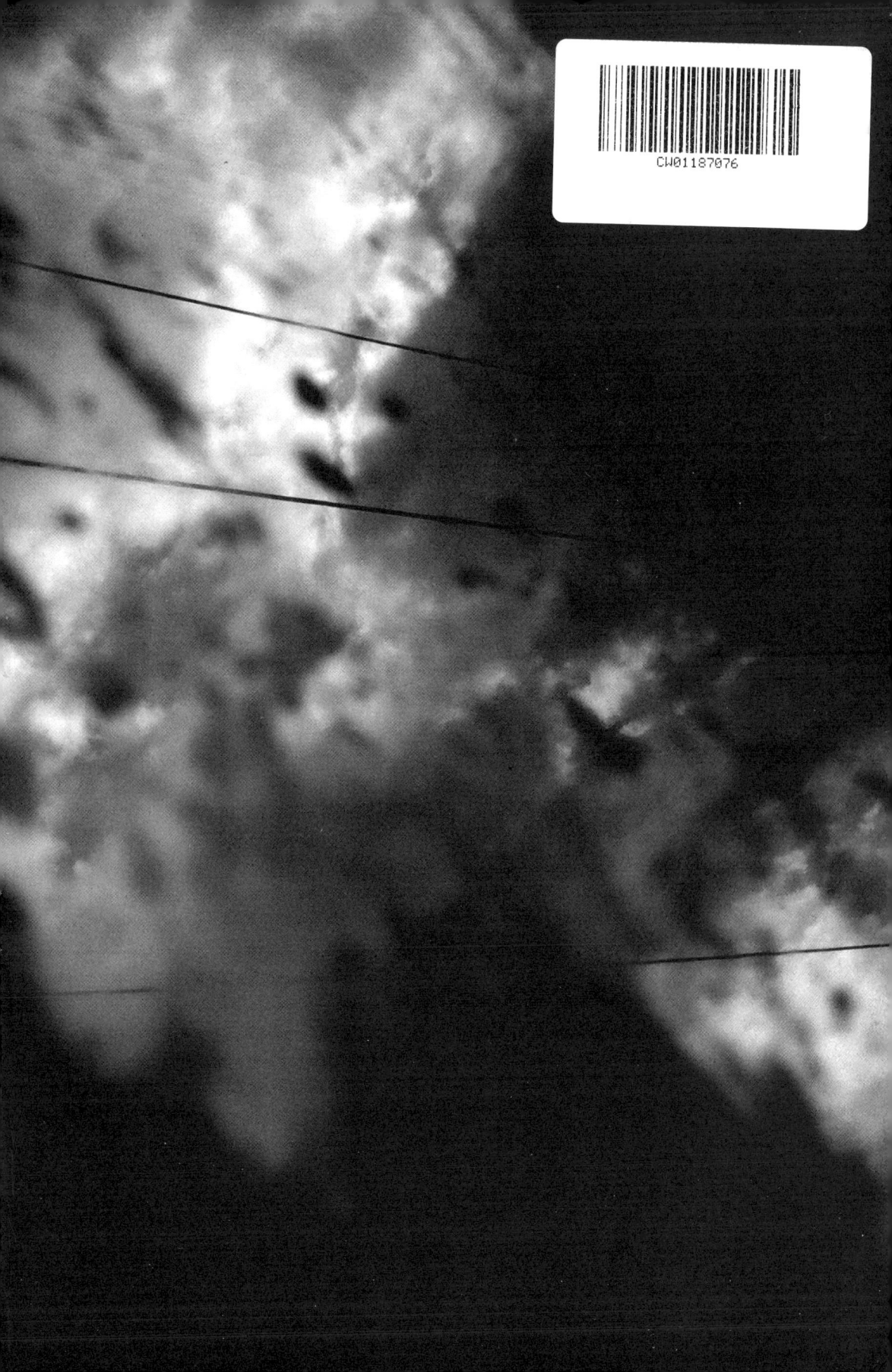

I AM DOGBOY

KARL HYDE

FABER & FABER

This edition first published in the UK in 2016 by Faber & Faber Ltd, Bloomsbury House,
74–77 Great Russell Street, London WC1B 3DA

Printed in China

All rights reserved
© Karl Hyde, 2016

Cover and design by John Warwicker

Photograph pp. 282–3 © Viktor Frankowski at the Royal Festival Hall, London 2014

The right of Karl Hyde to be identified as author of this work has been asserted in accordance with Section 77 of the Copyright, Designs and Patents Act 1988

This book is sold subject to the condition that it shall not, by way of trade or otherwise, be lent, resold, hired out or otherwise circulated without the publisher's prior consent in any form of binding or cover other than that in which it is published and without a similar condition including this condition being imposed on the subsequent purchaser

A CIP record for this book is available from the British Library

ISBN 978-0-571-32865-9

2 4 6 8 10 9 7 5 3 1

For my sister Karen
who told me stories to ease my fear of the dark

This is a book of interwoven threads that have evolved out of sixteen years of photographic and text entries of a daily diary that I began online on 1 January 2000.

In its nascent form, our website (underworldlive.com) gave a platform for me to be impulsive without adversely affecting the day-to-day activities of the band. The diary offered the freedom to publish art and lyrics-in-progress at will. It's been an addictive and compelling outlet for someone who has a constant need to create. Like so many of the major discoveries about myself over the past thirty-six years, it was born from an idea posited by my partner, Rick Smith.

The threads of the book are:

PHOTOGRAPHIC

Images as markers. Snapshots from along journeys as I map them. I've had a camera in my hand pretty much constantly since the early nineties. I've always been intrigued by the things that I find people leave behind, the things that catch my eye when I'm free from preconceptions. When I look back through these images, it allows me to glimpse what was going on in my own head at the time. It's a mirror to the past on any given day. The chance to catch that glimpse is the primary reason why I make art.

POETIC/DIARY

These are sections of specifically gathered words from the notebook entries that I bring to Underworld. Publishing them online every day focuses the text and allows me to hone it. They are excerpts from the raw material that I call on when working with Underworld.

AUTOGRAPHICAL

These entries aren't the truth – they are a version of a memory based on what I recall from my experience of events. Those events stretch from the very beginning to that eighteen-hour gig we played at Glastonbury, and the improbable rejuvenation of a band who threw itself completely into the molecules of a twenty-year-old album and re-emerged more vibrant and up for it than at any time in its existence. Some will remember it differently, recalling me with a disdain I almost certainly earned, while others will chuckle. If all their recollections were sprinkled amongst what's written here, you might have something approaching the truth.

MUSICAL

Nothing more or less than the sounds that have stuck with me. Musical map references; signposts by the side of the road along the way.

Karl Hyde, spring 2016

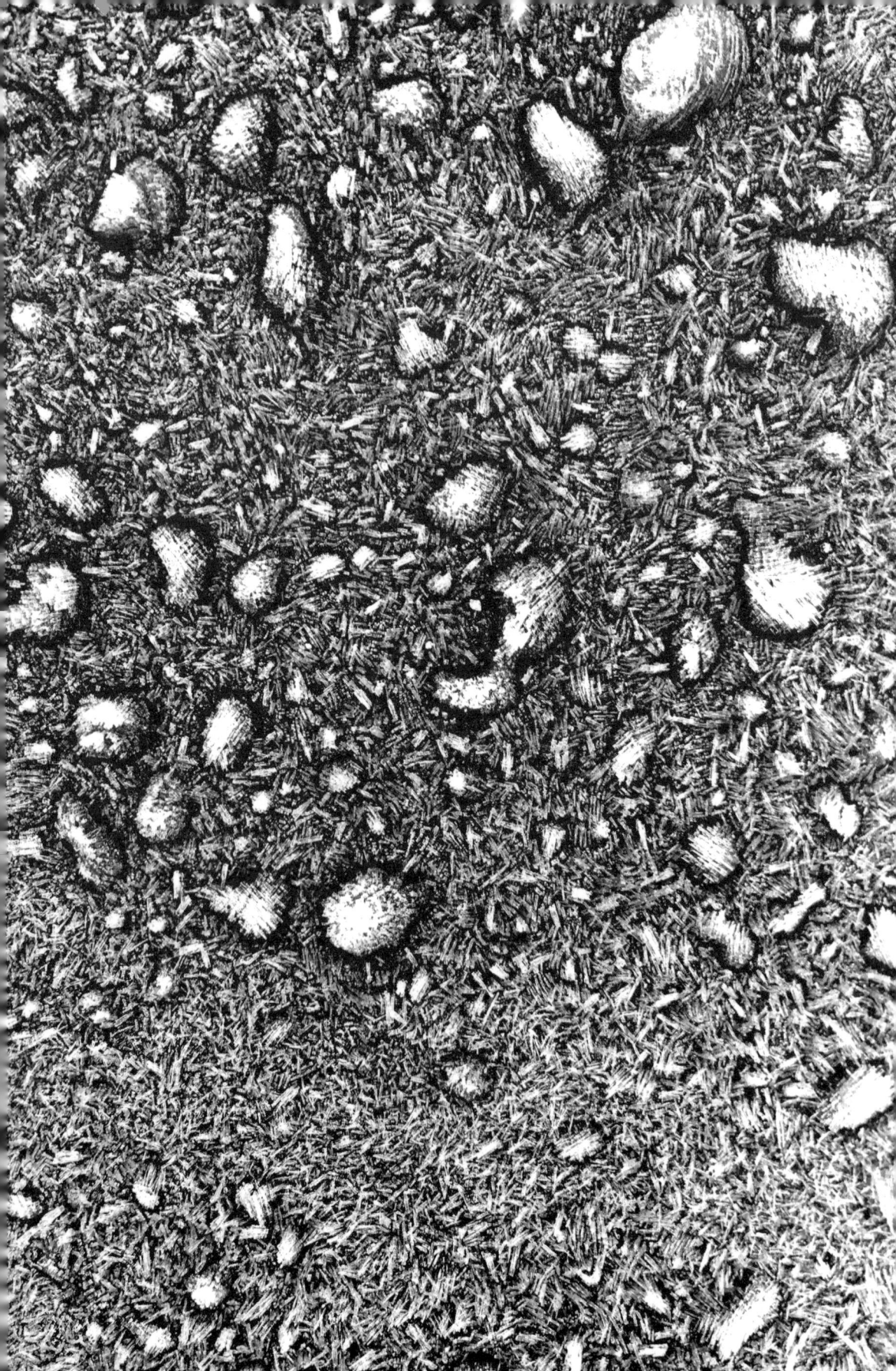

BACK TO THE END

Listening to Dylan with a phone in one hand, the sound of your voice, familiar. It broke out in sunlight as we locked ourselves together, answering your questions for our friends in Japan.
I was flicking through the master's poetry when I stumbled on the courage to write the way I feel. We've been making journeys by foot and film, the sound of your machine-gun tongue fuels such effervescent vision. Your passion is a beacon in the dark, your camera, the eye, you light the world – show me what you're thinking. Dylan glances back at me in black and white, concealed between the sheets of an old-school CD insert, Telecaster Blonde gun-slung casual across a shoulder, so easy with those words that cut a path through jungles of self-doubt and disbelief.

Tom Vek – 'How Am I Meant to Know?'

A TRICK OF THE MIND

Cold comes back to Essex on a guest-list direct to the bone.
We warm ourselves around fires piled high with fresh hedge
wood glowing orange, yellow-white. Smoke as thick as cream
clings to our hair and clothes, makes us smell good when we go
indoors, drifts across fields, languishing in valleys,
runs its phantoms through naked forests. We look at one another
smiling, clutching hands, warm, happy. Charcoal-hunting in a frost.
Woke up to a thin pink sky, lay awake listening to the wind whistle
Panpipes round the house.

Erik Honoré – *Heliographs*

WHEN WE ROCK WE RISE

The boys at Dagenham Roundhouse gather on Friday night, dress sharp for the part and ready for action, celebrating the glory of rock 'n' roll.

Møster! – *Inner Earth*

Darren saw it coming before I did. The 12-inch was spinning sweetly. Everybody happy, nodding, 'These guys are all right, we got 'em wrong.'

Then a hand reaches out of the dark. Eyes wild and wide. Grinning. Fingers on the speed control, twisting, up, up, up, cranking the BPM, the beats climb from Trance to Hardcore. We've been shafted!

We recoil, horrified. Darren shakes his head, 'I told you so.'

Our gear is in their hands, our precious stuff and dreams, OUR CROWD. What's going to happen to these beautiful people?

My blood runs cold. The stage and tower are infested with them, they're climbing all over it. We've got no backup, no security, no rescue plan. Red spiders are crawling in the rigging; we're alone at sea, miles from dry land and sinking.

Wild razor grins pushing us out, no space for us now, there are too many of them for us to handle and they're *ready for anything* …

Glastonbury '92

I was born in a three-room cottage on the edge of a small country town. Me, Mom and Dad, and, when I was five, a sister. We all slept in the same room. A single window looked out onto a lethal bend in a road that was the primary artery for trucks hauling steel from Port Talbot to the industrial heartland of the Black Country. Every Sunday afternoon in summer it jammed solid for hours with overheating metal and rubber rolling back to Birmingham from weekends at the beaches. Everything had to pass – regardless of class – through the eye of the needle of our little town. Built in stone by Thomas Telford, ours was the only river-crossing for miles.

Me and my mates would follow the snake of overheating machinery out west and back until it got dark, thrilled by the sight of so much throbbing metal, whose occupants were exotic zoo animals compared to us mortals. Once every hundred cars or so we'd get that unique rush reserved for a vehicle so special it lit us up to be close to it, to breathe in the smell of its rubber, its oil, its blood, feel its heat, grin at its passengers and wave. We knew we'd never live the fabulous lives they did. They were visitors from the future who'd come back to see how their poor ancestors once lived.

Our back garden was mostly clay. I'd dig it up to make crude pottery pitted with the imprints of little thumbs, leave them drying on windowsills, always amazed to be able to find such precious art material for free, right there in our garden. To me it designated our family as special and different, touched by the hand of God. A high wooden fence ran along one side of the garden like ramparts of a Western fort. I'd climb up onto it and repel the violent tribes of caravanners who holidayed next door, raining imaginary bullets down on their car park. Beyond that, a labyrinthine caravan site sprawled amongst apple, damson, plum and cherry orchards where my seasonal friends lived; sons of the transient working class escaping the terraces and back-to-backs of the Black Country. It was years before I understood why they disappeared at the end of every magic summer. When I did, it shocked me to realise they had other lives and homes made of brick. It was the first of the great betrayals in my life. From then on, whenever they left, I envisaged them having to change back into dull uniforms reserved for their civilian lives.

During those fabulous endless summers, we had a gang, a flag and a song. We carved our names in trees and raced our bikes on circuits of gravel tracks twisting between the caravans. We climbed everything, made dens in hawthorn thickets, dammed streams, filled jam jars with frogspawn, got soaking wet knee-deep in pools of stinking mud, and adventured for days through the vast forest that sprawled off the back of the caravan site, returning late, tired, hungry and satisfied, smelling of leaf mould, oak and pine.

Our house was cool in summer, freezing in winter. Mom and Dad lit ritual fires that never warmed us. We had no bathroom. When we were little all bathing had to be done in the kitchen sink next to an ancient grey gas cooker. All the rings were set to full to mask a chill wind that was always blowing through the cracks in a tiny Crittall window. When nature called, we used the public toilets on the caravan site. Every night before bed, Mom would walk me across an ink-black car park to reach the stinking brick building on the other side. Feet crunching gravel alerted every night-crawling carnivore and killer to our presence. She'd wait for me outside the door, torch in hand, talking softly through my crippling fear of the dark until, clutched close to her, we'd inch back across no man's land to the sanctuary of our little house and throw the bolt.

Granddad and Grandma rented a bigger house further down the road. It had three bedrooms, a bath in its own room, and toilets both inside and out! Bath times could be arranged there weekly to reap the benefits of total immersion. They had two types of tap in that house, *hot and cold*. It was like Christmas, but WARM! Granddad's toilet – outside in the yard – smelled of disinfected Woodbines. You'd hear the sounds of heavy coughing, spitting and the turning of the sports pages when he was in residence – never to be disturbed! Our landlord eventually built us an outside toilet, the most exciting thing that had ever happened in my short life. Built from modern brick, like the posh houses down the road, it was like a mausoleum at night, and still tested my fear of the dark as Mom followed me up the garden path, torch in hand, gently reassuring me through the door, 'I'm still here, don't worry.'

Mom and Dad's big double bed was positioned in the middle of the bedroom, bed head pushed against the wall. Mine was off to one side, half concealed behind a giant wardrobe harbouring the terrifying things that waited for me to fall asleep so they could slip out and drag me back inside. Every night I wrapped the bed sheets tight around my head so only my mouth was showing. Just enough to breathe, not enough for 'them' to touch me. Too afraid to move, drenched in sweat, my tiny body ached from contorting to breathe through the tiny air hole I'd made, unable to move until dawn. Mom and Dad bought me Beatles wallpaper to personalise my corner of the room, but I don't remember it ever being hung. The roof sloped low over my bed, catching the lights of cars driving into town. Taking that dangerous curve outside our house at speed, they cast arcs of light in rhythms that were underscored by the comforting screech of tyres. The rhythm of the traffic and the persistent scratching of mice in the roof were my friends. Some Friday nights, the drivers of those cars would be too drunk to make the bend. They'd mount the pavement and end up in our garden. Mom's flowers trashed again, the fence, the holly hedge too. Shattered fragments of windscreen and taillight were gathered up and kept in a shoebox under my bed. Every week, Dad would repair a little more of the front fence, rebuild the flowerbed, tack more boards to the gatepost to fill the hole left by another bit of uprooted hedge. The boards sounded like a marimba when I ran my knuckles over them; I'd sit for hours cycling melodic patterns on them with sticks. It sounded beautiful, though I had no idea what to do with it or where to take it. But the real music of my youth was the sound of squealing tyres, the shattering of glass and the dull thud of metal hitting immovable objects at speed; the muffled groans from discombobulated drivers and the slamming of broken doors.

Whenever I heard those sounds as a child, they would send me back to sleep, reassured that everything was as it should be.

Worcestershire, A456

Perry Como – 'Magic Moments'

THE ROADS ARE MADE OF

The charcoal marks between the fields turn grey.
Frozen black loses confidence, becoming less bold about town.
Green fields and the browns of succulent mud hide beneath
thin blankets of snow again, peppered by holes for
the earth to breathe. This latest deluge isn't so bad,
won't disrupt rehearsals, so I'm happy. It even looks
familiar, like the drawing winter always was to me.
Perhaps I found my muse again, watching late night
documentaries on Dr Feelgood, images of Canvey Island
and the seductive curves of concrete sea walls along
the Thames Delta. Wilko Johnson sends me to bed,
wide-eyed staring, on surfboards of staccato
Telecasters. I never thought I'd be a Fender man,
loved Marshalls and Gibsons too much. The 335S and 330S
of Big Brother and the Holding Company; the guttural
confidence of Eric Clapton's sound at Cream's farewell.

Clipped and confident distortion of overdriven valves;
Alvin Lee's 'I'm Going Home', Stevie Marriott's barroom stadium;
the Beatles waving goodbye on the roof. Terry Kath's SG on
'Free Form Guitar' and 'I'm a Man' on the *Chicago Transit Authority*
album, McPhee's Cherry Red SG.

Aspiring to own a Les Paul but knowing that I'd never have the money;
being allowed to hold one as a boy, a ton weight in tiny hands.
Going into Manny's Music, New York for an SG and asking the shop
assistant if I could compare it with, 'Maybe that white Les Paul next
to it.' Shocked I could afford it, walking out onto 48th like a king.
I never thought I'd be a Fender man but, then again, once heard,
Steve Cropper's solo on 'Green Onions' was forever in my blood.
So clear the road, load the Telecasters in the car, book of words,
diagrams of chords, faith in fingers and throat. Start the engine,
get the coffee on, I'm looking forward.

Kasai Allstars – 'Beware the Fetish'

'Are you going to play properly?' my grandmother would ask, exasperated.

'I *am* playing properly.'

'No, I mean tunes I can recognise.'

'I like these tunes.'

'Well, they aren't really tunes.'

'They are to me.'

'They're more like "noise", and it's giving me a headache.'

'It makes me happy.'

'Well, why don't you give it a rest for a while?'

'Being happy?'

'No, playing the piano. How about giving it a rest for a while?'

'Because I like the sound.'

'Well, I want you to stop now and give it a rest.'

'But I really like it.'

'I think it's time you went outside to play.'

'I want to play the piano.'

'Would you like me to teach you how to play?'

'I *am* playing.'

'No, you're making a noise, and it's getting on my nerves!'

'I didn't mean to do that.'

'I know, but you've been making that noise for a long time.'

'It's not noise to me, though.'

'And why do you have to put your head inside the piano?'

'It sounds better.'

'That's not how you play a piano.'

'But it sounds lovely in there.'

'Well, it's time to stop.'

Worcestershire, 1961

Ferrante and Teicher – 'Theme from *Exodus*'; The Everly Brothers – 'Walk Right Back'; The Shirelles – 'Will You Still Love Me Tomorrow?'; Del Shannon – 'Runaway'; Roy Orbison – 'Running Scared'; Anthony Newley – 'Pop Goes the Weasel'; Andy Stewart – 'A Scottish Soldier'; Lonnie Donegan – 'Have a Drink on Me'; John Leyton – 'Johnny Remember Me'

BLACK MOUNTAIN COLLEGE

Rode the early into the Emerald City listening to stories
from skinny girls with Scandinavian hair and sunken
cheeks. Must be the new look season. The light was
stark and bright, so I flicked on the latest app turning
colours into shapes, disarming the violence of the
morning, (where) everything (was) sculptural (and) inviting
in black and white. Down in the tubes they've got posters
for Merce, John, Robert and Jasper, the clan of the
Black Mountain College laying paper trails, telling me
this is the right road.
Popped out the hole at Oxford Circus, cut down to
Soho by back alleys, dodging the vibrations of pretentious
coffee bars selling luxury discomfort. My hungry phone doesn't
want to receive emails any more, it just wants to be a camera
taking pictures in black and white inspired by the masterpieces
Brother Warwicker captures of abandoned dust on the shop windows
of New Oxford Street. A master's eye, a genius of subtlety,
drives a silent car through barricades of derivative graphics
up the street of crocodiles.

Howlin' Wolf – 'Moanin' at Midnight'

Pre-school, back as far as I can remember, every weekday was spent in the sanctuary of Grandma's house. Mom at work in the drycleaners, Dad at work in the carpet factory, dirty shifts to pay the rent and feed us, my job was to drift and listen. Listen to the stories exchanged by old women sat on the kitchen step when they didn't think I was listening, drinking tea and spinning thumbs. Stories of when they were young, growing up, and life as it used to be in our town. Lay on the rug in the annex, I synchronised with the rhythm of Grandma's old mantle clock resonating through the sideboard like a drum machine, chiming quarters, halves and hours with chorused bells evoking desert blues guitars.

I listened every day to the whispers in the silence before the noon broadcast, radio dormant until the magic hour, the 'click', the warm-up, the words rising out of static. Distorted, thin and phased becoming rich and warm, valves glowing, glass dial illuminated with the names of exotic cities. *Listen with Mother*, the slightly mad lilt of a woman's voice telling stories of macabre puppet figures dangled on the ends of wires, and weeds that talked.

I listened – lying curled in the heat of the sun, floating between worlds on my textile raft – on Grandma's rug, where no one in the world could see me. Protected by the weave of its ritual patterns, I would lie motionless breathing dust from the pile, learning the signature smells of our family. I would be afraid to move for fear of disturbing the subtle music of the road outside, listening to the sounds of cars passing, rubber hissing, whispers kissing blacktop. The songs of wheels that rolled, relentless. I learned to predict with accuracy the frequency of their drive-bys in clusters of twos, ones and threes, punctuated by the dark rattle of open-backed trucks hauling huge rods of iron, snaking through the narrow streets of our little town.

I soaked up all these sounds, knew it was music, beautiful, abstract *and* harmonious. It was fabulous, but I didn't have a clue what to do with it.

The Hollies, Granddad's house on the A456

BBC Radio – *Listen with Mother*

ANY OTHER DAY

Starting at Barking Wimpy, coffee and tuna toasties, cellphone
to the ear, fielding calls from the far side.
Barking market, Barking Creek, River Road.
Squeezing between bent and rusted
gates, dubious items of clothing scattered along paths to the river.
A twisted pair of jeans next to a park bench,
a sports glove impaled on a security fence, walking boots
scattered drunk between discarded milk containers.
Polish fishermen smile in passing, wave, climb the sea wall and
disappear into tidal mudflats. Rust, decay, razor wire, blistered
graffiti – the beautiful marks you leave for me to find.
A chemical wind we breathe all day grows stronger with time.
Dagenham market, deserted except for a yellow digger scratching
holes in the black earth. Lunch at the Bata shoe factory,
post office, something wet with something sweet. Drive to
Coalhouse Fort, meet a river pilot, smile, shake hands,
telling stories of huge chunks of metal floating out to sea.
Bell buoys ring their lonesome chimes in midstream,
black dogs bark, fast-walking husbands dressed as security guards.

Plastic things washed up along the shore. Eroded wartime
concrete. Rotting timbers held together with wedding bands
of rusting metal. Standing in the marsh, our feet sink
into ooze, counting piebald ponies grazing feral on
landfill next to the power station. We slip our heads through
holes torn in chain-link fences and listen to the wind.
Gulls glide onto the surface of the river at sunset.
River as glass where concrete barges languish like the
half-sunk carcasses of animals at the end of war. Birdsong like
Trimphones, sunset like a rave laser, graffiti masterpieces
stencilled onto brutal concrete flood defences glowing in the
dying of a luminescent light.

1982 – A/B

WHEN LIGHT CAME TO DANCE

Yesterday felt like spring, walking dirt tracks
towards sunrise, so I let go and let the light in. Woke
this morning to Essex as a watercolour in greys and muted
greens. A gift, a good place to think, find a train and go
hang with the angels in the Emerald City. The charm of all
its vulgar rhythms jars (too long in the fields), but I'm
a sucker for the music of its streets, its poetry speaks
louder to me now than ever.

Melt – *Banana*

Summer, 1963. A grey Ford Consul, returning from a North Wales picnic. Two families inside, content, blissed out on the sweet smell of mountain grass. Tongues of gently babbling streams forded and dammed, balls kicked and laughter carried on perfumed summer breezes. The echoes of the season ringing softly in the ears as I slept on the front seat next to Dad at the wheel.

Then, the car flips on its roof. Everything inverted; the car rammed headlong into a signpost.

After showering the road in broken glass, we come to a standstill on the wrong side of the white line. The contents of our picnic dreams stripped naked and whipped out for the world to see.

I woke to snatch a glimpse of the roof as it hit me. Came to on the back seat in Mom's arms, sunlight on my legs, happiness smashed on the road. Shattered windscreen, rough as diamond rocks, glistening on the blacktop. Birdsong. Breeze. Afternoon sun. Unnatural calm. The violence of silence.

On the road from the Elan Valley dams

The Beatles – 'From Me to You'; Billy J. Kramer and the Dakotas – 'Do You Want to Know a Secret?'; Lesley Gore – 'It's My Party'

Mom was a brilliant, fully trained and qualified seamstress. For extra money she did alterations for the patrons of the little drycleaning shop she ran six days a week in Kidderminster. They were mostly men from overseas, come to Britain to earn enough to send back home to their families. India, Pakistan, Poland, Italy, the Caribbean. Their clothes exuding the aromas of exotic spices from around the world. It was completely unlike anything I ever smelled at home and it made Mom retch, snapping, '*Oh - my - God!*' as she marked up their jackets and trousers on the kitchen table as delicately as if they were wedding dresses.

Snipping, shaping, pinning and feeding each precious item with love and care, under the tap-dancing foot of her little black Singer until each garment was perfect. Every man who handed the few clothes they owned to my mom knew they'd be returned better than new. Mom was *that gifted* with a needle and thread, a true artist.

Most nights, I'd lie in bed listening to the rhythm of her sewing machine in the kitchen below. The 'chink' as the foot was raised. The crisp metallic scythe and 'snip' of her scissors. The 'chugga-ta-chugga-ta' of the wheel being cranked; the hiss of the cloth being guided, and the silences between as she tied-off and re-threaded cottons, wound bobbins, steaming and pressing with her iron as she went. Her precision-mending was so beautiful, Harley Street surgeons would have bowed their heads had they bore witness. I'd sit beneath the kitchen table on mending nights, soaking up the rhythm of her sewing machine until it went deep in the bone.

I could sing its grooves like a tabla player. When I eventually left home, a black Singer sewing machine was amongst the cherished parting gifts from Mom and Dad. For years I didn't grasp the importance of the groove Mom's machine sang, though I'm sure if I had, I wouldn't have known what to do about it.

That little black Singer sewing machine is the only thing I have left from that time. My first drum machine.

Under the kitchen table

The Crystals – 'Da Doo Ron Ron'; The Surfaris – 'Wipe Out'; Kyu Sakamoto – 'Sukiyaki';
Gerry and the Pacemakers – 'I Like It'; Jan and Dean – 'Surf City';
the Beach Boys – 'Surfin' USA'; Buddy Holly – 'Bo Diddley';
The Beatles – 'She Loves You'; Shirley Bassey – 'I Who Have Nothing'; the Ronettes – 'Be My Baby'

IN A CAGE OF PURPLE THORNS

The body truth
The buzz
The fall in love

Sewn on mother
Choral finger
Caught on camera

Global citizen
Alien agenda
Jumps in red
Like a hood ornament

Don't get her started
Super strident
Hot texture

'What you lookin' at?'
shaved heads uncovered in a freezing wind, hard stares.

Håkon Stene – *Lush Laments for Lazy Mammal*

My dad was a drummer in the Boys' Brigade. He reminded us every mealtime, beating polyrhythms on the table with his hands. Should've been a drummer, could've been a poet, looked after his family like a bare-knuckle saint doing jobs beneath his intellect (and knew it), never let on or looked down on anyone. But he couldn't contain his love of groove. It would burst out of him and make us smile, paradiddling on the table top until Mom would snap, 'Oh, Graham, will you please *stop* it! That's *enough!* I've got a headache.'

The music would stop. Awkward looks. Empty raging silences sucking light out of the room. At pudding time he'd grin, index fingers extended improvising drumsticks as he resumed his groove. To this day, I can tap out every one of those rhythms, they come out when I'm bored or stressed. They take me back to Dad making me feel good, drumming on the kitchen table, eyes sparkling, glancing across at me and winking.

Table, table

Sandy Nelson – 'Let There Be Drums';
Gene Krupa and Buddy Rich – 'Evolution', from the album *Burnin' Beat*

The Beatles taught my ears to hear differently.

Before that it'd been oddball stuff: 'Sparky's Magic Piano'; 'Big Bad John' by Jimmy Dean; tracks with heavy reverb … anything produced by Joe Meek, who created the kind of lo-fi soundscapes I loved.

And then I heard The Beatles and everything changed. The electric 'fizz' of their vocal harmonies vibrant, wild, relentless, bucking trends, cocky, 'getting away with it' and making it all look so cool. The past was over, the future looked amazing.

For the first time I had a sense that there might be a world outside of our little town. At five years old, still reeling from the shock of being abandoned to the constrictions of school, I had art and now I had The Beatles, twin lights at the end of a long tunnel I had to escape. They'd get me through. 'Love Me Do' woke my ears and 'She Loves You' nailed me. The Beatles laid a trail of breadcrumbs I could follow out of the forest.

Aged six, four of us lads started a 'band' that 'performed' Beatles songs in the playground every break, miming guitars with cricket bats, orange boxes for drums and cricket stumps for drumsticks. There was always a face-off for who was going to be Paul and John, and if you didn't get in fast you had to settle for George till next week. My mate Glenn, a great football player in his day, had the common sense to choose Ringo – it meant he always got the gig. If you were off school through illness it could take weeks to get back in the band (still feeling the pressure!). Girls would gather round to watch us shake our imaginary mop-tops, crowd the mic and imitate our heroes' iconic stagecraft. For a blink in time until the bell, our little grey shorts, jumpers and elasticated ties were mod suits, blue jeans and leathers; our tiny voices chipmunking the sex appeal of the Fab Four, the girls mimicked wild abandon and something clicked.

In the playground

Frank Ifield – 'I Remember You'; Pat Boone – 'Speedy Gonzales'; Mr Acker Bilk – 'Stranger on the Shore'; Bobby V – 'The Night Has a Thousand Eyes'; The Beatles – 'Please Please Me'

I loved the man. He was my rock, unwavering, benevolent, a gentle giant. The day would get special every time I saw him. I hung out with him from year dot and knew that no matter how crazy it got indoors, when he appeared everything bad would stop out of respect for him. My granddad was a coalminer. He worked with explosives, mining a seam under the river that cut through town. He walked with a rhythmic roll from a bad leg. He never complained and it never stopped him walking up the hill to the pub or downtown to the bookies. I don't remember him missing a day of work through illness. He would sit quiet, reading the racing form, chain-smoking Woodbines, sixty a day, hunched over the grate of an open coal fire, warming his shins and occasionally spitting coal dust into the flames. He couldn't stand injustice, would never tell anyone how to live their life until such time as someone upset a child. Then, running his fingers deep through his thick white hair, he would rise to his full majestic height. 'You mon't hurt that child!'

And that would be the end of it. Peace surrounded him, so I stuck close, knowing everything would be all right when he was around.

When Mom and Dad worked Saturdays, Granddad looked after me, either at his house or ours. He'd turn on the television and sit transfixed by the horse racing. Before the start of a race he'd take me out to the phone box over on the council estate to lay his bets, then settle back into his chair in front of the telly. He rubbed the arms of that chair bare with his excitement at every race. A pack of cigarettes always at his side, he'd turn to me, coughing, and point to the pack: 'Don't you ever smoke, lad!'

'I won't, Granddad, I promise.'

We'd watch the racing for hours (boring) then Saturday sport (I loved the singing at the start of Welsh rugby internationals, and the rich regional tones of the commentators' voices). Then the bizarre and exotic world of *The TeleGoons* (twisted, fabulous), *Juke Box Jury* (new music), *Dr Who* (dark, frightening, twisted). Sometimes he'd look after me weeknights, when the programming was weirdly different: stuff he would never normally have tolerated. One Friday evening we were watching *Ready Steady Go!* Some band dressed freeform and irreverent was kicking off, shaking it, going wild, turning it on for the cameras and girls. Maybe he could sense my excitement and saw my thrill, because, out of nowhere, he turned to me and in that same tone he'd put me straight about smoking, said, 'Promise me you'll never turn out like that lot, my lad.'

With all sincerity I replied (shocked he'd even *think* I'd ever turn out so degenerate), promising him, 'Never, Granddad!

The 1960s in front of the telly

Roy Orbison – 'In Dreams'; Welsh rugby fans singing 'Bread of Heaven'

Do you remember that first new dustbin you bought, galvanised, shiny and ribbed?

Remember how when you brought it home it rained? You set it out in the garden on bricks, on the dirt next to the path to the air-raid shelter. I thought it beautiful, exciting. Sculptural. I didn't want it despoiled or abused. It was perfect.

Remember it started raining and remember how you and me loved the sound of rain on the roof of the car, parked up, concealed from the world, eating fish 'n' chips cooked in lard with our fingers?

Remember that day? It was great. You let your mask down for a few minutes and we laughed, where the world couldn't see us. Well, that day the first new dustbin arrived you inspired me to ask, 'Can I go sit in it and listen to the rain?'

You didn't skip a beat, didn't even strike you as weird: 'Of course. Would you like a drink?'

I sat in it for hours, wearing the lid like a hat, lifted just enough to make a slit I could look through. Learning how to watch without being seen.

Remember when we got a coal bunker? That was so cool. A box built from brutal slabs of stone white concrete. The top was one great slab of wood, hinged for easy loading.

Remember how, before the first lorry load arrived, I asked, 'Can I go and sit in it?'

You looked at me and smiled and then it started raining, all the elements were in harmony. Perfection! I sat out there for hours on a little stool you lifted in, wrapped in a blanket, eating sweet fake tobacco, head lifting the lid just enough to watch without being seen. You'd come out the back door every now and then, look up the garden and shout,

'You OK?'

'Yeah, I'm OK.'

You understood how good it felt to be invisible.

Do you remember?

Cilla Black – 'Anyone Who Had a Heart'; Billy J. Kramer and the Dakotas – 'Little Children'; the Rolling Stones – 'Not Fade Away'; The Searchers – 'Needles and Pins'; Jim Reeves – 'I Love You Because'; Manfred Mann – '5-4-3-2-1'; The Beatles – 'I Wanna Hold Your Hand'; Gene Pitney – 'Twenty-Four Hours from Tulsa'; The Kingsmen – 'Louie, Louie'; Mary Wells – 'My Guy'; The Bachelors – 'I Believe'

When things got bad I withdrew into art. I was always making marks, drawing when the world got too much. My fingers itched to make the marks dancing in my head – screaming to be released – though I can't remember ever getting close to liberating them. It hurt to keep them locked inside. But what I drew never came close to what I imagined. I was always too considered, too controlled, too neat, too prim. Not enough 'let go'; not enough 'fun'. Even so, art provided a world I could escape to any time. I was in love with the smell of paper and graphite. Still am.

'He's a right little Picasso,' Favourite Aunty used to say. It lodged in my head, and the long-sleeved tops hooped with horizontal stripes appeared soon afterwards. Favourite Aunty lived deep in the forest that stretched for miles off the back of the caravan site behind our little cottage. She lived in a damp little gingerbread bungalow in an oak clearing, generating her own power from a giant diesel engine that choked and sputtered into life when electricity was required.

The neighbours were farmers whose house could be glimpsed on a hill through the trees. Like everyone in the forest, they had a generator too, and I loved listening to it pumping throaty beats, muffled by the trees, late into the night, watching house lights flicker through the leaves. At night the only sounds were the wind in the branches, the howling of foxes crying like human babies, the sonar ping of a lone pheasant, and the rhythm of diesel generators. It was outsider culture, off grid, all waste emptied into holes dug in the ground or flushed into weeping septic tanks concealed beneath giant rhododendrons (the soil around which gave off a constant stink).

This was the land of High Magic, the physical space I ran away to when life got me down and art alone couldn't fix it. Turning off the main road, you could slip through the back of the wardrobe, drop down a lane so steep it was near vertical, then up the other side between fields and withering cherry orchards where my dad pressed the butt of a shotgun to my shoulder when I was little and told me to squeeze the trigger. We left a hole the size of a cow's head clean through a cherry stump (modern art) that remained into my twenties. The blacktop snaked over a cattle grid, turned to cinder, then clay, became pocked with pot-holes stuffed with charcoal, ash and broken brick, passed through cattle gates and farm yards, across streams and brooks and eventually to the mouth of a grand avenue of pines that ran all the way down to the railway line, the steely twins that cut through the forest carrying coal from the mines to the coal yards in Kidderminster.

I've been obsessed with parallel lines all my life and it all started the first time I stood in that majestic avenue of pines guiding me to the gingerbread house in the woods.

Wyre Forest, Worcestershire

Field recordings of Wyre Forest

Sometimes when I look back, it feels like we lived in a Ray Bradbury novel about small town America. A place where the mundane was extraordinary and the extraordinary commonplace. Stuff we took for granted was weird to people who never grew up there. Stuff like the 'Rocket Station'.

Located somewhere secret in the heart of the forest, it was rumoured to be a test site for rocket engines, concealed in tunnels deep underground. At one o'clock every day for as far back as I can remember, a low sub-bass growl would emanate from somewhere in the woods. It echoed off the trees, creating a heavy Joe Meek reverb, evoking images of a vast animal raging alone in a subterranean prison.

I had no idea what a 'Rocket Station' was or did – I just took it for granted that we had one and that every day at one o'clock it would grumble to let us know it was still there, reassuring us all that everything was as it should be.

Wyre Forest

The Tornados – 'Telstar'; *The Quatermass Experiment* – 'Main Theme'

Every morning, the sound of a steam-train whistle would be blown on the wind up the valley.

Severn Valley

Elvis Presley – 'Mystery Train'

For my seventh birthday I was given a black guitar – a gift from a mate of Dad's who was in a band. It was something of a revelation as, until that point, it hadn't occurred to me that people in the real world, *this side* of the telly, could be in bands.

That small black acoustic guitar lived next to my bed, resting its head against the wardrobe that harboured dark things. Every morning, as I slid out of bed, the floorboards gave a little, making the black guitar rub against the wardrobe, amplifying its strings, which gently resonated like an Aeolian harp. Downstairs in the kitchen the radio would be accompanying the metallic beats of breakfast cutlery, but the sound of that sweetly resonating guitar was my private morning underscore. It was a beautiful soundscape, different from anything on the radio. I knew it had something to do with the path I should take, but didn't know what.

Six years later, I scraped off its blackness, stripped it of its uniqueness, flayed the skin off its back and left it raw – stained it with something fast and cheap and swapped it to get my bike back off my best mate. His parents took him away to live in New Zealand, where he rebelled, left the rails, carved himself a notorious little place in history then became a soldier in the Army of the Lord. Maybe the guitar died somewhere in the southern hemisphere; maybe it was recognised for the prize it was and lovingly restored by someone who to this day feels lucky. I still regret letting it go, and how I butchered it.

A bedroom in the 1960s

Millie – 'My Boy Lollipop'; Dionne Warwick – 'Walk On By'; Roy Orbison – 'It's Over';
Cilla Black – 'You're My World'; Doris Day – 'Move Over Darling'; The Beatles – 'Can't Buy Me Love';
Peter and Gordon – 'World without Love'; The Honeycombs – 'Have I the Right?';
The Shangri-Las – 'Remember (Walking in the Sand)'

SCOOTER IN A THORNBUSH

Rehearsing on the Essex prairies chasing demons like stray cattle.
Later, standing in a freezing wind along the touchline of a
floodlit football pitch, I lose my nerve.
The no man's land of a frontman without a band.
Robert Plant calls from Texas – sets me straight.
Two singers on the loose, escape the Black Country.

Marshall Allen presents Sun Ra and his Arkestra – *In the Orbit of Ra*

We moved to a new house on one side of the valley, with a view of the council estate. Unlike the first house, this one wasn't rented, it was *all ours*. Though now Mom and Dad had to break their backs and take on extra work just to keep it – a *real home* with hot and cold water in the taps, a bath and even a toilet *indoors*. Best of all, it had a telephone (cream plastic, pure 1960s TV cool) with a bell you could hear as far as the street so everybody knew we were on the rise.

My mate Budgie was the youngest of three brothers. He lived at the garage down in the valley below our house – the last petrol station out of town and the first one in. His dad had cleared the old wooden workshops to build a huge modern brick box with massive folding doors that roared when they opened, accommodating everything from bubble cars to trucks with ease. Pete and Keith, his two elder brothers, were the chief mechanics. They had strange Black Country accents, but were cool, driving me to school every morning in draughty old Land Rovers that rattled and smelled of oil – or big American station wagons with foot wells full of car batteries and receipts. Budgie was two years older, and my best mate before going up to the big school. We watched silent films on an 8mm projector in his attic. *Tugboat Willie*, *The Keystone Cops*, Laurel and Hardy; all with our own voiceovers. We always hoped the next time we ran them the characters would speak; we imagined what they did in the dark when we weren't around. We played with his racing-car track (a rare and exotic thing that rattled and sparked), flogged apples off his dad's trees to passing motorists, and every Thursday plotted up in front of the telly with a bag of Iced Gems to watch *The Monkees*. Budgie had a 7-inch of 'Last Train to Clarksville'. The A-side opened with a great hook, the melody was catchy, and it had an infectious vocal sound and style – but I preferred the other side because it ran backwards. The drums sucked instead of punched.

We rode our bikes, messed around in the workshop, became addicted to the smell of oil and rubber, and annoyed his brothers. Best of all, Budgie had a reel-to-reel tape recorder – a fabulous machine dropped into our world from another dimension. Every week we'd lock ourselves in his bedroom and record our own plays, comedy sketches, anything that made us laugh. We'd roar until it hurt, or his mom banged the door for us to shut up. 'You boys are giving me a headache!' (Headaches were popular in the sixties.)

We filled reels of tape with that magic stuff, no 'music', just hours of improvised dialogue and noises. I especially remember one of those 'life changers' when we discovered we could record at different speeds, unleashing our imaginations as we experimented with the mutated sounds everything in Budgie's mom's kitchen could make. We played back our recordings, slowed right down to reveal concealed dimensions: the lost world of Joe Meek, mutant animal voices, howls and grunts, electric creatures conjured out of spoons and mixing bowls. That little fat grey box with the Phillips logo, an object beyond my family's pocket, was the best thing I'd ever seen, and it sunk its hook deep into me. I lost myself every time I was with it. I couldn't get enough of it, but I also couldn't afford one, so any natural flow of ideas had to be curtailed, set aside. The joy, the freedom, the completeness I felt when Budgie and me were exploring sounds had to be completely let go of when I left his house. I'd been given a taste of something wonderful; peered through cracks into other worlds, but accepted I would never visit them. Dreams such as those Budgie and I created with his tape recorder remained 'sketches', never to be realised.

I seemed to be 'play-acting', going through the motions and then letting go, coming up to the line, but never crossing it. Nobody I knew had done anything amazing – never left town or been on the telly. Ours wasn't the kind of town where dreams became realities; those were things that remained in the head, to be laughed at when you got older, and considered the stuff of children. It was expected that you would eventually grow out of them, grow up, get sensible, get a proper job and tow the line. Magic was breaking through from the other side all the time – there were signposts telling me exactly where to go that I didn't know how to read. Everyone I knew in town had a regular job, and dreams were at best consigned to weekend hobbies.

In the culture I grew up in money was the issue. Security came with a steady income, and the wolf was too close to the door most of my young life to ignore the need for money. It wasn't something that was drilled into me, it was just something I picked up. All the adults in my life worked because they had to, and I never met anyone who could afford to jack it all in to chase a dream. A job equalled money, money equalled choice, and the more money you earned the more choice you had. No one lectured me or told me this – I came to this decision on my own. Without anyone to help me translate these signs and signals breaking through from exotic ultra-worlds, or anyone to show me how to harness the passion I felt for making 'stuff outside the box', I remained stationary, the forces of pull and push working in equal and opposite directions. I was a dog doing circles in its basket, an animal in constant turmoil. Without guidance I felt I didn't stand a chance, so why bother? I was trapped inside my head and retreating further inside. I knew I was never going to leave town. Sure, I could do stuff that my family thought was clever, but apart from being a minor local hero, was I ever going to amount to anything?

It didn't help that even the gardening teacher who I really believed in at secondary school told the class one day, 'Karl Hyde isn't a name that's ever going to be famous.'

1968

The Goon Show; The Monkees – 'Last Train to Clarksville'

'How long have you been in there?'

'All morning, Mom.'

'You're weird!'

There was a period of my life when you'd find me in the cupboard under the stairs. Lights out, door shut, slow breathing in the glow from the valves of Granddad's old radio. I'd turn on, tune in and escape into the clouds of chattering voices vibrating the airwaves that carried sound hundreds of miles to my secret hideaway.

That radio was my connection to other worlds. I didn't understand the tones of languages but I was drawn in, mimicking and absorbing their rhythms. I didn't care where they came from. I was engrossed in their groove, phasing in and out, intertwined with the music of cultures I had no knowledge of – yet became familiar with, resonating, calling to me.

Accordions, choirs, desert songs, opera singers, balladeers, crooners, cheesy heart bleeders, surfers, speech makers, news droners, twisting, writhing, haunting the airwaves, folding in on themselves, exposing their molecules, tattooed with fragments picked up on their cosmic journeys to the magic cupboard.

My favourite sounds above all were found at the ends of the shortwave dial, the scrambled barbed wire tangle of Morse code and Cold War coded messages carried in children's melodies and precisely repeated voice patterns. I listened to those fabulous broadcasts for hours as they floated on waves of phasing surf to reach my cocoon. They were my new *signature underscore*, carried on aromatic winds wrapped in electric dust. Jamming with Granddad's radio in the cupboard under the stairs lasted for years, but like every other 'out there' thing I did I didn't know where to take it, so I got bored and returned less and less to that cupboard under the stairs.

Late 1960s

BBC *Shipping Forecast*

When I was ten, Dad decided it was time for me to get serious about playing guitar or pack it in. God knows how he afforded it, but he found a guitar teacher and paid for private tuition.

Mr Wilson was an elderly gentleman who taught classical guitar from a smart and suburban semi in the posher part of Kidderminster. He greeted me every week with increasing weariness, knowing full well I hadn't practised the homework he'd set me and that my excuse would always be that I'd been writing songs instead. I'd play them to him excitedly before stumbling through another hour of painfully slow sight-reading.

I tried to learn, but was too impatient. I had too much music in my head that had to come out. The last thing I wanted was to bury it under shite renditions of 'Oh! Susanna' and 'She'll be Coming Round the Mountain'. At one point Mr Wilson tried to spark my enthusiasm, waving the manuscript for the Rolling Stones' 'Honky Tonk Women'. God bless him, but it was such an uncool thing to do. We spent an uncomfortable hour in the unspoken certainty that our two generations should never look for common ground in an anthem for a night of sleaze and barroom debauchery. Finally, on the day he announced that I clearly wasn't suited for his style of teaching, and that he could no longer take my dad's money, Mr Wilson concluded his last lesson by saying, 'I have something for you.'

From a back room deep within the house he returned holding two amazing things. In the one hand he held the most beautiful ebony banjo, inlaid with intricate swirls of Mother of Pearl, and in the other hand, a cheap red and white electric guitar.

'Both of these are for sale. They're both £8 10s, but you can only buy one of them. Which would you like?'

Even today, as I remember that kind, gentle man standing in the doorway of his front room, I recall how beautiful that banjo was and what a *sensible* investment it would have been, guaranteeing considerable financial return in years to come. I saw the crossroads clear as day, standing right there in the doorway of his front room, and without hesitating said, 'The electric, please.'

I secured ownership of that shiny red electric guitar – a Futurama II with a whammy-bar my Dad had rebuilt in the tool room at the factory. It sat in the corner of my bedroom between the toothless old black resonator and the new one with the nylon strings I'd picked out at Woolworth's for my tenth Christmas. The electric came with its own carry bag in cheap tartan plastic, which I'd hid under the bed so as not to embarrass all that fabulous Redred-ness. I practised leaning it in strategic places around the room to give the impression I was going places when my mates came round to listen to 'sounds'.

'It's not acoustic, it's *electric*.'

Kidderminster, 1967–68

Buddy Holly – 'That'll Be the Day'

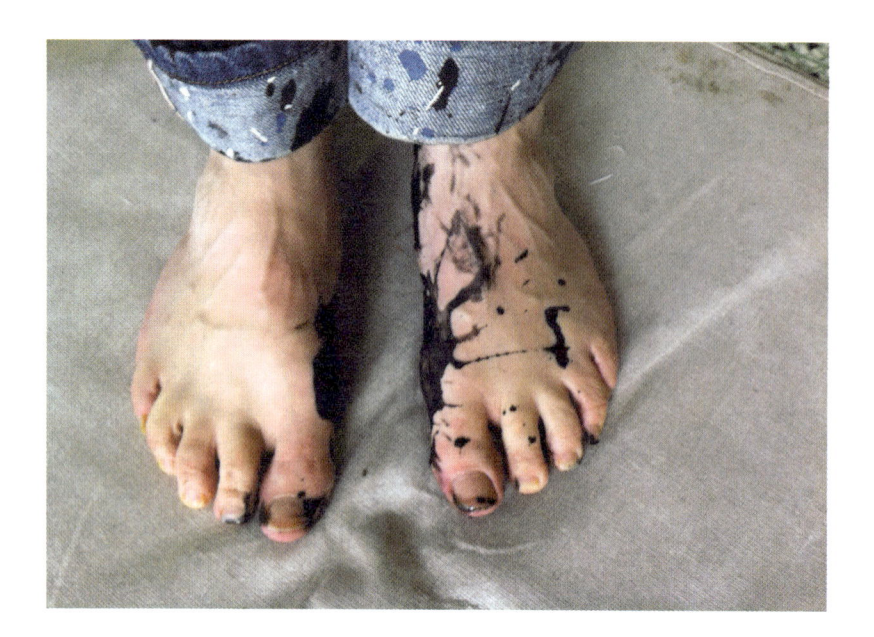

STRAIGHT

Ploughman cuts straight lines into corn stubble.
Copper turns to brown with grey whiskers.
I wave; raise a thumb, a hand, nothing.
Ploughman looks ahead, focused on a point
on the other side of the field, the future.

Chris Watson – *In St Cuthbert's Time*

DOG

Black, Grey, Charcoal, Black, Black, Brown (for colour), Slate, Black, Hunch shoulder Black, Dark Blue (to be different), Dirty White and Checked, Black 'n' Blue, Two tones of Grey (head down, shuffling), Black-Black, Black-Blue, Blue-Blue, Blue-Black, Biscuit (scuffed), Blue-Blue, Black-Black, Black-Black, Black-Black, Four tones of Blue (that don't sing), Black and Black and Black and Black and RED (a bag dangling, dancing, singing - no one listening), Blue (that's almost Black), Dusty Plumb, Black-Black, Blue and Black and Black and Black and Denim Blue (like a memory of summer), Pale Sandy Boots (supporting a stern expression), Black with glitter bits (fingers frantically tap the screens of small devices, skate across the surfaces of tiny ice rinks), Olive Green (combat) and Black, Dark Brown, Blue and Black, Muted Purples (to be different), Black and Dirty White and Black zigzags (so as not to conform), Greasy Dark Blue, Waxy Dark Blue and Washed-out Blue and Grey, New Turquoise (muted), Padded Pink (holding on to summer), Red and White polka dot bag (to be cheery), Dark Blue and Black and Black and Black and the Palest of Washed-out Yellows, Two Tones of Grey and Denim (like a memory of summer), Waxy Dark Blue (quilted), Two types of Camouflage (fashion), Black and Vibrant Blue and tight), Black Lycra (bouncing), Bright White Trainers (striding), Dark (almost imperceptibly) Blue, Black (on a bicycle),

Black (on a bicycle), Dark Waxy Blue with Black (slouching slowly), Vibrant Fluorescent Yellow (sweeping), Dirty White (arms crossed tight across the chest) Walking, Crisp Grey over Black, Black with a vibrant splash of Woolly Pink, an over-vest of fluorescent Yellow (pushing a bike).

Moskus – *Mestertyven*

THE PHOTOGRAPHER'S ASSISTANT

The photographer's assistant was a thoroughbred pony with
a fragile rider wearing a necklace of sophisticated gold and
a startled expression.

The Last Poets – *The Last Poets*

Throughout the sixties, I was in love with Tamla Motown. Vocals distorting the mics with pure acrobatic ecstatic melodies, the groin thrusts, gyrations and the cartoon motions; a new cool, a celebration, the total abandoned joy of groove. Hot-suited, glittered, glamorous, sharp, devotional motion cut loose in formation. I felt an instant attraction, soaking up every shake and shimmy. Then The Ikettes exploded on my eyes and in my head – powerhouse women who excited with a brazen confidence unlike anything I'd ever seen or ever met; sexual, never subservient, giving only what *they* wanted to give. Alive, in charge, electric and fabulous!

Next up, James Brown: the drop into the scissors, the bare-faced bravado. Confident, in control, fronting a looping groove that kept coming, punctuated with clipped snatches, the cool of minimal phrases, vocal tones, voice-noise. Brown was a singer who drew on the influence of brass stabs, but took them further, faster, wilder, over the edge, outside the box, stared you down if you dared look, hanging a full ten every time, surfing a relentless groove. It felt so *right*, made me twitch uncontrollably, moved my muscles remotely, got under the skin and into the bone, lay dormant, waiting for the right time. Then Sly Stone: deep, dark, hissing, moaning; leading the band on a journey into streetsoulfunk, laying the seeds of future rock, but keeping it tight to the one, maintaining maximum energy. A culture fusion, taking us all 'higher', cool-suited in rhinestones and diamond flashes, Superfly shades and rings. I soaked it all up, wide-eyed, not a clue what it meant, or how to respond.

I couldn't look away, had to keep coming back for more. Intuitively I knew all this would be important one day.

No need for a reason.

1965–69

The Temptations – 'Ain't too Proud to Beg'; Sly and the Family Stone – 'Dance to the Music'; The Equals – 'Baby, Come Back'; The Who – 'I Can See for Miles'

LEATHER HEART

Catch an early train in through the Emerald City
and out to the Edge. A day away from rehearsals,
walking streets of the forgotten East. Terraced chapels,
wheelie bins with numbers flaking, snooker halls,
scrap-metal dealers, hand-painted signs, hairdressers,
street names, the resting places of empire, pebble-dashed,
double-glazed outsider art. We'll count ponies grazing
in the lee of power stations, stroll to the river,
striding mud stones, rusting chevrons, dinosaur timbers sinking
under the weight of history where new faces arrived
with expressions of hope, fuelled on the promise of work and betterment
and Ten Pound Poms left in search of paradise.

sPace moNkey – *The Karman Line*

AT THE ELEPHANT

The boys courted the girls with blunt sexual bravado
and the girls reciprocated, laughing. The south
London boys carried cans concealed in black plastic
bags to set the blood fizzing for a Saturday night uptown.
The boys from Eastern Europe passed a single plastic bottle
round between them, swigging, laughing loud and shouting,
intimidating the theatre crowd.
The boys from south London drank alongside them as if
there were a wall between them, until the Eastern European
boys raised their plastic bottles in salute, touching it
to the rims of the south Londoners' cans.
'Yay!'
The girls crossed and uncrossed their legs, watching
with wild, excited eyes, dressed tight and revealing,
taunting winter's bitter wind with their relentless sexuality.

Studio One, Jump-Up

He turned up at school one day at the wheel of a powder-green Ford Anglia.

Even though we thought his wheels were a joke, the shoulder length of his hair elevated his status to 'icon'. From a worn leather briefcase he produced 45s whose labels bore his name – Clifford T. Ward – on vibrant orange paper discs embossed with the legend CBS. His lessons were fragile affairs, he wore his inexperience like a target, and we performed our cruel duty to the letter, testing and breaking him at times.

To stop our taunts, he would slip his records out and show us photographs of him as someone else.

A singer in a band. An alien ambassador from the land on the other side of the TV screen.

1968, Bewdley Secondary Modern School

Clifford T. Ward/Simon's Secrets – 'Keeping My Head Above Water'

The boys in the year above went unnoticed. If they weren't sports stars or thugs they weren't on the radar, so it came as a surprise when two twelve-year-olds stepped out of the fog and asked if I'd like to join a band.

'We heard you play guitar,' they said.

It was a random, tangential kind of thing to say to an eleven-year-old, but a piece of immaculate timing. Having messed around with guitars since the age of seven, I was now taking it seriously. It had never occurred to me that an improvement in my playing might actually prove useful. For the first time, I thought of myself as a guitarist as these guys opened a door for me into a world I had always thought was inaccessible. Despite a desperate fear of commitment and a crushing shyness since birth, I heard my mouth saying, 'Yeah, I do.'

Just outside the R.E. room, Bewdley Secondary Modern School

The Honeybus – 'I Can't Let Maggie Go'; Jimi Hendrix – 'Voodoo Chile (Slight Return)';
The Beatles – 'Hey Jude'; Joe Cocker – 'With a Little Help from My Friends';
Marvin Gaye and Tammi Terrell – 'You're All I Need'; Canned Heat – 'On the Road Again';
Status Quo – 'Pictures of Matchstick Men'; The Move – 'Fire Brigade';
The Lemon Pipers – 'Green Tambourine'; The Beatles – 'Lady Madonna';
Cilla Black – 'Step Inside Love'; Reparata and the Delrons – 'Captain of Your Ship';
The Showstoppers – 'Ain't Nothin' but a House Party'; Herb Alpert – 'This Guy's in Love with You';
R. Dean Taylor – 'Gotta See Jane'; The Foundations – 'Build Me Up Buttercup';
The Gun – 'Race with the Devil'

Through most of the sixties, all we had was 'the Light Programme'. This was before the BBC hired the young and exciting DJs who were broadcasting to grateful thousands from offshore pirate stations in the English Channel, before they invented Radio 1 and started transmitting programmes people under twenty-five could identify with.

The Light Programme was all we had, and it was for old people.

Occasionally it would *hint* that it knew what was happening in the modern world, but all we got was one song every hour tossed into a load of old people's music. The pirates connected us with music direct from America, musicians from *our* generation who were forcing change. They brought in the sound of *new* – a sound that moved at speed, came right up in your face and grinned. They let us know that exciting music was being made right *here* in the UK too! The pirates were how we got to hear anything more than the tidbits peppering the BBC. They were raw, unchained; they played by their own rules. Shows were hosted by DJs who understood us, knew what we wanted and delivered it on demand.

The problem was that these stations were out in the North Sea or offshore down south, invariably too far from Birmingham for us to receive. The only time we got to hear them was when Dad drove us down to Bournemouth for the factory fortnight's caravanning. Radio would soundtrack the journey, Dad would satiate his own hunger for what was new and happening, surfing the stations as he drove through the night to avoid traffic, radio dial illuminated, bathing the car in its benevolent glow, connecting me to the music of my tribe. The one station that was the exception, the one we could pick up even in our backwater river-crossing, was Radio Luxembourg.

Luxembourg was a commercial station, the tracks it broadcast were broken up by adverts (weird!), but this was worth enduring to hear stuff that was new. There was *no old people shit*. Head under the covers, ear pressed against the speaker of a tiny transistor radio, volume so low Mom and Dad didn't know I wasn't sleeping, I first heard The Doors, Crosby, Stills and Nash – the sounds of California calling. My one enduring memory is of listening to Luxembourg in a tiny caravan that Dad towed all the way from Worcestershire to the shores of Lake Geneva, the most extravagant holiday we ever took and the one Dad paid the price of for years.

Every night, with waves gently lapping on the quay inches away from our little house on wheels, the hissing of gas lamps underscoring the night, we would listen to CSN's 'Marrakesh Express' and The Doors' 'Riders on the Storm'. Those two tracks remain synonymous with the magic of listening to the radio with my dad. They evoke all the times I rode with him, dashboard lit up like cities of tiny lights passing beneath our wings. The Clay–Liston fight (the first and most important of underdogs I ever heard win), the '66 World Cup final, and hours of driving back roads with Dad, going nowhere in particular, just drifting, getting out of the house and heading west across the border into Wales, following snake roads between slate walls into the hills, through valleys, alongside lakes and beneath the massive Brutalist architecture of the Elan Valley dams.

All the time Dad would be tapping out his signature polyrhythms on the steering wheel, window down, breeze messing our hair.

'Let's give your mom some space, eh?'

Driving with Dad

The radio was always on somewhere, either in the kitchen or the car. Always tuned to music and always dreary, punctuated with random tidbits of 'contemporary thrill' to taunt us with what we couldn't have. On 30 September 1967 all of that changed.

I waited in the kitchen, listening to the countdown that launched BBC Radio 1. Life would never be the same. The pirate stations had been hounded onto dry land, their DJs bought and brought on board, welcomed into the bosom of an establishment that couldn't compete, so they hired them. The days of pirate radio broadcasts went on hold – at last we were given the music we wanted.

A year later, I heard a sound that felt so good I wanted to eat it. Desmond Dekker and the Aces' 'Israelites', a dirty, dusty, shuffling groove unlike any I'd previously heard. I wanted it, had to have it, it was the sound of a culture I craved to be consumed by. Singles in those days could take months to climb the 'hit parade' and, by my twelfth birthday, 'Israelites' was at the top. It was the best birthday present I could think of when Favourite Aunty asked what I'd like (*because I just don't know what to get you any more*'). I made it clear and simple: '"Israelites!" But ... if they haven't got that ...'

It was a bitter lesson – never offer an alternative if you're not prepared to take second best. On my birthday the world did a sick twisted tilt. How could I show my bitter disappointment at not getting the record I was desperate to play as I unwrapped Favourite Aunty's gift and got 'The Windmills of Your Mind' by Noel Harrison. The sonic road I'd set my heart on travelling had a dirty great hole dug across it. Miserable and alone in my bedroom, I struggled to come to terms with the sanitised psychedelics coming out of my record player. I was being dragged back into a culture I was desperate to escape – a music approved by the elders, the sound of 'acceptably weird'.

What I wanted was reggae played on cheap guitars recorded on knackered tape machines, the sound of lo-fi dust and enough fizz to make me go blind. Pure sound, no skin, no colour, a music that felt right deep in the blood, pumping out of crude boxes whose subsonic vibrations I could feel all the way from the dancehalls of Jamaica. I hurt bad to see it come so close, look me in the eye, then slip away.

Twenty miles up the road the Birmingham reggae clubs were playing even deeper beats, filling dancefloors with boys and girls cutting wild abandoned shapes. Meanwhile, my mates were into rock, and it was the only diet on offer to a twelve-year-old white kid living on an island a million miles from anywhere cool.

1969, an island

The Band – 'Rag Mama Rag'; The Move – 'Blackberry Way'; Martha Reeves and the Vandellas – 'Dancing in the Street'; Glen Campbell – 'Wichita Lineman'; Sam and Dave – 'Soul Sister, Brown Sugar'; The Righteous Brothers – 'You've Lost that Lovin' Feeling'; Desmond Dekker and the Aces – 'The Israelites'; Marvin Gaye – 'I Heard it Through the Grapevine'; The Temptations – 'Get Ready'; Junior Walker and the Allstars – '(I'm a) Road Runner'; The Isley Brothers – 'Behind a Painted Smile'; Bob and Earl – 'Harlem Shuffle'; Glen Campbell – 'Galveston'; Thunderclap Newman – 'Something in the Air'; the Beach Boys – 'Break Away'; The Temptations – 'Cloud Nine'; The Isley Brothers – 'Put Yourself in My Place'; Mama Cass – 'It's Getting Better'; Fleetwood Mac – 'Oh Well'; The Upsetters – 'Return of Django/Dollar in the Teeth'; The Pioneers – 'Long Shot Kick de Bucket'; Harry J. Allstars – 'Liquidator'

By 1969, me and the two boys from the year above had formed a band called Miggerspinnel Pumpkin. We started working on our 'sound' after school every night in the music room, where the cleaners frequently burst in on us to complain about the noise.

Paul Mountain (who everyone called 'Mont'), having conceded I was to be the guitarist (because I already had an electric guitar), went one better and bought an impressive Hofner bass – blood red and black. It played like an ox but looked 'serious', giving him the gravitas befitting a thirteen-year-old. This image was undermined by the ancient valve radio he'd hot-wired into using as an amp – previously, throughout every rehearsal, it had faded in and out punctuating his bass lines with cricket scores. Mark Howell beat a primitive groove on a junk-shop drum kit of glitter red, which had the singular idiosyncrasy of having *real calf-skin* drum heads that required entire drums to be 'sent-off' for a new skin to be steamed and hand-stretched every time he broke one.

I had been more fortunate. Dad had asked around the factory and found me a *proper* amp, a weird triangular thing in cream and turquoise livery with gold knobs – a Watkins Dominator. Like my £8 10s flame-red plank of a guitar, it looked like it had been plucked from a sweet shop but it made me feel serious. A couple of years later I swapped the Dominator for a louder, bigger, blacker, more 'fake alligator' thing, and have regretted it ever since.

Our music was basic, a primitive beat repeated under bass and guitar looping in unison – we hadn't a clue how to do anything else. There was no mic, so no need for a singer. It was painfully limited, but had we any knowledge of music beyond the old-people fodder we were fed by the radio it would have been obvious we were writing surf music.

Every evening we met to play the same thing over and over, a sub-Shadows sound that went on for the whole of the summer term. When school finished we relocated to Mark's bedroom for the holidays – lugging gear up three flights of stairs, training for the years to come of hauling our own gear when we were too tired to even dribble.

Our sound was going nowhere. We needed help, a guide. A guru.

Mont found the ad in the newsagent's and our music took a dramatic upturn. Between washing lines of drying nappies, in a tiny damp wooden shack on the edge of town, on the other side of the railway tracks, we learned how to play the blues. Tony (Fruit) Hill, a legendary bluesman from twelve miles down river, had relocated to our little cul-de-sac of vibe and, finding himself suddenly responsible for a new baby and low on gigs, he needed extra cash fast.

In exchange for the money our parents paid him he handed us the key to our future. Fruit had a sparkle in his eyes that belied his true age, and that remained until we lost contact in the eighties. There was a boyish cheek about him, attractive to men and women alike. He was a gifted blues guitarist, should've been famous, touring the world like a lot of the great players from our neck of the woods. The West Midlands used to feel like the arse end of the world, and if you had any talent at all you used it to get out. Back then the escape route was either through music or football – turned out I was crap at both.

Once a week, Mont and me would lug our guitars up that long country road (I'm really not making this up) to Fruit's shack and hand over our cash. Surrounded by the sweet, damp, soapy aroma of drying nappies, we learned basic blues licks. It must have been demeaning for him to have to spend his time in the company of kids, but he sparkled and smiled through every visit with warm enthusiasm, inevitably breaking into anedotes, frustrated bursts of genius riffing, before pausing to turn us on to old blues records. Then he'd turf us out into the dark for the bleak walk home.

Grey Green Lane

Savoy Brown – 'Train to Nowhere'

The first time I saw Richie Havens on the telly is what did it for me. The thrill ... the raw intensity, the uniqueness grabbed me by the throat. It was a joy to see him every time he cropped up on whatever stuffy TV shows he was invited on to. God knows why they booked him. He was always out of sync with every show I saw him on, way more dynamic and honest than everything else, even when suited and booted to tone down the rawness of his energy for the folks at home. His performance at Woodstock was the one that really nailed it, plugged me into the national grid. He was the real deal, more honest, passionate and visceral than any musician I'd ever witnessed. It was like he opened himself up and laid himself bare, right there for the world to see, in an act of disarmed love, transmitting a powerful positivity that set him apart from every performer I've seen before or since. To this day, he remains at the core of what drives me.

Playing lead guitar was too much effort for too little reward. It was too truncated a style, confined to its little slot – told when to start and stop, like the family pet. There's something about soloing that's too remote, perched up on its mountain, alone and exposed. Guitar solos speak a different language to the groove in my head. I've tried, honestly I have, right up to the albums I recorded with Brian Eno, but I just couldn't see the point – lost interest a few notes in – and even Brian was shocked to admit, 'You really can't play lead, can you?'

Rhythm guitar excites me. At its purest, it's inclusive and generous. It's an invite to the best party: 'Come on in, I promise good times.' Rhythm guitar got to me through Richie Havens, then funk, Afrobeat and highlife. Rhythm guitar is the backbone, the rails, the tracks laid down for the train to groove on. Rhythm guitar is the source of energy, the fizz that lifts a track, drives it along, takes it higher and keeps it 'up'. I learned this listening to James Brown records – take out the rhythm guitar and there's no thread to link the pearls. Put it back in and the body starts dancing all on its own.

No offence intended – 2015

Captain Beefheart – *Ice Cream for Crow*

Every Saturday through the summer of 1969, me and Mont would cycle six miles to visit Guru #1 – Cliff. Since he had revealed his true identity to us we had been captivated, drawn to his flame, enthralled by his stories of a secret life as a pop singer in the Emerald City.

Was it a moment of weakness or an act of charity that inspired him to reveal his address?

Either way, we took it as a green light to drop in any time, which was basically every Saturday.

He lived in a modest semi on a modern housing estate in Kidderminster, built on the tennis courts of a demolished grand pile where Mom and Dad used to play back in the day. Me and the boys had expected a more esoteric dwelling, but guessed he must've bought it as a cover. The powder-green Ford was always parked round the back, but strangely disappeared soon after we knocked on the front door. It was a big deal to find him gone, our hopes of stretching out on his fabulous orange leather sofas, a Revox reel-to-reel perched on the shelf next to a quality turntable playing the latest releases (in 'stereo') from Island Records (who he was now signed to) and stories of recording sessions with legends in the great city in the South – all of this was crushed on the days his Ford de-materialised, but we never gave up.

Cliff was our only link to a world we craved to be a part of as we drooled over *Top of the Pops* every week, the only connection I had to somewhere I was desperate to live.

Kidderminster

Led Zeppelin – *Led Zeppelin II*; Chicago – *Chicago Transit Authority*

WRONG TURN AT ELEPHANT

From the train to the tube, following the boys from south London,
I take a wrong turn at Elephant and end up in an alley between the
shopping centre and skeletons of street stalls. It's the kind of place
I used to haunt dark corners where the dirt sings 'Hallelujah!'
I sink back into my 'Beast' and adopt 'the stare', but if anyone looked
twice they'd see right through it. Move fast, with extreme purpose,
register all exits, look ahead but listen behind. With a gang of
zigzag girls wailing wide-eyed and ready, covering my rear I move
swiftly to higher ground, drawn by the sound of traffic and the
comforting glow of a London Underground sign. Sanctuary in the
smell of dust and electricity sucked out of the tunnels beneath us.
The warm air hits me in the face and I inhale the skin of millions.
The lifts are rammed; eyes stare back at me, blinking. I take the
stairs instead, keep moving, remain out of sight of the sparking boys,
sounding loud and up for it just ahead.

Invisible Conga People – 'Can't Feel My Knees'

SOUTH OF THE RIVER

Ride the train back to Peckham, recording words,
a bag full of scripts, a camera, notebook, something to
scratch marks on paper for the gallery in my head.

Tanx – 'Car Song'

SLEEPLESS

Awake all night in Peckham, longing for big Essex skies.
I watch Karlheinz Stockhausen documentaries, manipulate the volume,
mix in street sounds. The mind plays games to simulate adrenaline,
the arms hang limp and ache. Stockhausen fizzes and honks, slipping
radio dials across stations, fragments of random conversation, Morse
code, frequency harmonics – the ears blur in sympathy with the symphony
of the eyes, the thighs tingle silently inside the jeans. The nice lady
smiled as she showed me my sunlit room. That was yesterday, now it's
dull, dirty-orange after midnight in the glow of designer street
lamps. Bill paid and empty. In the room of edits and mixes the kettle
remains the constant, coffee on maximum rotation, whistle whistling,
underscoring Stockhausen's oscillations. The walls are covered in
words describing scenes collected on the journeys I've been on, and
Stockhausen is still lecturing as I snap back into consciousness about
the state of 'not thinking'. My skin begins to itch, the texts and
emails stopped hours ago, everyone I know has gone to bed.

Vaughan Williams – *Fantasia on a Theme by Thomas Tallis*,
conductor: Sir Neville Marriner with the Academy of St Martin in the Fields

ON LEAVING PECKHAM RYE

The shadow kid in the hood who lurched towards me mumbled, 'Sensi?' swerving fast as he caught my eyes. Slip the ticket out the pocket, slide it into the slot and ride – one continuous motion. Just enough time for photographic evidence of the magic train swinging low to carry me home. Who knows when I'll pass this way again? The hoods in the carriage keep their heads down, nodding with the rhythm of the rocking. The mall at the Elephant smells of cleaning products, printer ink and perfume. Girls giggle, stumbling arm-in-arm. On the pavement outside, the stench of meths rises from a pool of broken glass, hits the back of my nose like a dirty knife. It mingles with the perfume of the girls and exhaust fumes from buses parked outside to reassure me I'm going home. Women in lingerie smile down from illuminated billboards as I slip my ticket in and slide between the barricades.

Nic Jones – 'Canadee-I-O'

NO
BUSES SERVE THIS STOP.

FOUR TO THE FLOOR

Fat contrails converge above a demi-moon, dissipated on the wind in a clear blue sky. Below, the earth is a caramel crust dusted in frost, inviting me to crunch it. In Madrid, where riots give way to artworks and Goyas to backstreet coffees, drunk men sit at tables taunting a simple boy. He's bad robot dancing, learned from bitter experience to play the fool, that when they're laughing they don't use their fists.

Little Walter – 'My Babe'

One day, in the summer term of 1969, the old firm – Atty, Mark G, Andy M, Willie G and me – were given a tape recorder in music class and told to score a poem of our choice. You have to understand, this was an extraordinary task to be set in a school which was perceived as being no more than a holding pen for kids who would ultimately work on farms, in the forest or in factories; a school which could in no way ever be misconstrued as progressive in its teaching practices. However, on this one freak day, we encountered a glitch, a door into a parallel universe. By some unknown twist of temporary insanity the music teacher (who had up until this point quashed my love of music) told us we had to choose a poem and recreate it with sounds only.

'We'll need a recording studio, somewhere quiet!'

'How about the chair cupboard in the hall?'

A few hundred chairs later, we had an empty, soundproof room and set about scoring my favourite poem, 'Jabberwocky'. The sounds still vibrate in the bone, an extraordinary day. Then gone.

Bewdley Secondary Modern School

the Edwin Hawkins Singers – 'Oh Happy Day'; Jethro Tull – 'Living in the Past'; Fleetwood Mac – 'Man of the World'

THE RETURN OF WEATHER AND HIS MINIONS

Woke to the one sight that makes me go, 'Oh no!'
Snow!
A light dusting by comparison to some, as parts of the world
mobilise daily on fat tyres and heavy insulation, but here,
on the prairies of Essex, we like to wake to the green stuff.
Throw in a little sunlight, grow a few buds and watch me dance.
Took a different tack today as the sun hesitated to show its
face. I covered myself in goose grease and ventured out.
If you can't beat it, turn it into art.

Jo Stafford – 'Allentown Jail'

The best guitar shop in Dudley sold quality instruments. Not like the one in Kidderminster that displayed its guitars amongst washing machines and assorted domestic appliances. Real 'heads' in serious bands shopped at Modern Music on the edge of town, opposite the entrance to the zoo, just before you got to the sad penguin enclosure.

I'd sold my Futurama (that first electric) to a local kid for twenty-five quid and went straight to Modern Music where they had a blood-red Hofner Galaxie for exactly the same amount. The Galaxie is a bells 'n' whistles guitar, fashioned after a Fender Stratocaster, but with none of the finesse and five times the switches. It weighed a ton, had a neck like a tree trunk and a little damper device you could press up against the strings if you weren't capable of damping them with your hand. I loved that guitar, it came in a shaped case made of pressed cardboard with red velveteen lining and leather straps – proper pro – and smelled great.

Years later I saw Dave Hill's 'Super Yob' ray-gun guitar for sale in the shop. It had been custom built for him by John Birch when Slade were at their peak, taking up permanent residence on *Top of the Pops*. We were grateful to Slade, partly for keeping the Midlands on top of the charts (and by default making us less of a joke to the rest of the country), but mostly for giving us material we didn't mind covering, perpetuating the myth that we were a band aware of current trends and therefore 'one to book' for your Saturday night out down the working men's club or the village-hall brawl. It saddened me to see 'Super Yob' up for sale and I never forgot that feeling. Next to it in the window there was a beautiful Zemaitis, with that signature filigree engraving on its metal fascia that I remember seeing Ronnie Wood play with the Faces on *Top of the Pops*.

Maybe Modern Music was the back door into the charts? I kept my Hofner polished and ready.

Dudley

David Bowie – 'Space Oddity'; The Equals – 'Viva Bobby Joe';
Zager and Evans – 'In the Year 2525'

The day I wrote my first song I took it straight to Guru #1 and played it to him. He sat on the edge of his luxurious orange leather sofa and listened intently: 'Did *you* write that?'

'Yes.'

'What, *all* of it?'

'Yes.'

'Lyrics as well?'

'Yes,' waiting for some disapproving remark, like I'd been listening to too much Kinks and not enough Joni.

'That's a really good song!'

I was shocked. It felt like I'd just been handed the keys to the executive toilet, a door to a secret society opened, sweet perfumed air wafting out.

'Have you recorded it?' he asked.

'No, I don't have a tape recorder.'

'You need to get one if you're going to be a songwriter, Karl.'

'We can't afford one.'

'Wait a minute.'

He left the room, the weight of a blood-red Hofner electric heavy on my legs. I was keen to play him the song but just as keen to show off the new guitar, a matching twin to Mont's bass. From the hallway under the stairs I heard him in conversation with someone on the phone: 'Could we come now? Great! See you in ten minutes.'

We rode in the pastel Ford – a rare privilege for one so newly inducted to the inner circle – across town, past the carpet factory that'd provided Dad with the money to buy me the guitar that was lying on the back seat, past the hospital where I visited him after his throat operation, both of us tearing up as we waved to each other on leaving. The same hospital we'd visited weekly for the bowing in my legs to be rectified and to have the gash in my seven-year-old forehead stitched with an enormous curved needle. Past the police station that was too big and too grand for such a backwater town, and into a suburban cul-de-sac of smart middle-class semis with bow-fronted windows and garages for cars with names like Rover and Riley and Vanden Plas, whose interiors smelled of polished leather. At one of these a man, of similar age to the Guru, answered the door: 'Is this our songwriter?'

'It's his first song, and he needs it recorded properly.'

Kidderminster

The Kinks – 'Lola'; Joni Mitchell – 'Big Yellow Taxi'; Skid Row – *Skid*

I followed the Guru's mate upstairs to a converted bedroom – festooned in chocolate quilts, a sepia four-poster structure, a medieval throne room.

'We've had a full band in here,' beamed the engineer.

'Set the drums up right there in the bay.'

Him and the Guru went back years, a history of recorded works from album demos to comedy sketches, an expansive library of unreleased comedy improvs intended for radio but never pitched – legend only to their closest friends. The song I was there to record was written for a BBC schools competition in support of the charity Shelter. They would have liked it to have been about the plight of the homeless, but as I didn't know anyone homeless I thought about 'houses' and how the beautiful cherry orchards I'd grown up with had been ripped up to build new estates. It was a kind of protest song, inspired in part by listening to Donovan's 'Universal Soldier'. The song was based around a simple, stripped-down rhythm. A top line melody played over an open droning string, like a Link Ray riff performed by the Shadows. No drums, no bass, no dressing up – just my voice on top and a little reverb to sweeten the mix. The end result reminded me of Adam Faith at his most melancholy. His was a sound that spooked and thrilled me when I was little. The engineer knew exactly what I liked.

'If it's for the BBC, it has to be top quality, it's important,' said the Guru, settling back in a corner seat, turning 'producer' on me.

A greenery park
And the sound of a lark
In a nearby tree

Are drowned out
By moving earth
And a JCB

The Green Belt's cut back every day
Just so the architect can get his pay
Just so that we can see the day
When there's no more country

It went down in one, perfect. I had a song with a sound, *the* sound that had always been in my head. The pastel Ford took me all the way home and dropped me off at the end of the road. I floated through the door, skipped into the kitchen, beaming, clutching a tape with my name on, the first one I ever had, desperate to play it to Dad so he could be proud of me, but unable to because we couldn't afford a tape deck. It sat on a shelf in my bedroom, gathering dust, before moving to the bottom of a bigger box that travelled a lot and remained unpacked.

Bewdley

Harpers Bizarre – 'Witchi Tai To'

GOIN' HOME

'Alvin's gone, man!' said the voice on the phone.
It shocked me, shook me, worse that I never heard it on the news or in the radio obituary. I'd been watching him a week ago, playing 'I'm Goin' Home' at that festival of festivals, the gathering of the free love tribes that signalled the end of beautiful times.
Him with his famous red guitar, fingers in overdrive.
That 'Ban the Bomb' sticker inspiring me to personalise my guitar like his.

I've always had a problem with abusive authority. What happened after I played my first ever recorded song to the music teacher at school summed it up. The engineer had sprinkled a little fairy-dust on the track to sweeten the mix. He'd even managed to make the old Hofner sound good. The music teacher listened to the recording.

'That's good, but you'll have to record it again.'

'What? Why?'

'Because some girls from the year below are entering a song in the competition and all entrants from each school have to be on the same piece of tape.'

'But this sounds really good. Can't we just send it in anyway?'

'No! We've arranged for you all to go to a recording studio at Birmingham University where you'll do it again.'

'But why? It sounds great. Why would you want to do it again?'

'That's the rule!'

And there it was. The *rule*. Phase one, welcome to the world. When it came to the rules no one gave a shit about art.

We drove up to Birmingham in a rented coach to record our songs for the BBC in a studio that felt and looked like a laboratory: cold and white. The walls were covered in peg board, the kind that looks retro cool at Abbey Road with The Beatles strumming, laying it down in black and white, but back then in the austere surroundings of that 'laboratory' studio, they snuffed the light out of a twelve-year-old boy with a blood-red guitar. The engineers wore alarmingly smart jumpers, were impatient, kept telling us how little time we had and that we needed to get it right first time. They were shit at setting the vibe for a young musician to turn it on, didn't give a damn, and let you know it.

'There won't be time to *re-do* anything!'

I opened my guitar case, to let it breath and impress the girls, but they were too busy practising their song, a sweet unison refrain, wrapped around a stripped-down bongo groove. They couldn't care less about my shiny red thing. The engineer caught sight of it.

'Oh! Were you thinking of using *that*?'

'Yes, it's my guitar. It's what I use.'

'Well, I don't think we have the right cables to plug it in. In fact, I *know* we don't, so you'll have to use something else.'

'But it's my sound. Can't you find the right cables?'

'You should've told us you wanted to use this before you got here. Have you got something else?'

The music teacher had been ahead of me all the time, had my demise all worked out. She'd brought the school guitar, a lump of rough-hewn wood with strings like girders and the action of a suspension bridge. She grinned, almost clapped with glee as she handed it to me.

Nowhere exciting, 1970

Ash Ra Tempel – *Ash Ra Tempel*

SUGAR HITS THE SWEET-SPOT

Talks-fast woman
In the night
At the edge of the world
Wreckless
Nervous
Unseen

Fish cracker
Pink linen crown
Half-moon
Half-thong
Half-rice
Half-chips
Mirrors on the ceiling

Blow the whistle on me
Wear it like a penalty
With benefits

No ice
Honey-day laughter

Cinnamon erection
Birds
Make me different
Enjoy

Shangri-La in the rain
Dodgy and all that
For years

Sugar hits the sweet-spot

The Boswell Sisters – 'The Music Goes 'Round and Around'

Back in the gloom of the music lesson, we gathered around the big old schools-issue radio with the industrial veneer, waiting for it to warm up, impatient to hear how our songs had got on. Then, when the results were announced, I got my first slap in the face from the cold hand of injustice. The girls in the year below had won with their wispy-voiced bongo drone.

What shall I do?
I've got nowhere to go
Nobody loves me
No one wants to know …

And something about '… *an electric cooker and fridge* …'

I got the runners-up prize, a record token to buy anything I wanted … *for the school*. I wondered how come both entrants from our school got first and second prize, if anyone else had even bothered. At the record shop there was loads of stuff that I wanted and more whose sleeves promised exotic thrills, but none that were appropriate for a music teacher intent on killing one's love of music. I dumbed down and headed for a record shop (there were record shops everywhere back then and they were always busy) where I remembered old blokes in tweed who pondered sleevenotes and stroked their chins. I selected a compilation of classical guitar recordings (it was actually really *good*) and handed over my precious record token, the only proof I had that I'd *made it* onto national radio. The music teacher smiled thinly, 'A very good choice,' and stuck it at the back of the cupboard, where it remained for years after I left.

The non-music room

Walter (Wendy) Carlos and Benjamin Folkman – *Switched-On Bach*

Mark Howell eventually got bored and left the band. Mont stashed his bass under his bed and the band folded. But I'd got the bug. I had to have a band, then remembered this lad, whose mom had been on at my mom for years for me to come hear her son play the drums. I'd always said, 'Tell her, "No,"' but maybe now was a good time to check him out. He'd been practising in her front room for years; he must be OK, right?

Paul Harris was a blond looker, reminiscent of Steve Harley with a cheeky twinkle. He lived down the hill from the carpet factory where Dad worked, drove a bright orange Mini Cooper, and had the biggest gold-sparkle kit I'd ever seen – bingo! I sat in his mom's front room and listened to him play. He was really good. I couldn't believe my luck and cycled straight over to Mont's, where I talked him into dusting off his bass and giving it another go. Then there was Mick, the son of a mom that my mom knew, who played guitar with swagger and a cheek that girls loved (another twinkler), so we drafted him in with his black Les Paul (copy) and his AC30 amp (the real thing).

Mont decided that if we were ever going to do more than rehearse we should learn other people's songs – that way we could at least get gigs. The four of us formed a covers band, starting with the Faces' 'Maggie May', called ourselves Talisman Wood, and toured the village halls and working men's clubs of the West Midlands for the next five years. Me and Mont also wrote songs which were slipped into the set whenever we could get away with it, though mostly we were required to play what was in the charts at the time (from Glam through to 'A Glass of Champagne') with a few rock 'n' roll classics to dig us out of trouble. I don't remember how or why, but at fourteen I found myself fronting the band with a thin little voice that wasn't ready for the job.

'Our kid doesn't have a strong enough voice,' my cousin Ian once said when he came to see us with his gang (a phrase that's dogged me ever since).

Mick left, a keyboard player came and went, as did a saxophonist who got stage fright before his first gig and disappeared. One evening, Pete Lambert, a reclusive guitarist who drove a cool Mini Moke and lived literally across the road, knocked on our door, an outsider vision with his wild shoulder-length hair and gentle bearded smile. (His dad used to run the scout camps in the forest where Favourite Aunty lived. I can still sing the roundels from those campfire sing-alongs about animal fairs and a monkey's alarming anal escapade.)

'I hear you're looking for a guitarist.'

By thirteen, I was the only boy in school with hair long enough for the teachers to insist I wear headbands for PE. I was terrible at football and worse at cricket, but, weirdly, had an aptitude for hockey that fast-tracked me to school captain then on to play for the county, and then for a local team that was a feeder to the England squad. For the next five years, weekends went like this:

> Friday nights, the band played at one of the local clubs. Ride home in the van, unload and be in bed by 1.30 a.m.

Saturday: up at 8 a.m. Cycle three miles to the hockey club, play a home match or travel with the team (mostly men who brought 007 blondes in furs and knee-length boots to watch, jig and offer promise of rich reward from the sidelines) all over the West Midlands. We'd sink a couple of beers at the clubhouse then I'd cycle home in time to load the van for another gig. Play, then home, unload the van. In bed by half-one.

Sunday: up at 6 a.m. Cycle around town delivering the Sunday papers, hauling the heaviest bag of the week (and the best-paying).

For a while, on Saturdays, between the hockey matches and the gigs, I added industrial cleaning at Dad's carpet factory to my CV, crawling under looms in my home-made headbands to scoop out 'shoddy' (fluff). Needles of waste yarn stuck to my hands and arms like pincushions, and I kept up this punishing regime until my body eventually collapsed. It taught me a useful lesson about physical limits, but I also learned that the adrenaline from playing in a band could get me through pretty much anything.

1970–72

Osibisa – 'Ayiko Bia'; Redbone – 'The Witch Queen of New Orleans';
Bob and Marcia – 'Young, Gifted and Black'

Because of Radio Luxembourg I still can't listen to a clean copy of 'Riders on the Storm'.

It sounds too 'nice', too precise, too clinical. I want to hear it fade in and out; hear it twisting, flipping and phasing, get thin and barely audible just as the best bit kicks in then filter back up to something rich and full. I want to forget that any second now all that richness will be sucked out of it, drawing in white noise and radio static, maybe even some random voices and a little French accordion (there's always a French accordion drifting around on the AM dial). That was the first way I ever heard it, the only way I ever want to hear it. Years later, a mate would play me the *The Doors* album and I wouldn't recognise it.

For my birthday he found me a rough old 7-inch in a junk shop that had come out of a jukebox, gave it to me wrapped in newspaper, no sleeve: 'I think you'll like this.'

When the needle slipped into the groove, it crackled, popped, jumped, jiggled and, out of a cloud of static and scratches like a voice calling me through a crack in time, Ray Manzarek's hypnotic left-hand bass line transmitted 'everything is fine'.

The sound of the storm, back where it belonged.

AM radio noise, 1970s

Faust – *Faust*; Stomu Yamash'ta – 'Red Buddha'

In 1971 I got my first taste of stereo when Mont invited me round his house to hear his dad's new headphones. I'd never worn headphones before, only seen them in Bond films, and had never heard 'stereo'. Mont was offering a free taste and it made me nervous, like I was about to do my first drug. His family always seemed a few rungs further up the ladder to me, not better than mine, but they definitely had a bit more cash. The fact that you had to take your shoes off when you walked into their house made them seem sophisticated. His dad was a draughtsman, or something cool like that, and there was an appealing artiness about him. Mont lived in the upmarket bit of the council estate on the east side of the river (the other lot), and, though he knew all the local gangs, his passion for music kept him off the streets. The headphones were classic 1970s hemispheres, white and bulbous, clinging to the ends of a black leather arch between delicate fingers of chrome. They were connected to a tower of illuminated boxes (trimmed in silver and wood) by an ultra modern curly lead, a style of cable that was becoming all the rage. I walked in. Mont was lying on the floor, eyes closed, trancing out, a thin sound emanating from his ears.

'You gotta hear these things!' He grinned like he knew he was about to change my life. *Split*, the new album by a band called the Groundhogs, was on the turntable. The cover was strategically positioned for me to see - a seductive black and white picture of a guitar legend having some kind of transcendent experience; head back, eyes closed, mouth open. I got down on the floor and lay back. He put the needle into the best groove and grinned as I slipped the headphones on. What I heard confused me, it was unlike anything I'd ever heard, but didn't sound right, felt unnatural. It was too contained, had no air around it and failed to blow me away. I faked a thrill. 'Yeah, great!'

The sound was too close, too synthetic, an approximation of natural spatial information, a caricature of nature, it made life sound smaller - interesting, but *less* than real life. I was going to have to relearn how to listen if I was ever going to feel the buzz he felt.

'Innit fantastic?'

'Yeah, it's ... mmm ... fantastic.' I swerved, buying time to learn how to enjoy it, remembering the first time I tasted beer I'd hated it but knew I'd have to learn to love it if I wanted to be a man.

Wribbenhall council estate, 1971

the Groundhogs – *Split*

Birmingham Town Hall. The queue of 'heads' goes round the block smelling of petunia oil. Combats, loons, freak-flags fluttering in an evening breeze. Mont and me spilled out of his dad's old black Ford dressed in 'version' threads – too clean for the scene, feeling conspicuously crisp as we skulked to the back of the queue clutching our tickets. I was fourteen. It was my first gig – one week after hearing *Split* for the first time in Mont's living room, I was about to see the Groundhogs in the flesh. His mom had managed to buy us late box-office tickets – seats up on the balcony, left side, overlooking the stage. Starched ushers drew themselves in as we entered, recoiled, ripped tickets with dexterous fingers. A fabulous sea of hair stretched out below us; plush velveteen seats wrapped the full way around the auditorium. The great town hall organ pipes – symbols of dour council power – frowned down upon us; parallel lines of brass towered above the stage.

And that stage! Filled with the backline of *three* bands, no room to move. A cityscape of speaker boxes rendered in orange amps, their white-faced hieroglyphs teetering atop sandy-coloured 4x12s, two at a time right across the stage. The beauty of that vision made me gasp, '*Orange amps, here on Earth!*' Three bands for 10 shillings. The first two – Quicksand and Glenn Cornick's Wild Turkey – each with its own orange barricade, freshly funded from record advances. Both performances were a cacophonous, reverb heavy mess of distortion that bounced round the cavernous town hall, peeling the gold leaf rococo and igniting seas of flailing hair. I remember vividly there was a girl with a mane like a whip that she cracked relentlessly in time with the kick drum. Tony McPhee, Mr Groundhog himself, was standing serene in the wings taking it all in. Mont nudged me, 'That's him!'

Break to the bar. Lemonade and beer. Feel the electric petunia tension, glances of kindred spirits coiling.

'It's time.'

When we got back to our seats everything had changed (I love it every time that happens). No orange, that's kid's stuff. Big boys' toys now: stacks of Laney, grey to the horizon, like granite blocks, no fuss, stripped down, simple, confident. Bass, drums, guitar. The house lights went down, a deafening roar went up. The volume of the crowd distorted my ears. We rose automatic as one, my legs had been hacked and something primal had taken control: face lit up with involuntary grinning. I didn't understand it, but I was gone!

'Stick your fingers in your ears, it'll sound better!' shouted Mont.

Then we're surfing, lost in the genius of 'TS' McPhee; his guitar screaming, wailing and moaning, slabs of howling cascading sparks pouring molten steel into the dark. I didn't know how to like it, but I was determined to learn.

Brum town hall, November 1971

Deep Purple – 'Fireball'; David Bowie – *Hunky Dory*; Isaac Hayes – 'Theme from *Shaft*';
The Doors – 'LA Woman'; Sly and the Family Stone – 'There's a Riot Goin' On';
Emerson, Lake & Palmer – *Emerson, Lake & Palmer*; Chicago – *Chicago III*;
Osibisa – *Osibisa*; Hawkwind – *In Search of Space*

I was fourteen when the maths teacher got the boot. He was our favourite, the one who got us hooked on a subject that had always been a drag – he made it cool and we took to it like fish 'n' chips. Guru #1 had set me on course and now the maths teacher ensured there was no turning back. His name was Miller, but we called him 'Windy' after that little animated fella in the kids TV programme *Camberwick Green*. He was small, vibrant, younger than the rest, and we welcomed him like one of our own.

It all started when he took a bunch of us eleven-year-olds camping in the holiday, pitched up on the grass at the back of school – a week of miserable rain, soaked to the skin. He got keys to the school hall and let us in to watch TV on the permanently padlocked industrial unit that I'd previously never seen working. He bent the rules for us, made us feel like his mates, had our loyalty for ever. We played table tennis and scared each other with ghost stories, huddled in our sleeping bags up on the stage.

And then he took us to the cinema – how cool was that for maths? *2001: A Space Odyssey* was showing at Kidderminster ABC. I'd seen the poster and tried impressing girls with my fake knowledge of the plot, but I was dying to see it and was resigned to having no one to take me. Nothing prepared me for the life-changing experience of seeing that film. Did my mates see what I saw? Maybe not. They went on to be farmers, mechanics, engineers and bikers, but that night I heard things I'd never heard before, or thought possible: the choral works of György Ligeti. I made my mom take me to see it again later in the week, bored her to death with the longest film on earth, just to sit in the dark, life forever altered by the sound of those beautiful discordant voices. Bought the soundtrack and played it on a loop. Built my first installation in the wardrobe, emptied it out, installed a seat, a flashing light, drew the bedroom curtains to make it dark and, with Dad's go-kart racing helmet on, shut myself away in a virtual world, record player pumping Ligeti on a constant loop into my eleven-year-old bloodstream, imagining I was floating above the Earth unseen, anywhere but here.

One summer term, the annual staff–pupil cricket match was played on the town pitch in front of school on the last day. To rapturous cheers, Windy strode out to the crease dressed as his stop-motion alter-ego: straw hat, wellies and a farmer's smock. He raised his bat and grinned, fully aware of the message he was sending out to the whole school, making it clear whose side he was on. He was one of us and we loved him.

At the end of the third year, we heard Windy was gone, booted out or asked to leave for some rumoured indiscretion we didn't believe – a storm of whispers. He stood at his classroom door as we lined up, shook every one of us by the hand, looked us straight in the eye and murmured personalised messages to each of us. It was too painful, I couldn't bear it, wanted to run, throw a desk through the window, cut across the fields, swim the river. But then he had my hand, looked me in the eye and whispered, 'Don't give up the music.'

Through the wardrobe

2001: A Space Odyssey soundtrack; John Kongos – 'He's Gonna Step on You Again', 'Tokoloshe Man'

POTATO MAN MEMORY

Sheltering from a bitter wind in a high-stool chain café,
a wind so cold it bypassed the bone and went straight to
the soul. Bloodless knuckles clutched collars high round
sinuous summer necks, isolated stares in throaty wools.
A twenty-minute lock-out at Oxford Circus. Crowds huddled like
Antarctic penguins without the etiquette of instinct to rotate
outsiders to the middle.
I watched an old potato, shrivelled like a man, wrapped in every
garment he had, held together like a cartoon with string around
the middle. I saw a man take solace from a tiny bottle, poking
its head out like a tortoise from a ragged paper shell. Potato man
rises, pushes a slow greasy bundle towering on a barrow up the
wind-bleached pavement in front of a long stare. Hello, is that
me with his lips around the glass teat like a newborn? Was gratitude
ever so cheaply forgotten, sheltering from a bitter wind on a high-
stool chain café?

Transmit – 'Who'

Summer holidays were spent down on the south coast or up in North Wales, always in caravans. Though North Wales had originally been with the family, we'd gone upmarket and relocated to Bournemouth, towing a rented four-berth. The North Wales location had moved from Black Rock Sands outside of Porthmadog to a site with its own clubhouse and bingo on the cliffs just south of Aberystwyth. This trip was taken with Favourite Aunty in one of Uncle's strange Eastern European vehicles that smelled of dog and leaf mould. Life on the caravan site was never dull, as me and cousin Tim dipped in rock pools, walked into town along the cliffs, told ghost stories and played football until we'd hit every caravan. In the evening we played bingo, pinball and table football at the clubhouse, flirting with girls high on Vimto and crisps. Most evenings Uncle's little black and white portable telly would flicker, perched precariously on a chair and tuned exclusively to BBC (there was, no doubt, some cultural snobbery at work).

My family preferred ITV, so this obsession with 'the other side' broadened my horizons and got me hooked on a world beyond *Crossroads* and *Corrie* - a weird, exotic posh world of award-winning dramas and middle-class comedies. Unfortunately, we also had to endure the BBC Proms live from the Royal Albert Hall - not exactly *Top of the Pops*, not even *That Was the Week That Was*. I remember the night of 13 August 1970 started with the smell of cooked fish - a miserable evening that was dark, and damp. No bingo for us. While the girls went off to flirt with future husbands, we would have to settle for the drone of another orchestra, imprisoned with our painful hormonal urges, jerking pinball flippers. The orchestra shuffled in and did their thing - 'Triple Music II' (world premiere) - David Atherton conducting the BBC Symphony Orchestra, my will to live ebbing away. Then suddenly something shifted - a rip in the fabric of time - and in burst an ensemble so unlikely, so raw, that my uncle was caught off guard. It was too late for him to turn the TV off before he realised it had all gone horribly wrong. The picture tilted, froze, jag-jumped, dynamic angles cut the screen, vulgar sounds. A box van careering round the outside of the hallowed hall like a Beatles film on steroids. It was bringing change, delivering revolution. 'Soft Machine' - Elton Dean, Hugh Hopper, Mike Ratledge and Robert Wyatt - unleashed their irreverent cacophony upon my poor uncle's ears, as I relaxed back against matching cushions, cocoa in hand and voodoo whispering, 'Don't touch that dial!'

Sonically, the album *Soft Machine 4* has remained with me since then: something I always try to slip into the playlist of every radio broadcast I make.

Morfa Bycan caravan site, North Wales

Soft Machine – 'Virtually, Parts 1–4'

FAT FLAKES FALL

Even the sky doesn't want us to leave Essex, emptying snow
onto us and putting on a light show more beautiful than I recall,
in salmon pinks and dirty chalk purple cloud fingers. They part,
revealing blue sky as hedgerows glow orange, facing sunrise like
deckchair holidaymakers on Southend Beach, why would I want to
leave? The excited, happy Mexican voices on the phone last night
reminded me. Time to grow wings again and cut clouds, time to
dance and celebrate the union of happy faces. People gathered
to give good energy, exchange a smile, raise hands in hallelujah
and let the light in. Oh yeah, now I remember.

Huntsville – '(AGE)'

No contest. The best music teacher I ever had, the one who had the greatest influence on me, was John Peel.

From catching moments of *The Perfumed Garden* on holidays where the pirate stations could reach us, to his late-night shows on BBC Radio 1. No stereo, no bass. Two hours of exotic escape.

Every night his show was a door flung open on to worlds I never knew existed, planets orbiting light years away from our house, seemingly unattainable – but at least I could glimpse them through my little radio. I'd tune in knowing something new was about to happen, not knowing or caring what, just excited by the sound of his voice and the records he dropped. There were times in every one of his broadcasts when I loved what he played, but more that I hated. Most of it was pure noise to me and yet, most of that 'noise' became the music I came to love, and John's show changed how I thought about music every time I tuned in.

Sweating under the sheets, I imagined him in the basement of Broadcasting House in a tatty studio, lights on low, crouched over an old mixing desk. At his side, a stack of records teetering. Just like Wolfman Jack in *American Graffiti*, getting off on sharing his love of music with a generation hungry to hear *new stuff* (twenty odd years later I'd broadcast from the studio next to him, discovering to my joy that I'd imagined everything exactly as it was).

After all those years of intermittent signals and police busts on light ships in the Channel the BBC had got the best of the pirates under contract, and John Peel was amongst them. Many of us growing up as teenagers in remote little towns and villages were desperate to hear something fresh, eager to find other people like us – a tribe that we could identify with through the mutual love of a band, a sound, a groove. For those of us who followed his show religiously, Peel was the best music teacher in the world.

Under the covers again

A REMEMBERED LOVE OF DANCE

Down at the stadium last night the hairs on the back of
my neck stood up as 'Cowgirl's kick drum dropped.
Robbed of oxygen by altitude. This height above sea level
always leaves me breathless, the head can't really believe
a city could be so thin on breathable molecules.

I love soundchecking the night before a festival,
watching forklifts distribute refrigerators to beer stalls,
lone skateboarders glide across the arena floor like kings,
clouds of dust rise up from besoms, drovers of dirt,
choreographed to clean, do their dance across the arena
herding crap with love and care to make everything
right for the feet of thousands.

Riggers the size of hills push enormous metal barriers
with ease, reducing tons to matchsticks. Hands that could
snap me like a twig tap in harmony with the high-hat,
feet move in time with the snare, bodies swaying in the
breeze of a familiar sub-bass groove, everybody smiling,
everything gets easier as the mood lifts us closer
to the time.

Mischa Bakaleinikoff – *Film Scores*

Driving in Dad's car through Bournemouth, a roundabout festooned with summer blooms, Roxy Music came on the radio. 'Virginia Plain' put a full stop on everything that had come before. A few bars in, Dad reached for the off switch. 'What a bloody row!'

'Don't!' I yelled from the back seat, the first time I'd ever stopped him.

I'd got goosebumps. Never heard anything so fresh. I knew it was great because Dad thought it was bad, and for the first time our musical tastes were completely different. This was a noise that talked directly to me, music written just for people like me, born out of the clatter in my head, arranged in a fabulous cacophony of squeals, honks, howls and croons.

Everything wrong.

At the same time *right*.

When I caught them on the *Old Grey Whistle Test* a few weeks later they were dressed head-to-toe in fake furs and satin spangles, tripped out on sci-fi ballroom chic.

'I'm havin' some of that!'

Dad's car, 1972

Roxy Music – 'Ladytron'

The school careers advisor greeted me with a tired smile and a weary handshake in the gloom of the first aid room. The room stank of Photostat chemicals that made me feel like a lab rat as I sat down at his table.

'Have you thought about what you'd like to do when you leave school?'

'Yes, I'm going to be a musician.'

'I see. We don't have many pupils wanting to do that.'

'...'

'We did have one lad. I think he's still going, but overall it's a very precarious career path.'

'Yes.'

'Have you considered any alternatives?'

'No.'

'I see you're good at art. There's a very good career to be had designing carpets for a student with your talent.'

'...'

'Had you ever considered that?'

'No. I'm going to be a professional musician.'

'Classical?'

'No. In a band.'

'Well, I'm not sure there's anything I can do for you, though if you change your mind about carpet–'

'No, thank you, I'm going to be a musician. But thank you anyway.'

'Well, I'm sorry I couldn't be of more help.'

'Oh, believe me, you've helped.'

'Good luck!'

Long before he'd finished talking, I'd left the room, the building, the town. The dreary entrapment of his most prudent suggestion scared me shitless. He'd showed me the best I could hope for if I stuck around - he'd helped the shyest boy in school grow the balls to leave. It was the most inspiring careers advice anyone could've given me. I just wish I'd had the chance to thank him.

The medical room

David Bowie – 'Suffragette City'; Deep Purple – 'Highway Star';
Alice Cooper – 'School's Out'; Santana – *Caravanserai*;
Lou Reed – 'Walk on the Wild Side'; Jimmy Cliff – 'The Harder They Come';
Wishbone Ash – *Argus*

She was the teacher I fancied the most, wore the best leather miniskirts in town, and therefore had my complete attention whenever she walked into the room. We were in the library during a break and she was fixing me with a threatening stare: 'What are you going to do after school?'

'Er, well, my dad wants me to design carpets at the carpet factory.'

'What!'

'Well, it's because I'm good at art.'

'Are you kidding me?'

'What about art college?'

'What's that?'

'Haven't you ever heard of art college?'

'No.'

'Oh my God! I'm going to get you the prospectus and YOU ARE GOING TO ART COLLEGE! If you go to work in the carpet factory I'll never speak to you again!'

My blood ran cold, I didn't have a clue what she was talking about, A-R-T college ...?

'What do they do at "art college"?'

'*ART!*'

'What, all day?'

'Every day.'

The pennies began dropping as the miniskirt faded into clouds of swirling brush-strokes – oh my God!

'Wait, you mean there's a place where all you do is art all day ... and they let you?'

'That's art college, and I'm going to get you the prospectus if you're interested, and if you're not you're crazy.'

'Yes! Yes! I'll do it!'

And right then I would've done anything, not for her miniskirt, but for the new world I could see opening out in front of me. A place where you made 'art' *all day*.

Nothing, nothing, nothing would stop me now. The best leather miniskirt in the world had spoken, with a voice like a bell. The path out of town was revealed and I was already on it. There was just the small matter of convincing Dad ...

The path, the way and the light

Rod Stewart – 'You Wear It Well'; Hawkwind – 'Silver Machine'; America – 'A Horse with No Name'; Mott the Hoople – 'All the Young Dudes'; Alice Cooper – 'Elected'; Blackfoot Sue – 'Standing in the Road'; Al Green – 'Let's Stay Together'; Tyrannosaurus Rex – 'Debora'

From the age of fourteen I spent most Saturday nights loading gear into Transits and leaving town, while other kids were kicking footballs and riding bikes. Sometimes we'd drive south to towns with working men's clubs, sometimes east to the nightclubs of Birmingham and the Black Country, and sometimes west to village halls along the Welsh border.

The clubs smelled of sour beer, stale cigar smoke and cheap perfume. Your feet stuck to the carpet as you walked in. Black Country nightclubs were organised. They had bouncers and dressing rooms, they were efficient, unemotional, smelled of disinfectant and air freshener and did what they said on the tin. They delivered professional entertainment that commanded a high ticket price.

The village halls smelled of a time between the wars. They guaranteed a fight and spilled blood – nothing serious, just violent enough to get a rush on and claim some turf. The other lads in the band were a few years older than me, but when a fight broke out age didn't matter, it was all about etiquette. You didn't touch the 'turn'. The sons from the farms would watch the sons from towns stroll in like they thought they were the dog's bollocks, dressed sharp and strutting. They'd watch them pose at the bar like they were taking over, let them settle in, spend their money and drop their guard. Somewhere around the halftime break, somebody would say something to someone or touch up somebody's girlfriend, and the word would go around. You could feel the ripple from the stage, an energy shift in the room, and it was 'on'.

I never saw any one specific signal – the dancefloor would be packed, everybody mingling, getting down to the groove – then suddenly it would turn. Fists, feet, teeth and broken glass, the floor awash with beer and blood. On the door, farm boys with hands like shovels would run in to break it up, then one of them would take a punch and it would turn serious. You had to keep playing or risk getting *noticed* – keep believing no one touches *the 'turn'*. I remember stopping only once. A geezer paused mid-punch, turned to the stage and yelled, 'Keep playing or you'll get a clout!'

We started back up and a bloodied face tore away from the mob screaming, '*If you don't stop, me and my mates are gonna wait for you outside!*'

My dad (who always came to gigs in those early days) sensed the crossing of a fine line of etiquette and stepped up, 'Is this bloke bothering you, son? That's a lethal weapon in your hand, lad. [To me] If he tries anything, hit him with it!'

The bloke looked Dad square in the face and seeing the serious intent in his eyes, winked at me and went back to the fight, 'You're all right, kid!' he smiled.

Far Forest Village Hall

A nightclub, early seventies. Small stage, a few lights, acoustic tiles on a low ceiling. I'm hauling in Laney cabinets (the same as Tony McPhee). The man behind the bar says, 'You won't need all them boxes, boys.' Clusters of tables and chairs fill the room, a small dancefloor close to the stage is covered in the marks left behind by the passage of feet escaping the week. A door at the back of the stage leads to a small nicotined room. No windows, a few old chairs, a table, a mirror, a fluorescent light, a plug socket and a door with the sign FIRE EXIT. We push it open for some fresh air and calm before another perfumed night oozes in off the street. There's a tiny strip of dirt, broken glass, discarded things blown in by the wind. Four feet away, there's a chain-link fence to stop us escaping. It's got the vibe of a miniature prison yard. We hang onto the fence, looking out across a car park to a waste-ground, push our fingers through the holes. The drummer stares through the wire taking a drag on his cigarette. 'What a shit hole. Who booked this gig?' he spits with familiar disdain. I say nothing, seething (it was me who booked the gig and he knows it), follow him back inside and walk on stage. The MAN is sat two rows back – flanked by respectful girls in short evening dresses, pendulous earrings and lashes; everything in curves – a jacket draped around his shoulders, silver hair and rings.

'That's him, then?' the drummer whispers, concealing a raised eyebrow as we start the set, trying to act the part, but feeling dirty. One song in, word comes back. 'The MAN says it's too loud.'

We dutifully notch it down, we're on his turf, we lay it back, thin it out, Radio 2 it. The MAN nods in recognition. Everyone relaxes.

He controls the night.

Later, outside the club, our Transit is parked up on the pavement, back doors wide open for the load-out. We have survived an ugly night, ferrying equipment out through the front of the club to the annoyance of the manager, who huffs and wants us gone. He stands at the door, trying to distract his regulars, greeting the cheap suits and short-short dresses, smiling to loosen their wallets and purses, encourage a little heavy spending at his over-priced bar. The bouncers are tolerant, we bonded on the way in, so they conceal their shrugs and winks, 'Just be as quick as you can, eh lads,' they whisper.

The boys in the band leave the van unattended, something they maybe could have done back home in the village, but here it's just begging for it. I'm shocked, pissed off, wondering what world they're living in tonight. You may as well give the gear away for free if you're going to leave your van unlocked on a street like this, so I sit on the bonnet looking blasé, faking unfazed nonchalance as young gangs cruise and sniff around, glancing back, calculating the odds. I stare back like I know something they don't. Bricking it.

In the early seventies you could do stuff like that and not get killed. Pull a double bluff, carry it off. Looking back it seems so quaint. How sweet – a fresh-faced country boy in his late teens, shoulder-length hair and loons, facing down the local wide boys while slouched on the bonnet of a two-tone Ford that still smelled of fish from a previous owner.

Your Turf

After every gig, from the age of fourteen to eighteen, I'd come home to a silent house. Mom, Dad and my sister would have long gone to bed; a solitary light would remain on in the kitchen, with a spread of cold food left out for me. Unable to sleep, I'd make a plate of snacks and switch my head off reading the small ads in the back of the *Kidderminster Shuttle*, listening to the house settle on its bones, alone with hissing ears. Sounds that were terrifying to me as a small boy were now reassuringly homely, providing a comforting solitude.

In the morning Mom would walk in – 'Urgh!' – then reverse rapidly, recoiling from the stench of her favourite son, rancid from another night in another acrid club. 'Put your clothes straight in the wash when you get up!'

We didn't have a shower back then. Bath time was exclusively reserved for Sunday night, when I'd fill it high, turn crocodile, sink low into bubbles right up to the eyes, secure in the knowledge that the world couldn't see me.

Wyre Hill

Feeling deeply alone. The only one like me. An outsider – special and different, superior and crushingly inferior, out of sync with the rest of the world. These were normal everyday emotions for me. I didn't *get* the world at all. It was like I'd been off sick on the day the instructions to life were handed out. *You* all knew how to do life; I didn't, and it got worse. I just wanted to withdraw, get out of it, and run. Stop the pain, make it go away.

Every Christmas, I'd be given a little nip of sherry. I'd feel the warm glow seep through me and take my breath away momentarily. It scared me in a chemical way that I liked. One Christmas, I hit the advocaat hard. I was doing Mom and Dad a favour, saving it from going off at the back of the cupboard. I kept pouring large glasses, wiping them out with a finger, sucking it clean, going back for more until it was all gone. I'd sit glowing at the back of the living room, the *Morecambe and Wise* special on the TV, while I sat just watching the backs of Mom and Dad's heads. They didn't have a clue I was completely out of it and, finally, blissfully happy.

At last I'd found my soulmate; my sweet solution.

Semi-detached

LOVE THAT JET-LAG BOY

For the past two nights I've been waking every hour.
A ragged and noisy head. My old familiar whispers,
'Come down the hole again.'

I've got vibrating skin, stinging body, blurry eyeball.
I'm getting tetchy, a long way from home.
Such a fine excuse for a flip out - impatience feasting on the cheese of exhaustion,
I'm justified and grandiose, but, look ... here comes the sun.
everything gets easier as the mood lifts us closer
to the time.

asamisimasa plays the music of Øyvind Torvund – *Neon Forest Space*

HOME

Essex looks more beautiful than I remember, even after sitting
in a jam on the M25.
Although sunny, I got hailed on as I stepped from the taxi.
Was it just stupidity behind my grinning, or genuine happiness
to be home on the prairies?

Mexico City, a joy, everyone we met made us feel good, from crews
to audiences who travelled miles to pay hard earned cash.
(But) it's good to be breathing sea-level air again.
This smile inside fuelled on the cracks and colours of Mexico City,
sucking 7-Up through plastic straws, dipping chips into homemade
guacamole as skins shed winter in the sun.

Until we see each other again I'm lying in the long grass watching
rainclouds fold their fingers in the sky.

Hawkwind – 'Brainstorm'

LATE-NIGHT SHOPPING

The twenty-four-hour store smelled of skunk, everyone looking sheepish.
I choose to remain a different kind of out of it
not catch anyone's eye. The place felt 'on edge'.
Confirming the
absence of dark chocolate Bounty bars I reversed out the door,
leaving fellow shoppers at the checkout sweating beneath the weight
of family-sized corn-chip bags.

Far East Family Band – 'Parallel World'

I left school at sixteen for a two-year arts foundation course in Stourbridge, but first Dad insisted I get a job and earn money.

As ever, he was thinking ahead, planting the seed, showing me how it was done, though I didn't think so at the time.

All my mates were still at school, in post-exam euphoria, playing barely legal pranks on the staff, enjoying the fun we'd earned, while I was long gone and working on a timber-mill production line.

Every morning at 7 a.m. I waited down in the valley for a lift in a battered old ambulance driven by a hippy. All summer I worked on the crate-packing line with a frisky gang of women, who hit on me with relentless innuendo. It was a dangerous job for a kid fresh out of school, bundling stacks of fruit-box components, with a machine that bound them in loops of wire; a machine that was like a giant circular cheese-cutter capable of removing a man's hand if he were unlucky to have it there when it malfunctioned (as it did daily).

I made it through summer by calculating what I'd earned at the end of every day, counting down to the London trip we'd planned, in Pete's Mini Moke, to buy new guitars. When the end of the last shift on the last day of the last week came I wasn't sad, didn't bid the ladies on the line a fond farewell or shed a tear. I legged it out of that Godforsaken hole, stinking of sweat and sawdust, and, as soon as I got home, showered the dust out of all the cracks and washed the elephant off my back.

The drive to London was sunny and euphoric, the sides off and the top down, our long hair flapping into knots around our eyes. It felt so cool to ride in Pete's machine, everybody we passed smiled and waved. We were happy, driving south with money in our pockets and guitars on our minds. In the early seventies, the back pages of the *Melody Maker* said Shaftesbury Avenue was *the* place for guitar shoppers, so that's where we went (parking up in a multi-storey on the corner of Lexington Street, Soho – a few yards from and twenty-plus years before what would become the Tomato building). We cruised the street, window shopping, but never quite seeing anything that looked right or affordable. The entire summer's work had rewarded me with the princely sum of £110. I'd had to endure abuse and embarrassment for that money and I wasn't about to blow it on the first guitar on the street. Somewhere up near where the fire station is now I saw a vision, a mint green Gibson SG, with three white single coil pick-ups and a price tag of £120. Pete, being a qualified metallurgist at British Steel, had enough wedge to help me out, so I slipped into the store, buzzing.

'Could I try that SG in the window, please?'

The nonchalant hairy regarded me with disdain from his slouch against the counter. 'What are you looking for, son?'

Now, remember, I was sixteen, left school, just finished working at the timber mill, and this 'twat' is calling me 'son'. I remained pissed-off-calm as my mates sucked their teeth and looked away.

'I'd like to try the SG in the window, please.'

'Yeah, y'see it's not an SG, and I know what you're looking for, and that doesn't sound like it.'

'Could I just try it anyway, please?'

'Well, y'see, I don't think it's what you're looking for, if you get what I mean?'

'Well, I'll tell ya. I've driven all the way down from the Midlands today to buy a guitar, and I'd really wanted to try *that* guitar, and I've got the price of it right here in my pocket but you just blew a sale!'

I strode out of the shop, headed to nearby Rose Morris, and spanked my hard earned cash on a brand new Ned Callan Cody electric like the one I'd dribbled over in *Guitar* magazine that month. It was nowhere near the class of the Gibson, would never acquire a vintage sound or value, but that day was the turning point where I decided I'd never spend money in anywhere run by assholes.

Shaftesbury Avenue, summer 1973

David Bowie – 'Life on Mars'; Medicine Head – 'One and One is One';
David Essex – 'Rock On'

'Ahhh, look at 'im, 'e's so cute – an' look, 'e's blushing. You embarrassed, love? No need to be, I'm not gonna bite ya, you can 'ave a look. Go on, 'ave a look, y' mates are 'avin' a good look. Doncha fancy me? Oh look 'e's embarrassed, 'e's so sweet I could *eat* 'im!'

The other lads in the band all looked, the drummer made suggestions that she rebuffed with professional ease. I was her target, her fun-time plaything, a little light relief before show-time. Our dressing rooms adjoined. She'd left her door wide open on purpose, feather boa and sparkles and a little shiny string. I was unprepared, scared, looked down, afraid I'd turn to salt, folding myself outside-in so no one could see me. Long before she'd stopped toying with me I was already a million miles away, boxed off and hiding in the imaginary room I'd escape to every time I was out of my comfort zone.

Birmingham nightclub

Ike and Tina Turner – 'Nutbush City Limits'; Thin Lizzy – 'Whisky in the Jar';
Free – 'Wishing Well'; Nazareth – 'This Flight Tonight'

Age seventeen, I bought a boot-making kit from an ad in the back of *Melody Maker* and built myself a pair of flimsy suede knee-length numbers that laced all the way up the front. They had long fringes dangled in a ring around each knee, to which I added beads to make them dance and flick as I pranced about. They took ages to put on and were the butt of dressing-room jokes. The soles were made from bits of lino. They were thin and gave no grip; they'd slide around all over the stage, forcing me to remain rooted to the spot or else end up on my arse. Inspired by Zal Cleminson (guitarist with the Alex Harvey Band, who painted his face like a cat-suited Joker), I bought grease paint and made myself up like a clown from a second-rate circus. On every gig, at the halftime break, I'd slip into 'clown mode' and, with the band peddling the opening riff to 'Jungle Rock', I'd re-emerge, dancing in from the back of the room, through the open-mouthed and by now drunk audience, shaking a pair of maracas I'd fashioned from two washing-up-liquid bottles stuffed with dried peas. An alarming vision of a demented clown clad in a painter's boilersuit and two-tone Docs.

Because Mom was such a fabulous seamstress, I pushed her to make me new and ever-more ludicrous outfits every few weeks, setting her increasingly impossible tasks to create slim-fitting jumpsuits out of old workwear and second-hand flying suits to ape the skintight glamour of Ziggy, Alice and Eno. No matter how stupid my ideas were, Mom always delivered, never let me down. My performances grew more theatrical every week. I experimented with reciting poetry on stage (off-the-cuff rubbish) while shredding images torn from the tabloids – shallow politicking on the fly, all image, no content. The band didn't like it so I dropped it. We went back to playing strictly covers only, and I withdrew the 'art'.

During this brief period of flirting with gender, sexuality and just having out-and-out fun I was influenced by the cultural icons I identified with: Ziggy, Eno, Alice, Steve Harley, the Droogs from *A Clockwork Orange*. The one who was head and shoulders above them all though was Zal – something about that unfazed clown-face grin chilled me, made me want to live in his world, in his head, walk in his shoes, see through his eyes, be him – pulling cool shapes in his sleek bodysuit, with that incongruous iconic rock guitar (a fabulous cherry-red SG!). When glam rock was in the charts – making money and making girls scream – it was deemed kind of OK for a boy to send out mixed messages about his preferences as long as he kept it on stage. It was obviously not OK on the streets of a conservative little country town, though, so I reserved it for weekends and gigs until I liked how it felt too much to hide it. You'd have to ask my mates how they felt about me turning up at the pub in jewellery and make-up, but that happened a lot later, and I was too far gone to care.

Jumpsuit, 1970s

The Sensational Alex Harvey Band – 'Faith Healer'

We were on a typical night out, driving pitch-black back roads between the fields, pub-crawling. My mate Haggis at the wheel of his Ford, a car full of the usual faces, out on the lash. I was in the back seat, pissed, head lolling back, staring at the stars, cheap stereo cranked up to distortion, pumping out something hard and heavy – Motörhead, or something German. Haggis said, 'Hey, check this out.'

He killed the headlights – no streetlights in the countryside, total blackout – then he floored the accelerator and chuckled. Everybody in the car started yelling: 'Turn the lights back on you twat! You'll kill us!'

But not me. Nobody noticed me smiling, lost in the numbed-out bliss of booze and metal, willing on the end for the first (but not the last) time, whispering, 'Take me now, Lord. I'm truly happy and I don't want to wake up tomorrow.'

Worcestershire, between the fields

Amon Düül II – *Amon Düül II*; Robert Calvert – *Captain Lockheed and the Starfighters*; the Rolling Stones – *Goats Head Soup*; Deep Purple – *Made in Japan*; Stevie Wonder – *Talking Book*; The Who – *Quadrophenia*; Roxy Music – *For Your Pleasure*; Steve Miller Band – *The Joker*; Roxy Music – *Stranded*

Had my first drunk blackout aged seventeen at an art school party. Came round momentarily to watch myself trying to eat a turd I was being offered as a sausage. Ended the party wrapped around the porcelain, white Levi's streaked from the waist down like a butcher's apron.

Stourbridge Art College

The Isley Brothers – 3+3; Sly and the Family Stone – 'Fresh'; Hall and Oates – 'She's Gone'

On 1 November 1974, the radio broadcast music from another planet.

Kraftwerk sounded like outsiders. 'Autobahn' was the calling card of a band playing by its own rules. The sound they made referenced nothing but itself, and I loved that. They were from Germany, a country whose music I'd come to know as original, extreme and underground, thanks to those nights under the covers listening to Peel. He fed us the voice of Berlin, a fortress of creativity marooned in a grey Eastern Bloc ocean, where artists exiled themselves voluntarily to escape the mediocrity of Western pop. When I thought of Berlin, I imagined a city where people smelled different, dressed dark and wild, and were committed to being *deadly serious* about everything they did. It scared me.

Autobahn was my bridge into that culture. It was made with instruments I couldn't imagine or afford, so there was no point in me even trying to emulate it. Just listen and imagine. In my head I was *only a guitarist*, condemned to play music from the past. Kraftwerk generated sounds from the future. The nearest planet I had been to was the one inhabited by the mutant voice of Walter Carlos's 'March from *A Clockwork Orange*', a soundscape I'd fallen in love with the second I heard it. These sounds were new but felt like home. I wanted to live on their planet, but it was a long, long way from Bewdley. How the hell could I make sounds like that? I didn't know anyone who could show me. When 'Autobahn' came on the radio, something extraordinary happened. It was revolutionary, a signal that a new direction in music had broken out. A rocket ship was waiting to take us to that other planet, but there was no room for pale imitators.

One Sunday in March 1975, I'm winding down in my bedroom, listening to Annie Nightingale on the BBC, when she puts on Tangerine Dream's 'Rubycon, Part One' and the sound stops me dead. I sit there, motionless, head left the building, floating in succulent German chemical soundscapes. This music was from the same tribe as Kraftwerk, Hawkwind, György Ligeti, *2001: A Space Odyssey*, tripped-out electric soul. Seventeen minutes later, she lifts the needle off the record. 'My God! The *whole* of one side of an album!' I'm electrified, shaking, open-mouthed at the barefaced *balls* she had to do that. Never heard a BBC DJ play more than one track off an album before. OK, this album has only two tracks ('Rubycon', parts one and two), but it still blew me away that she would play *the whole of one side*, no fades, no conforming to rules. That day Annie demonstrated you *had to break rules* if you wanted to turn people on. That one, seventeen-minute broadcast whispered in my ear, 'Step outside the box, little boy,' and I loved her for that.

For me, it put her up there with John Peel. But as the thrill of the message in the moment cooled, reality was already taking back the wheel, chuckling through its teeth, 'You don't have a clue what to do, do you?' (yet).

The bedroom above the kitchen, 1974-75

Kraftwerk – 'Autobahn'

Back in the band, our luck changed. We got a residency playing only our own music at a pub in Brierley Hill, run by two brothers who took a shine to us. We packed the place out with crowds of hairies, eager to see us. One memorable night, after taking a ton of money on the door, the brothers hugged us: 'Lads, when you're famous, don't forget us!'

They had big plans – started booking bigger venues, promised to take us with them. We transferred from sell-out nights at the pub to first on the bill at the Brierley Hill Civic Hall – the biggest gig of our lives. Trapeze headlined that night, it was the zenith of Talisman Wood's career – sharing a changing room with musicians who had actually toured America and had a *real American conga player* whose belly wobbled up and down in sync with its master's groove.

We were going places, people liked our songs, paid money to hear us play them. The endless, depressing weekends playing covers in working men's clubs were over. I felt a new impetus to write songs – we had a reason now, an audience hungry to hear us. I felt strong, clear, focused. I could feel opinions forming, had something to say at last. It was like the cork had been taken out of the bottle, and I was set free. The gap between us and faces on the TV was getting shorter. We were closing in on the prize, getting ready to cross over to the other side. I started planning to buy new equipment, researching, expanding my knowledge, feeding off this new surge in electricity.

Then something happened, I don't know what.

The brothers called one night with bad news – they'd have to stop booking bands, there would be no more gigs at the pub, or anywhere for us with them. They'd lost a mint on the Civic Hall gig and suddenly we were alone again, naked in a world that didn't want our music. The light flickered and died. We were back playing covers in working men's clubs.

Brierley Hill, mid-1970s

Most of our gig money had gone into buying a van. Then a bigger one. Then a PA and lights, and we had hired roadies who brought their girlfriends who made us look good. The band had been gigging every weekend, earning decent money, all of which went straight back into running the band, and for the five years that we remained together none of us had a weekend off, nor a Christmas nor New Year's Eve. We were always working, doing it for the band ... very occasionally for 'fun'.

Once a week, we rehearsed 'loud' in a community centre in the middle of a housing estate over in Kidderminster. We'd learn new covers in Pete's front room (occasionally we'd try new songs from me and Mont). Pete's hobby was making homemade wine – he had gallons of the stuff all over the house. Favourite Aunty had previously introduced me to the afterglow of an evening on her homemade wine, so I had to see if Pete's brew was up to scratch. The trouble is, that once I started I just couldn't stop, and I would get progressively more drunk until I couldn't play any more and the rehearsal had to be abandoned. Pete would stick on blues records that sounded like old man's dust to me. John Mayall, John Lee Hooker, Savoy Brown, Chicken Shack. Couldn't stand them – not the sounds and definitely not the songs: 'Take it off or find me another bottle!' (I got drunk a lot at Pete's.)

Then, eventually, as always happened, I was worn down and drawn in. The blues hooked me and it was inevitably the Groundhogs who did it. The track that reeled me in was 'Groundhog' off *Split* – a song I'd deliberately ignored for years. The guitar and voice wouldn't let me go – still hasn't. I remain a devoted disciple.

We siphoned off a few quid from buying vans and PAs and bought a day in a basement studio under a music shop in Worcester. The engineer seemed disappointed and pushed for time when he heard our songs, one each from me and Mont. Mine was vaguely 'rock', based on a droning string with a melody that moved against it. I didn't have a clue what to sing, how to express myself, or even that I had anything to express, so I wrote 'Self Conscience Pomp':

> *Go tell all the nation how to see,*
> *Go tell (something, something) about being free*

And then something, something about something ... with a *guitar solo*.

I recall Mont's song was much more sophisticated, the lyrics were about 'food'. Having had the confidence in the sound of my own voice knocked out of me by cousin Ian, I tried other people's voices. Ian Anderson of Jethro Tull (circa 'Love Story') was my flavour of the month back then.

We paid for enough time to cut the two songs live, no overdubs, before we were booted back out onto the street. Dazed, we wondered if it had actually happened – a huge build up of expectation, with a massive anticlimax (the pattern of future recording sessions). I don't remember much of what happened to the tape we were left clutching – did it get sent somewhere? Did someone turn it down? How many record labels did we try, and which ones? I left it to someone else, because I didn't have a clue what to do with it. There was a dense cloud of mystery surrounding how you got a record deal. I could only imagine as far as making a recording, because that's what I'd been shown. No one had told me what you do next, and I didn't think to ask the Guru. None of the local rock stars ever dropped into the pub to pass on their experience – they'd all buggered off and left the rest of us to work it out for ourselves, which we never did. After the recording session, we went back to playing covers and never tried that hard to break out again.

When I eventually moved away to art school in Cardiff I travelled back every Friday to rehearse, missing out on all the student action and leaving my beloved girlfriend to party in my absence. It was in Pete's front room in 1975 where I recorded our last band meeting. A four-man breakdown in real time caught on C120 – it was so raw I based my thesis around it. Mont and Paul wanted us to focus on becoming a better covers band – we'd grown lazy in keeping up with the current chart sounds; and I'd lost interest. They wanted to play better cabaret clubs, for better money. Their argument was that we were never going to be discovered doing our own material (this was a fair point; it was rubbish), but we could still slip in the odd original song when it was appropriate. They figured we'd stand a better chance of being 'discovered' by a record label if we played the top cabaret clubs instead of the places we played, at the bottom of the pile.

The band had peaked and was in decline. Pete and I were in agreement that we'd had enough of covers, so we argued for dropping them altogether to focus on strengthening our own material. And that's where it ended. Mont and Paul formed a better covers band that played better cabaret clubs for better money and did well for years; Pete (who had a few years on us) took voluntary redundancy as a metallurgist at British Steel, bought a tractor with his severance pay, slipped his vintage SG Junior under the bed, and became a contented farm contractor. I headed back to Cardiff in search of a band and a drink.

In search of a drink

Savoy Brown – 'Vicksburg Blues'

I thought I was such a star until I went to my first art college.

It was clear from day one on the foundation course that everybody knew more than I did. What the hell had I been taught at school? Somehow I made up for all the art education I had never been given, and thanks to the luxury of two years on the foundation course I crammed my way up to being 'not bad' by the age of eighteen, just in time to apply for university.

It was the most fantastic two years of my life, just making art all day, every day.

There was just one scary glitch, though, when Dad found he couldn't afford to support my studies any more and it looked like I was going to have to leave and get a job – but Favourite Aunty turned fairy godmother and pulled cash out of thin air. She discovered that years ago our town guild had set aside a pot of money to fund the education of the 'apprentices' of the town. No one had called on it for decades, so the guild very generously gave me what I needed to complete my studies.

In the process of getting a more rounded art education I'd also got myself a girlfriend – a biker with her own set of leathers. I was attracted to her wild energy, but was sure she would turn me down if I asked her out, so I asked her to sing in our band instead. I had no idea if she could even sing, but I fancied her like mad, and something about her electricity said 'dark horse'. I told everyone in the band to leave her alone, no one was to hit on her and everyone stuck to our agreement until the night of that particular rehearsal when I got customarily drunk on Pete's homemade wine ...

After that we were inseparable. She introduced me to her Technicolor, widescreen world: Janis Joplin, Roxy (sans Eno), Ann Peebles, Bruce Lee, *Fritz the Cat*, *Emmanuelle*, *Serpico*, *Midnight Cowboy*, *Straw Dogs* and, most important of all, *Woodstock*. We saw bands in clubs all over Birmingham, riding night buses piloted by stone-faced drivers protected by metal cages. After two years at art college in Stourbridge, the girl decided that Cardiff was the place to do her degree, so I followed like a lost dog, ignoring every tutor's advice to pursue a career in the much more sensible 'graphic arts'.

Through her I'd discovered Fine Art was where the fun was. Shock of shocks, we both got in to Cardiff. Early on, the college sent me to an obscure annex called 'the Space Workshop' where I was to become a part of a unique department called 'the Third Area' (based on the philosophies of the Black Mountain College in North Carolina). I was taught by two extraordinary tutors who helped me find something locked away deep inside myself that I never knew existed. They gave me a space to play and access to four-track tape machines, quadraphonic sound systems, theatre lighting, video cameras, film cameras, microphones, performance art, installation art and a suitcased EMS Synthi (exactly like the one Eno used with Roxy on the *Whistle Test*) to take home whenever I wanted. It was like being back in my wardrobe again and yet, here in the Space Workshop, it was like that all day, every day.

For the next three years, I cut loose in paradise.

Stourbridge to Cardiff

Ann Peebles – 'I Can't Stand the Rain'; Janis Joplin – 'Ball and Chain'

Things started out well at university but soon went downhill. Entering college as a star – in my head at least – I hit the ground running then lost the plot. I didn't have a clue what I was supposed to do and was hauled up before a tribunal that read me the last rights. With the band at home over, a stalled feeling was starting to spread like weeds through my teenage life. It was looking like the boy from the Midlands was on his way back, when the one young tutor who was loyal to me (Chris Monger) intervened to buy me some time to prove I deserved to stay. Perhaps it was the twee little installation I finally built or just Chris's powers of persuasion, but I managed to scrape through to the second year.

Everything changed that summer. The penny dropped and I started building artworks out of industrial waste like my life depended on it. Year 2 and this new-found drive and direction landed me a prime spot in the sculpture department, along with my drinking buddies under the sceptical watch of sculpture tutors who couldn't believe they'd let this weirdo into their manly fraternity. It was all welding, casting, drilling, and hauling heavy stuff.

I set about building man-traps with broken glass, shards of wood, death-trap corridors, mazes, nightmare spaces. This evolved into Zen gardens, where I ritually executed stick figures, studied tribal ceremonies and shamanic fetishes. I built a large hut with a floor of sand and a Japanese paper sky where I worked all day, then set about setting fire to stuff. The dean paid a visit to praise my work, but asked if I would consider not starting fires indoors. I was flying.

Vivid nightly dreams were transformed into reality by day. I began working with early video, black and white ghost images. I'd create installations with quadraphonic sound, build ceremonial pits that incorporated sawdust, candles, wax, crudely painted scraps, sound systems and video monitors. I wrapped myself in bandages (begged for from hospitals), painted myself red and yellow, pinned on button-hole carnations, built ham-cloth chapels for the marriage of tiny bones, wrapped animal bones in delicate coloured wires and wedding rings. I bagged myself in plastic, wrote stories about animals that could talk and which stalked me – while walking on two legs. I filled display cases with fictitious ceremonial artefacts. The speed at which I was producing art was limited only by the speed at which I could work. Everything was possible. My muse was on fire.

And then the girlfriend left me.

I couldn't blame her. My prospects weren't great. I was playing in another cabaret band; I'd only just managed to not get kicked out of college, and I was still very much a small-town boy fantasising he was something more. I'd spent my short lifetime judging myself by my intentions – the rest of the world was judging me by my actions (and they were only just starting to bear fruit).

She found somebody older, with drive and vision.

I ground to a halt. Downed tools. Devastated.

Cardiff, 1976

Stevie Wonder – *Songs in the Key of Life*; the Rolling Stones – *Black and Blue*;
Steve Miller Band – 'Fly Like an Eagle'; Tom Petty and the Heartbreakers – 'American Girl'

I drank to escape, but also to stop myself being *ordinary*.

I knew that if I remained the way I'd been, I'd be condemned to working in the factory for the rest of my life. So I drank.

The more I drank the more unfettered my thoughts became, so I carried on drinking, adding a pen and bits of paper to my night trawling, documenting everything that the booze let loose in my head. It worked.

Straight, I was ordinary. Drunk, I wasn't.

I did a deal. Drunk me did the research every night. He then handed over those results to straight me who'd turn it into the *real stuff* that would go on to help secure me a first in Fine Art. That process gave me a practical solution to being handicapped by being nice and ordinary and timid and too afraid to follow through. Drink removed inhibitions and I liked me better that way. I wanted the drunk me around all the time, so I did my best to let him loose whenever I could.

I was hooked. I never did drugs for fear of becoming an addict, blind to the fact that I was already a full blown alcoholic at seventeen.

Staggering out of a Margate pub two years earlier, a little kid had run out of the night and stuck a flyer in my hand before disappearing. The flyer was all about how alcohol causes brain damage.

'Bloody cheeky little shit!' I shouted as I lobbed it back at him.

When I was eighteen the guys two years above at university carried me home one night. One of them, Marty St James, told me, 'You need to slow down. You've got a drink problem!' It made me proud that at my tender age I was able to shock them. I lost the use of my legs that night for twenty-four hours. Twenty-fours spent laughing as I crawled around the flat, shaking.

One night, after tortuous days of being unable to get over the ex, I became so depressed I got ragged beyond my customary 'staggering' drunk and decided to end it. The road to Butetown was low enough on hope to be perfect, a romantically glamour-less place to die. I was returning to an empty flat every night, damp, cold and desperately alone. One second I was stumbling home, the next I'd had that 'one clear thought': 'Cross the road without looking.' A fast car would do the rest. In that fraction of second I let go, gave up, turned left and stepped out into the road and the oncoming lights.

Cardiff in the dark

When the girlfriend left me my world collapsed. I couldn't make art any more and left Cardiff, instinctively drawn back home to that small backwater town I had been desperate to leave. There I discovered the family waiting for me was completely different to the one I'd escaped from.

They listened, gave me space, watched me slip out to the pub with my old schoolmates to anaesthetise myself with booze, and said nothing. They heard me stagger home drunk every night and never judged me. Just gave safe harbour and a gentle space for me to gradually open my shell.

I was shocked to find parents who were cool, a Dad who *understood me* and a grandmother who let me into the wildest secret of all, that she'd been 'young once too'. I never looked at my family in the same light again. They loved me, could actually see me, and I'd never known how much they cared until I thought I'd lost everything that was important to me – my girlfriend. The memory of this astonishing discovery has stuck with me ever since, but I re-wrote history when it came to some crucial facts about my musical lineage. Twenty years into the future, when journalists asked, 'Do you come from a musical family?' I told them, 'No,' imagining myself as a gifted freak, the first in family history to buck the trend and against all odds find escape through music.

But that's not the truth.

Grandma had a beautiful singing voice. She sang in the church choir and played piano at home for the family. Granddad sang music-hall songs to me all the time ('To Market, to Market, with My Brother Jim', 'Underneath the Arches', 'Daisy, Daisy').

Mom (their daughter) sang in the church choir from a young age, with a reputation for having one of the most beautiful voices in town. I grew up listening to her singing hymns in the kitchen on Sundays and carols round the house at Christmas. She made a sound so beautiful, so confident and pure it scared me. Mom could've had a career as a professional singer but she reserved that talent exclusively for solo performances in the kitchen.

Every summer, Favourite Aunty took me to singsongs around the fires of scout camps deep in the forest. To this day, their infectious roundels are earworms to me.

Dad could've been a drummer, should've been a poet. Beats still spill out of him, and when he writes letters it's with a natural, unassuming, incisive style I can only dream of. It remains one of the greatest crimes that he spent most of his life working in the factory, and yet without his 'patronage of the arts' I'd be working at the factory too. It was Dad who gave me my first guitar, bought me my first electric and traded his car for something he could help to transport our band equipment in. It was Dad who made sure music was on the radio at home all day, every day, and on in the car every time we drove together. He bought me my first record player when I was ten, my first two singles, 'Build Me Up Buttercup' (The Foundations) and 'Race with the Devil' (The Gun). He brought records home that had a 'sound' which stood out, picked up on bands that passed me by and kept me in touch with what was happening. Dad had got me started and kept me going. He saw something in me that I didn't, and that's an amazing thing to do for a kid who didn't have a clue.

I've spent years carping on about the local superstars who never helped us kids with our music when we were desperate for guidance, whilst every day my dad was always there, helping me to keep going (as well as being swift with criticism and ready with an opinion to conceal his pride in his son).

For the record, I come from a *very* musical family.

Bewdley

By the end of the week at home I was ready to return to Wales, pack my stuff up, leave art school and get a job. At least I felt strong enough to walk streets still infected with the memories of a relationship I never thought would end (never once thought to sing about it, though). Back at college, sitting in the shaman's hut I'd built and moved into down in the sculpture department, ankle-deep in sand, I reviewed the quaint little objects I'd made in the life before she left. It all looked like valueless crap now. How sweet, how safe – and nothing to do with the *real world*. What had possessed me to waste time on such childishness? I sat there in the gloom, angry at every tiny detail of that hut, feeling nothing but disdain for art and the tutors who thought I was worth teaching. I wanted to set fire to it all, walk away sniggering and not look back. An hour passed, I didn't move, listening to the sound of laughter outside, life continuing, business as usual, oblivious to my pain. Another hour passed. There was a collection of wooden balls in front of me; it was a game I'd been working on before the crash. They waited, half-painted, watching me to see what I'd do next, holding their breath. By rights I should've shovelled the whole lot into the bin and got out of there. Instead I decided to finish them first. Picking up the first ball, turning it around, it told me what colour it wanted to be and I dutifully obeyed – my shitty life turned around.

A hut in the sculpture department – Cardiff School of Art

Eddie and the Hot Rods – 'Do Anything You Wanna Do'

Between 1975 and 1978, the best parties in Cardiff were over at the Punk House, a condemned building full of art students that someone collected rent on. It sat rotting above the rag 'n' bone shop on Lower Cathedral Road. Cathedral Road 'proper' was lined with grand Victorian homes, so large that some were run as small hotels. They were genuinely posh, nestling behind lines of leafy London planes. The other end – Lower Cathedral Road – was strictly low-rent, one rung above the gutter.

I aspired to live in the Punk House and always hated leaving at the end of a party, but it wasn't the kind of place you could live with most girls. The fact that I (then) had a girlfriend ruled me out of ever living there: bare floorboards in every room, minimal furniture, the bathroom smelled of fermented piss, soaked into old *NME*s strewn about the floor, which were a kind of rock 'n' roll litmus paper. My mates in the sculpture department lived there – two lads from up north, who rolled their own, loved wood, hitched up their sleeves and hauled entire trees into college every week. One of them brought a battered Martin acoustic all the way from home, a crazy thing to do with something so precious. I'd never even seen a real Martin, let alone one that was left lying around a condemned shithole to be fallen on by drunks. He was a fantastic guitar picker: he could play all the hard John Martyn bits note perfect and did an impressive version of 'May You Never' without thinking anything of it – a mere party trick. Hacking lumps of wood was his real thrill. The fact was he had more talent than me as a guitarist and yet wasn't at all interested in being a musician made me feel like such a loser. Like everyone else in the house, he slept with all his food to protect it from rodents and random scroungers.

On the rare occasions that nothing was happening, the merest suggestion of a party would start an all-nighter at the Punk House. My mate Marcus was the other northerner, who spent all the second year building a 'Cow Table' with country scenes carved between its cow legs. All year he worked on that thing, though I don't know if he ever finished it (he called me once out of the blue, years later, when I was living in Romford and Underworld were in the news. He'd given up sculpture, retrained as an English teacher and moved back up north where he had a sideline as a respected dealer in punk records). These two were my inseparable drinking buddies, we could be found singing round the piano in the Old Arcade or slumped over pints at the Westgate, drifting into oblivion on a sea of Brains dark. The old drunks were always pleased to see us. They took a shine to us and we included them in all our rounds, so they tolerated our art bollocks. All this time I kept a wad of paper in my jeans and a pen for when the beer inspired me. Most mornings I'd wake to find a fresh stack of drawings flung across the bedroom floor, ideas for installations that would eventually bag me my degree. The booze was my sweetest muse.

There may have been a couple living right at the top of the Punk House, but we didn't see them much, though there was always a lot of giggling coming from behind their door. There was a tiny room next to theirs at the top of the stairs, where my mate Les lived. He used to live on the other side of town when he had a girlfriend, but she left him, automatically qualifying him for a room in the coolest house in the city. Les was one of the *alternative* crew to which I belonged – 'the Space Workshop' lot, the outsiders from the 'Third Area', the weird ones. He was a filmmaker of extremely long 'art-films' and a creator of cerebral performances that involved the wearing of coloured robes and the strategic banging of percussion. I liked him, he was part of our extended drinking circle, an 'OK bloke', though he stole the girl I fancied after I pointed out her uncanny resemblance to my favourite *Blue Peter* presenter.

Les took pity on me and I was invited to share his tiny room up in the roof. Our beds were made from two fire doors rescued from a skip, resting on house bricks for legs. Every morning we would squat on our doors and cook breakfast over a one-bar electric fire. In the gloom of the tiny landing outside the room, I stored a sealed jar of bones from the last Sunday roast I'd had with the girlfriend. She'd since moved in with her new bloke and was living in the house next door. It hurt for a week, but I soon drank that feeling away and lost myself in art.

There was another important occupant of the Punk House. A transient who came and went, and nobody ever knew where or why. He'd show up either fresh faced in a new tweed suit or sock-less and unwashed, still wearing the same suit and looking dazed. The rumour was he came from a wealthy family, had a drink problem and that they'd soon come looking for him, drag him back to rehab, dry him out and put him back on his feet. Then he'd run away and start the whole thing over again. During his bombed-out phases he would turn up at the Punk House. I think he'd been hiding here since before our time. When he was sober he was lucid and bright; when he was 'on it' I'd find him alone, sunk into a ravaged armchair in the middle of the barren front room staring motionless into the fireplace. 'There's a mouse living in there,' he told me once. 'In that hole. I saw him stick his head out. Don't ever light a fire, he's my friend.'

Looking back on it, he was the guy I identified with the most. It took me another twenty years to work out why.

Abandoned

Sex Pistols – 'Anarchy in the UK', 'Pretty Vacant', 'God Save the Queen'

BACK IN THE BAND

Bursting into spontaneous laughter.

Early driving in the sun to clear the head
I loop back past the sign that reads
WELCOME TO ESSEX.

Gets me every time.

Fire! Orchestra – *Enter*

As I recovered from being ditched by the love of my life, the first real guitar of my life walked in. One of the young lecturer fellows offered me his old electric, needed a quick sale (something to do with a girlfriend). It came in a really old battered case with squeaky latches, like a family heirloom, and as he opened the lid I stifled a gasp.

'How much do you want?'

'I've been thinking. I don't know that I want to sell it any more.'

'How much?'

'This is a really special guitar for me, the first good guitar I ever owned.'

'How much, then?'

'Hundred and fifty?'

Even in its sad, decayed condition it was worth double.

'I'll give you one-twenty – final offer.'

'Done!'

It was all I had, cleaned me out, but I knew I'd just bought the crown jewels. I didn't even have to hear it plugged in – just looking at it I could hear its voice loud and clear. Walnut brown, peeling varnish, metalwork corroded and fabulous – it smelled like the history of rhythm and blues. A 1959 Guild Starfire, original Grovers, twin P90s and a Bigsby tailpiece, this guitar was everything I'd ever wanted and it had just walked into my life and *adopted me*. But oh, when I plugged it in … hallelujah! The first truly great guitar I ever owned, a real problem solver, a guitar I'd be turning to for solutions into the twenty-first century.

I never thought I'd own a guitar as mature as this one, so I cherished every second that I played it. That guitar has never disappointed anyone. I saved some money and took it to Dave Dearnley (the sinewy frontman of local bar band Eager Beaver who always wore a shark's-tooth earring). He'd just started building and refurbishing guitars and handled my precious child with a respect I recognised as the mark of a great luthier. He dismantled it, cleaned it, stripped off its decrepit trench coat and fitted a fresh set of wheels – cream bodywork with ivory trim, inspired by a photograph I had of Brian Jones at Madison Square Garden. Connoisseurs would step back and whistle, studio engineers would nod in admiration when they heard it, and I'd feel happy every time I played it.

The sculpture department, Cardiff School of Art

I found him hanging around the stairs outside the damp little flat she left me in down in Butetown. Suit jacket and skinny jeans, walnut 335 – the real thing, but left-handed – with a Beatle cut and a cheeky eye.

'Are you Karl? I'm Ross, but you can call me *Ross*.'

Ross Grainger was a fast-witted Welshman, Cardiff through-and-through, and easily the best never-to-be-famous songwriter in the city. He turned up on the first day I'd woken up without a band since I was eleven. He didn't want to do covers, only original material. The bass player from a cabaret band I wintered with pointed him in my direction. I'd been making a fortune with that band, playing clubs up in the valleys through Christmas and New Year. Men would queue up to stack tenners on the stage to buy one more tune for their girls. I got kicked out of the band as soon as they worked out how much more they'd each make without me – the singer prided himself on his pulling power.

I was sick of playing covers, and wasn't all that good at it, to be honest, but Ross made it clear he just wanted to play the songs we wrote. He loved Americana, picked guitar like Appalachian moonshine, and introduced me to Neil Young, Little Feat, Dylan and The Band. He hooked me on the thrill of lock-ins in basements of after-hours record shops that dealt in under-the-counter bootlegs.

'This guy's all right, he's with me,' he'd smile. He'd usually slip in a joke about the English, before adding '... but this one's OK.'

At the end of every Jack and Southern Comfort all-nighter, as hallucinations began to crawl the walls, we'd stagger into sunrise clutching one more reel of tape filled with new songs, before wrapping it in tinfoil and brown paper and slipping it between the ruby lips of the nearest post box safe in the belief that *this was the one*.

Cardiff

Little Feat – *Electrif Lycanthrope (Be-Bop Deluxe)*

The Jack and Southern Comfort ran out at 2 a.m. Ross and I had filled another reel of tape with songs. The light was thin and flat as the sun began to rise. Reluctantly we agreed it really was time to stop. Lying half-clothed and stinking on a mattress in the spare room sleep came fast and deep, but when the wake-up call came three hours later I went into the shakes as a cheese-wire was slowly drawn through my head.

A woman's voice like a school-run mother was singsonging my name, face peering round the door, already dressed and smiling. It should've been a pleasant start to the day, Ross's wife was pretty and kind, but in my condition the wake-up was grotesque – all I could see was the face of a pantomime dame. Without thinking, I got up fast and regretted it, instantly nauseous, unable to stomach even toothpaste, but managing a sip of water while declining the milky tea on offer for fear of immediate regurgitation.

Slipping into the smell of a familiar overcoat I followed her out the door to the bus stop. Did she notice me shaking, holding onto anything that didn't move like a man on the deck of a rolling ship? Resting my forehead against a concrete fencepost at the bus stop, its cool rough texture made me feel a little better – a sweet kiss from an old friend. On the back seat of the bus I focused on her voice, a sound that came from the outside of a glass bubble. It was the only fixed point I could latch onto, everything else was in constant motion, swirling around me. I felt poisoned and I couldn't stop shaking. Her voice sounded nice, and 'nice' was what I needed, the antidote to another night on the lash. Halfway into town, I began to chuckle.

'You've perked up,' she giggled.

'Do you see anything odd about the inside of this bus?' I dribbled.

'No. Just people going to work.'

'Oh!' I chuckled, as thousands of fluorescent spiders scrambled over everyone but me and her.

At the bus stop by Cardiff Castle I waved her goodbye and headed down Queen Street to college. The precinct rippled like the back of an enormous scaly reptile as spiders big as dogs scuttled into alleys to escape me. This was getting interesting.

On a bus to Cardiff

Neil Young – 'Like a Hurricane'

THE THING'S NOT MINE

On a train, on a seat, sat no one. A folded newspaper in the place of a person. A woman gets on, looks at me, looks at the newspaper, then back at me. I shake my head discreetly to let her know the thing's not mine. Stooping and flipping it open in anticipation of distraction she recoils to see a feather lying in the crook of a crumpled cigarette packet. I don't let her see me watching, not wishing to embarrass her as she flops it onto the floor. Something voodoo about the combination makes me withdraw my feet not wishing to touch it in case it's bad magic.

Alexis Zoumbas

THIS TIME LAST SUNDAY

Strange to take to the stage without my brother, without the safety
net constructed from years together. No familiar glances, dances or
cycles of beats. Strange to greet the day without him and yet,
the thrill of a high wire without a net feels right.

Kraftwerk – 'Europe, Endless'

DUMP THE DARK STUFF WITH THE BINS

Knee-deep in bad news radio morning, a heavy sheet of negativity
drawn over our nation again, again.

Some mornings I can laugh off this obsession,
some days it feels like I'm going down with global
dark-stuff flu. Held down, feel the bad vibes, beaten into submitting
to the gloom, infected with fear and suspicion.

I don't seek negativity, don't crave it to justify my
insecurities. I gravitate towards positivity, people who raise
themselves up, face towards the light.
Spring bursts out the ground and does the same thing - it must be
natural. Being pumped daily with bad news is against nature,
marathon running in lead boots.

I take the bins out, crunch through morning frost in the sun, buds erupting to meet the light. Knuckles numb, I slip a camera out and look around, see the world for the first time, again, again, count my blessings, sober, still alive, shower off this dark radio dust and go in search of the bright stuff. In the back of a car, east London bound, production rehearsal, pre-Dubnobass ... tour. The company of friends, old and new, riggers, truckers, sound and lighters.

All pulling together to transmit good news ... people still coming together to celebrate what's good about people. Watching Essex out the window, slip past easy in the sun.

Goran Kajfeš Subtropic Arkestra – *The Reason Why, Vol. 2*

LIGHTS ON IN THE HOUSEFUL

I've been sat here all morning trying to write how I feel.

Body trashed like a hangover, but this smile in the mirror reminds me something good happened last night.

Howlin' Wolf – 'You'll Be Mine'

After art school, I should've moved to Berlin, like everyone I knew with any balls, but I was too scared. Berlin was too real for me and that put me back in my place – somewhere small and safe. Somewhere like Cardiff.

    I used to have a hunger to move on, but after art school I lost it. Like a full stop to a liberated phase of my life, I did one major exhibition that turned out to be my last. I was invited to be part of a group show for students who'd excelled that year, held at the Arnolfini in Bristol. I built an installation that was 'safe'; it fell some way short of 'pushing it'. A stained white boilersuit hung limply on a wooden thing in a white room like an industrial Jesus, underscored by the white-noise hiss of black and white TVs tuned to static. Every time I called in to check it, the gallery had turned the sound down, which pissed me off and made me want to stop working with galleries. Art, as far as I could see it, was too exclusive for what I needed. Galleries were too intimidating for the millions of people I wanted to reach, so I decided to make 'radio' my gallery. Music would become the sole art form through which I'd speak.

    Stop moving. Settle down. Start a band.

Bristol, 1979

Anita Ward – 'Ring My Bell'

Through the sale of his unfashionable records, the Guru had up-scaled to a large country pile set within its own parkland on the Welsh border. Arriving up the long curving drive in Ross's old Hillman Avenger the sheer opulence of his house made us burst out laughing. We'd never known anyone so rich who would invite us 'round for tea'. 'That god-awful punk has put music back twenty years!' he moaned, knocking back another vodka from a cut-glass tumbler and firing his shotgun at the squirrels in his oaks.

Castle Weir

Clifford T. Ward – 'New England Days'

We saw his ad in the Cardiff papers and found him behind the door of a remote cottage hidden away in a corner of the Ffawyddog on the hill above Crickhowell. Squeezing past a dismembered VW van, cowered by the smell of the outside privy, we were greeted by a hairy face: ''Ello, men. Cuppa tea?'

    And so it was two city boys found themselves clutching mugs of geological stains, huddled round an open fire as a drummer skinned up and assessed us through faraway eyes.

Up on the Ffawyddog

Nils Lofgren – 'Cry Tough'

After the Punk House, I'd upgraded to a rat and flea infested room in a house alongside the Taff, from where, one afternoon, Ross picked me up in his old Avenger and we drove north, leaving the oppressive monotony of the city behind, heading for the hills, for clean air and the sweet grass of the Ffawyddog. It was dark when we reached the cottage.

I don't remember our motive for being there. Maybe Ross was troubled about the way the band was going, all of us holed up every weekend for months in that primitive cottage on a steady diet of pot and magic mushrooms on toast (for some; rough cider for me). The alcohol drove me mad, leaving me to curse their hippy weed.

The kettle whistled on a loop, tea without milk, the rich soporific aroma of burning wood. Primeval and reassuringly good. We sat in silence, clutching mugs of hot black water, breathing in the woodsmoke of an open fire, watching pictures in the flames. It was strange to be there in the week, almost like we'd caught the house without its trousers, unprepared for our rude arrival: 'It's weird to see you guys here. What's up?'

'It's Karleeto's birthday!' Ross suddenly announced, breaking the deepening ice between us. 'Twenty-one!'

'Wow. Twenty-one!'

The drummer sounded almost normal as he said it, bursting into a genuine human smile, his shiny eyes framed by hair in multiple directions. 'I haven't got anything for you, man. I'm sorry, if I'd known ...' he trailed off. 'Wait a minute ...'

He disappeared into a back room where he dried the harvested storks of his personal crop and returned clutching an LP: 'Haven't heard this in years, used to love it, played it all the time when I lived in London. I was going out with this girl ... I've no idea if it even plays any more.'

He slipped the vinyl out, finger in the hole, thumb on the rim, with a respectful delicacy that I'd never seen in him before. Then he handed me the iconic sleeve, a lo-res image of a crotch shot, a pair of jeans with a working zip alluding to delights on the other side. Holding it for the first time, I felt the electricity of its dark lineage jumping up my fingers, whispering promises, offering fantasies of cool sleaze if I crossed the line, promises of magical dirt and night streets alive with twisted thrills. The sounds that came off the record were nostalgic, decadent, inappropriate for the two-fingered punk era we were living in, but I didn't care. All that punk shit was so serious, so angst ridden, try-hard, and most of it was theatrically fake.

The Stones rolled on, didn't give a toss. Their sepia-tinted, cigarettes-and-Jack-fuelled sound was reassuring – it held me like a baby in a soft warm blanket, a guilty pleasure, drug of choice. I could fall back into the ooze of languid guitars and let go. The Stones hit the sweet-spot, as I blissed out on something bottled, let myself drown in that one song going round and round, identifying with the sad and broken like that scene in the opium den from *Once Upon a Time in America* where Robert De Niro takes a hit on that sweet stuff and grins.

'Wild, wild horses couldn't drag me away ...'

Up on the Ffawyddog

IN BRUSSELS

For the past two nights I've been waking every hour.
A ragged and noisy head. My old familiar whispers,
'Come down the hole again.'

I've got vibrating skin, stinging body, blurry eyeball.
I'm getting tetchy, a long way from home.
Such a fine excuse for a flip out - impatience feasting on the cheese of exhaustion,
I'm justified and grandiose, but, look ... here comes the sun.
everything gets easier as the mood lifts us closer
to the time.

Boredoms — everything they ever did

SMILES AT AB

Sunlight hit the rooftops of Brussels as we ate breakfast remarking it was reminiscent of sunrise in San Francisco years ago where after watching T.O.W.I.E. all night we forgot where we were, disappointed to discover it wasn't Essex.

Slim Harpo – 'I Got Love if You Want It'

The studio in Cardiff was a thing from another time, decorated in the style of 'during the war': quaint and fake, like rationing was still going on. Classical columns lined the walls, fashioned from corrugated card, a dusty perfumed smell in the air clung to the back of your throat when you sang and stuck to your clothes for days. The musicians we'd pulled together for the session knew the engineer from prior experience. They sniggered as he excitedly drew me to one side and asked, 'Would like to see my photographs?'

He showed me pictures of blokes striking pseudo religious poses, lost in rapture, immersed in spiritual transcendence, gazing towards the heavens with doe eyes while squeezing fat candles. I politely declined, 'Perhaps another time.' He winced, deflated.

Clutching another set of precious tapes we made our escape. Hoping we had captured magic this time, we were energised by a new drive to go public with our songs. It was time to let the world hear how good we were. We wanted to see the lights beyond the edge of town, beyond Newport even, across the border into the badlands of England and right into the belly of the Beast. Scouring telephone directories for names we recognised we cold-called all the record companies we remembered from our favourite albums. Most of them told us, 'We don't do appointments, but if you send your tape …' We knew their tricks now. Pub legend had it that they copied your tape, got some other artist to cover it, called it their own and made a million. You were left with nothing. No way were we getting suckered by that one. They all got struck off the list as we assembled an impressive meeting schedule of two appointments.

We were off to London, where we'd knock on every door until someone let us in. It was going to be legendary. People would talk about it for years, like Dylan riding freight trains into Manhattan.

In the absence of a box car we chose the milk train – the night train, the slow ride to London that stopped everywhere and parked in sidings. We would be able to stretch out on the seats and sleep before hitting the streets fresh, just as the city was waking. We'd find a café, wash our faces, comb our hair, and then, fuelled on tea and fry-ups, we'd unleash our strut on a music industry so unprepared for our sound that they'd hail us as the next big thing and fight over our signatures.

Cardiff Central to London Paddington

Neil Young and Crazy Horse – *Rust Never Sleeps*

LAST NIGHT'S WOMAN

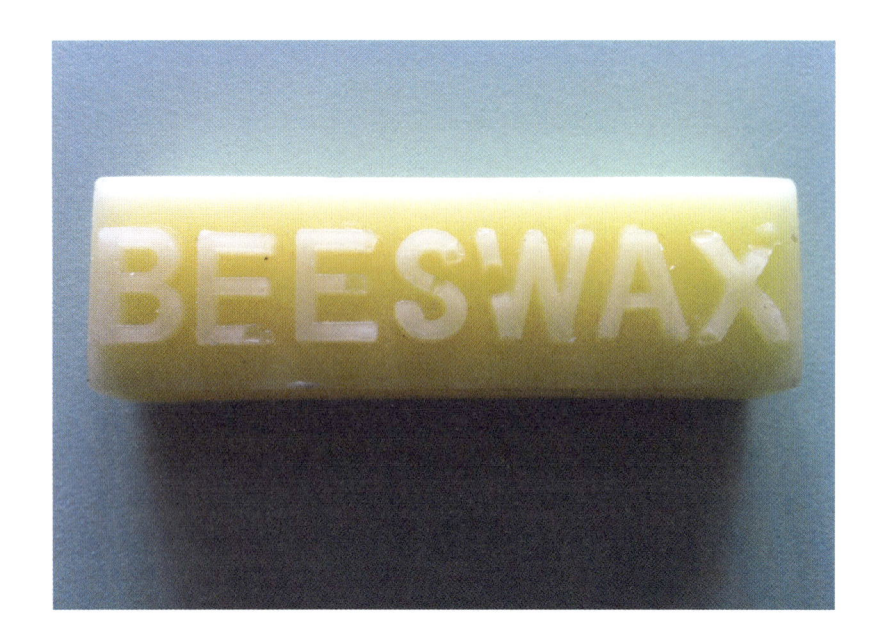

Last night's woman wore a giant bear, a fake fur barricade,
an enormous orb of fashion brown, a gargantuan hat.
She blocked out the light in the Albert Hall.
Was she there to watch them or just check her Instagram?
She stood up, turning round to see who was in tonight, left,
returned with no recognisable rhythm, mildly distracted by the music,
all the while clutching her cellphone like a lifeline.

Espen Eriksen Trio – *Never Ending January*

The train pulled into Paddington at 1 a.m. The plan had already turned to shit. The milk train was a myth. Two Billy No-Mates from Cardiff – local stars falling out of heaven, fresh meat for the dogs.

Walking the backstreets around Paddington station, rain was seeping through our clothes, cold and straight to the bone. London was strewn with strange dirt, the detritus of a foreign city piled at the edge of curbs. Drunks and night crawlers performed their rituals, dancing to a relentless rhythm. We were exposed. On the telly it had all looked so great, a glorious vibrant parade.

Shivering in the rain, London felt threatening and hungry. We were dog-tired, needing to be off the street, to get somewhere safe and get some sleep. Ross had the number of a mate who'd just moved up to London to be a roadie. He'd promised us a place to crash 'any time', so we found a phone box.

The lights were out, the receiver still warm, the acrid stench of cheap perfume.

A piss-puddled floor in which we paddled, huddled close for warmth and dialled.

'Oh ... damn!' said the voice on the other end.

'Well, the thing is, it's my brother's place and he doesn't want anyone just turning up.'

'But you said, "Any time".'

'Wait a minute ...'

Silence. Voices in the background. Hungry faces circling the phone box, hunched shoulders, fists in pockets.

'How long will you be?'

'About half an hour. Can't afford a taxi: we're walking.'

'No, I mean how long will you be staying? Y'see my brother really doesn't want you here.'

'He doesn't know us ... we're very clean.'

More mumbled voices, faces pressed up against the dirty glass, a boot kicked the door. 'Much longer, mate!?'

'OK, he says you can come and get warm, but you can't stay. You can have a tea if you like. We haven't got any milk.'

Notting Hill

The Stranglers – 'Peaches'

LOVED BOX

Glorious day,
Southend-on-Sea,
A stroll along the promenade,
Walking in rhythm with the melodies of East-End conversations.

Dog-walkers smile as we light up to see them,
Cut along pavements like seasoned skaters.
Families,
The old with the young,
Converse in cafés.

Casinos and online gambling,
Gleaming groomed motors cruise,
Fish 'n' chips,
Pots of tea,
Plates stacked high with doorsteps of crusty white buttered bread.
Life gets no better.

Sun Ra and his Arkestra – *To Those of Earth and Other Worlds Beyond*

CHOCOLATE RABBITS

Slipping away from the crowd I found you in a giant brush stroke.
A liquid arc (substance unknown),
Bold and confident.

Hunting heavy papers,
Everything's too delicate,
Too 'domestic' for what I got in mind.

Scratches on walls,
Perfect stains and scuffs.
The vibrant red dust of rust singing in the rain,
Succulent as beach pebbles.

In backstreet silence,
Two figures dressed in black,
Think no one's around,
Transform into musical notes,
To dance like crows over the cracks of empty pavements.

Change the Beat – *The Celluloid Records Story, 1979-1987*

At 3 a.m. we were ejected back onto the streets of Notting Hill. It wasn't posh back then; hardly a place to be lost after dark. We were hit on by drug dealers and junkies and shadowed by curb crawlers.

Our first appointment was at 10 a.m. so, with knuckles deep in our pockets, arms tight to our sides for warmth, we started walking, walking, wet and freezing, hunting warmth and shelter or a smile.

Around 5 a.m. we reached the rim of Soho. A little café appeared through the rain like a mirage on Charing Cross Road (it's still there). Bright lights, mirrors, high stools, Formica, a transistor radio playing something familiar. I remember the overwhelming presence of yellow.

We shuffled in, glancing back over our shoulders for wolves, rattling our change to count out what little we had. Yesterday's cakes and ready-filleds were watching us, fat and wrinkled behind glass, hopeful for a little company, looking for trade. A colossal Gaggia squatted and fizzed behind the counter. Clouds of steam billowed from its chromium bulk, rising in snakes that curled across the ceiling, falling as a warm, welcome mist. Ross and I found the two stools furthest from the door. The mirrored walls looked back at us, our sunken eyes set in faces ten years older than they'd been the day before. We said very little and made two teas last an hour.

101 Charing Cross Road, London

Little Feat – 'Willin'

APRIL

The spoon drops to the floor
No one outside the window
Voices
Flowers
Sugar in the bowl

Painting of a girl in a red dress and crown

Morning
Call
Everything in 3D

The Last Poets – 'Mean Machine Chant'

No sleep, rain-soaked, steamed and crusty, we started walking to the first appointment, up in Camden. The Bronze label was known for hard rock – they had Uriah Heep, Motörhead and Girlschool signed – but they'd let us in and we were very grateful. Crumpled, stinking and exhausted, we took a 9.30 lift ride to the A&R floor. A disdainful sideways glance between two junior A&R men – the first rancid stain on my 'music industry' memories: 'God, they've started early today!'

We deposited our tape and left, walking seven miles across town to our next meeting at Island Records in Chiswick. Island had released my favourite John Martyn album, *Inside Out*; it was long renowned for championing outsiders. In the corner of a quiet square of slick town houses we shuffled through the burnished portals of a gleaming white palace. It smelled of coffee, chrome, polished wood and perfumed secretaries.

'Excuse me, lads, coming through.'

The first gentle voice we'd heard since leaving Cardiff; Burning Spear's flight cases were rolling into the studio. We'd arrived – paradise! The receptionist smiled and offered sustenance. Hot and cold sanctuary.

'He'll see you now.'

Heaven! Rising as anointed sons of Wales, we ascended the lustrous staircase to the wizard's office and sank back into the tender leather caress of his luxurious couch.

'Have you got a tape for me, boys?'

That rumour about A&R men nicking anything you sent them might have been our fear once, but by the time we got to that office we were way too trashed to give a damn. They could take our songs if they'd just let us sit and soak up all this 'fairy dust'. Maybe a little would rub off on us. Ross slipped the tape out of its ragged paper sleeve.

'Reel-to-reel, eh? Don't see so many these days …'

'Better quality.'

'Nice.'

That tape had taken the last of our savings and our futures were riding on it. Press play – 'click' – first track, weird to hear it here in Island Records, sounding not so bad, even better than I remembered. Second, third and last, the wizard listened to the end of the final reverbed decay. We'd done it! There was no way he would've sat through all that if he didn't like it – we had a label hooked on the first attempt. We were going home to the green-green-grass in style, welcomed back across the Severn like heroes, next generation superstar Welsh.

'Well, that wasn't what I'd expected. I really wanted to like your music, boys. I saw the state of you and thought you looked in need of a rest, so I didn't have the heart to kick you out. I really wanted your music to be good … but I'm afraid it's not. I've heard it all before and better. It doesn't sound original, it's too much like a lot of artists I've heard already. Damn shame, boys, I really wanted to be blown away and help you, but I'm afraid it's not for us. My advice is this: go home and write something original, then come back. Best of luck, boys.'

Undefeated, indignant, full of it, we went back to Wales to write more generic songs. We never paid to record them and we never crossed the Severn to try our luck together again.

Island Records, London

Burning Spear – *Live*

TUESDAY MORNING, 3 A.M.

Driving empty roads beneath stars, connecting the lights of solitary houses.
It's the time of day when the world is temporarily returned to us.
The lights of the dashboard illuminated, mimicking the stars as the windscreen
turns into a film.

Bly de Blyant – ABC

DRIFTER'S DREAM

Trucks unload behind my bug-eyes. I'm hiding behind black glass
so you can't see me. Arranging stones, the broken bones
of consecrated buildings, making good the things that fell to pieces.

Shock-haired lobster woman, posing for trade, window dressing,
catch your eye, draw you in, basket bicycle lying smashed on
the pavement, nobody stopping, step around, don't look, walk on,
shadows sing a cold song.

The Fall – *Hex Enduction Hour*

LANDED IN TOKYO!

Seeing double through sleep deprivation.
Covered in warm rain, wandering familiar backstreets hunting
the noodle. People smile at us, stop us, shake my hand.
Others whisper in passing, glancing. 'Is that him? Yes it is!'
Outside the venue, watching fish leap from the water trying to
fly, we photographed one another to prove that we're actually
here. My body and head hunger to walk and soak up the rhythm,
but I feel like someone's stirring my brain with a dirty spoon.
My eyes ache like they've been doing press-ups on their knuckles.

Swans – *Soundtracks for the Blind*

Bute Street. The long road to the docks. In the future this place will be called a 'marina' and we'll split our sides, remembering the nights we stumbled down here, after closing time, in search of more. It was a desolate place. Even alleys were friendless, an occasional figure waiting beneath a streetlight for a slow car. If you dropped the right name you could drink down here till dawn behind locked doors in walls. Knock and a flap would open, a face squeezed into a square would appear, eye you up and down: 'What?'

'I'm a friend of–'

'Wait.'

Slam! Muffled voices, music underwater in another room.

'What did you say your name was?'

Locks, keys, chains, bolts. A crack in the wall, a yellow light, a single bulb hanging from a naked flex squealing, 'Help me!' weakly – half-man, half-fly. Pass beneath it down a dirty corridor to a back room/front room/kitchen, a stripped-out space lined with sunken faces waiting for some action, hoping it's you.

'Two beers, please, mate.'

A makeshift bar serving beered-up water in dirty glasses, handed over with hang-dog disdain at the back of the gloom. A drink so soulless you get sober from the despair that hits the back of your throat. A floor with bare boards like the Punk House. It feels like home.

After-hours drinking den – Butetown

Rose Royce – 'Love Don't Live Here Anymore'

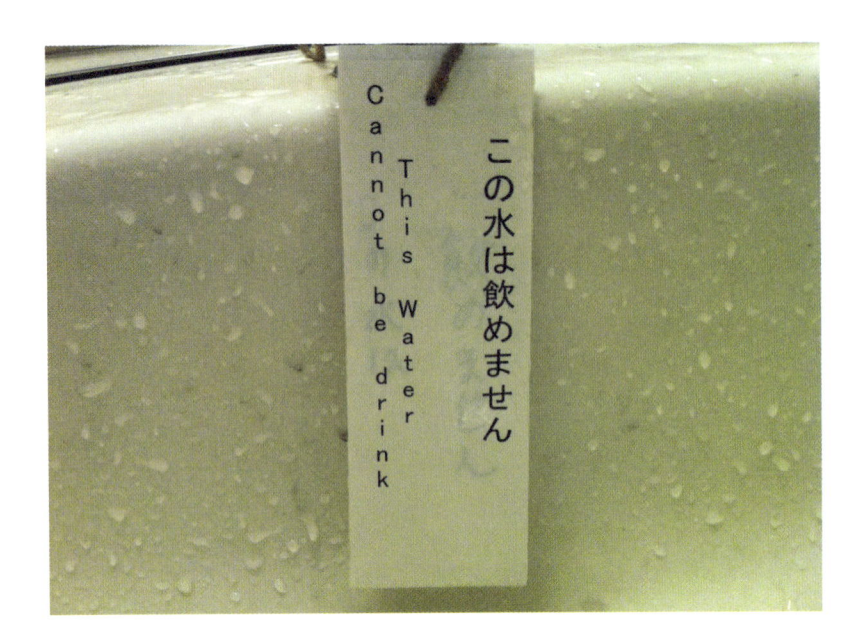

OSAKA MAXIMUM JOY NIGHT

Riding late night in the back of a taxi with lace-covered seats.
We spill out, laughing loud, rejoicing up Osaka alleyways.
The lights of the city shimmer, dripping off buildings, liquid
as rain. Perfect girls clutch themselves, delicately dressed and
cold on corners, chaperoned by sharp-suited Manga boys as we weave
between them, too much in love or lust to notice us.

Mark Kozelek and Jimmy LaValle – 'By the Time That I Awoke'

The end was inevitable.

Ross and I had formed a band – the Corsairs. As usual, as the band eventually crept out into the world, I was thinking more about 'the look' than 'the sound'. We found ourselves playing clubs in the valleys – that's where the *heads* sheltered from the threat of punk, playing bingo, high on cider and weed, listening to bands that still flew the flag of rock.

Relationships were increasingly fractious; maybe the potency of the weed had changed or the literature the hippies were basing their lives on had grown darker, but the drummer finally threw us out of his cottage and we were forced to join the human race and pay for a rehearsal room like all the rest. There was one half-derelict place in Cardiff, with just a dirt floor and one plug socket hanging on wires that we ran all the amps off.

There was another in a community centre up in Blackwood – clean, with toilets, electricity, windows and heat. The only problem was its proximity to gangs of bored kids. One lot broke in and started threatening to 'do' us. Remembering something I'd read in a sociology book about recruiting your enemy to police your back yard (OK, it sounds nonsense but we were desperate), I stepped up to the biggest, baddest looking of the lot, took him to one side and whispered, 'Do you wanna stay in here and watch us rehearse?'

'Yeah.'

'All you have to do is chuck your mates out, then you can stay. You'll be like our security.'

'All right, then. Ta!'

He chucked his mates out and we got our rehearsal, but had to beg a van off a bloke down the road to haul all our gear out fast before it was nicked by our head of security.

The old VW van that had rotted on the drive at the cottage for years was weak but back on the road and loaded up for the final show. The drummer was angry about something we never quite understood. He just wanted us out of his life, but the gig at Tonypandy Royal Naval Club still went ahead. The band had gone through a few personnel changes – mostly bass players for some reason – since it first rehearsed at the cottage in the hills. In its final incarnation, it included new boy, Alex Burak, on bass (a man who would go on to play a significant role in the future of UK electronic music).

But before that, there was the small matter of bingo, cider and weed.

Tonypandy-Blackwood-Tonypandy

Neil Young – 'Cinnamon Girl'

NOT HIT BOTTOM YET

Fake
Snake
Singer
Face
Tied up
In tiny horse ropes

Eyes closed
Fingers
Sticky-taped to the wall
Broadcasting flowers

I feel no pain
I'm numb
Addicted to your cuts

Unknown Mortal Orchestra – 'Necessary Evil'

... AND BEAUTIFUL

Two hours sleep before breakfast and the 8.30 lobby call for work, but you can't call this work.
Mining is work, weaving carpets in the factory is work, this is exhausting fun, so it's with ragged-arsed features I step once again in front of the camera and answer your questions.

Kevin Coyne – 'Good Boy'

The flat on Riverside had the best view in town, right into the open end of the Arms Park (the holy-of-holys for Welsh rugby), providing us with the finest sound system known to man when, on international days, we would open our windows wide as the home crowd sang from their hearts, reducing me to tears with hymns and arias.[1]

There was a lot I loved about that flat. It was another shit-hole, but it was close to town and none of my housemates complained about me writing songs at the top of my voice all day. My mate Tim Diggles lived at the front of the house. A dedicated filmmaker and graduate of the same art school as me, he was devoted to Radio 3 and obsessed with François Truffaut. I was woken every morning by classical music at high volume. Directly underneath my room lived a couple who rowed on a regular basis. Their violent outbursts would culminate in them having sex, which would always be followed by the playing of Fats Domino's 'Walking to New Orleans' on an old wind-up gramophone.

The old woman upstairs had moved out, but we'd had to seal up her flat because of the fleas left behind by her flock of mangy cats. I set up my recording gear in the through room to the kitchen, where rats and mice holidayed to the smell of cooking fat and kitten shit. I loved that flat, but knew it was time to move on, try something different. I'd grown disillusioned with Fine Art, there was no fight left in me.

My new girlfriend came from a world outside of the arts. She was the best thing that had happened to me since I'd run away to art school, so when she asked me to follow her I did. She had a good dependable job in the city, hated student squalor, had family in Penarth and didn't mind the short commute. I, on the other hand, had a degree in something I'd fallen out of love with, was signing on, had no band again and was directionless. All I had was a love of punk. Penarth, a genteel suburb to the south of Cardiff, seemed as good a place as any to die. I stepped off the shuttle from Cardiff Central and blinked into the quiet gloom of tree-lined streets, aware of a powerful sensation of the light being turned down. No danger, no cars, no wild dark dockland club nights, no stench, no drunken student parties, no loud music blaring from boarded windows, no tribe I could identify with.

I began to atrophy.

The flat we shared was a dingy three-room cell at the back of 17 Victoria Road. It could only be reached via a crooked little corridor under the stairs. It had no bedroom, rather a double bed swung down out of the wall with your bedding strapped in place,

---

[1] Listening to the hymns sung from the Arms Park was a tradition for me going back to when I was small and though we had no connection with rugby in our family international days were always spent with my granddad watching *Grandstand* on telly with commentary by - of course - Eddie Waring. The Welsh home games always stood out for me as the singing was like that of no other gathering of fans. It was hymnal, transcendent, not of this world. Even at that young age it always moved me to tears.

like living in a caravan that never went anywhere. When the boredom got to me, I drank myself numb on sherry. In the summer, a silent stream of ants found us, snaking their way in from a crack by the front door into our flat and up the wall behind the bed. My girlfriend freaked and couldn't sleep, but I was usually too drunk, too tired or too lacking motivation to care. I dumped my sculptures under the hedge in the back garden and turned an old pair of PA speakers into a spare bed at the end of the kitchen. The toilet had to be unblocked with coat hanger wire regularly, and the only view out of the living room was of a brick wall.

Penarth, 1979

Miles Davis – 'Bitches Brew'; The Mothers of Invention – *Uncle Meat*, 'Ian Underwood Whips It Out'

I'd been really inspired by the Robert Johnson band performing tracks from their album *Close Personal Friend* on the *Whistle Test*. Johnson's style of playing was nothing like his blues legend namesake. It wasn't laid back or down and dirty. The Robert Johnson who lit up the TV that night played with a high-speed frantic energy solely based on speed-rhythm guitar and high-octane bass gymnastics driven across the top of a brittle drum groove. This guy was a direct descendent of Richie Havens, reconnecting me with my love of playing rhythm guitar. The faster the better.

So I searched for the hottest, fastest young bass player in town, and was introduced to a guy called Pino Palladino – a gentleman with a soft Welsh voice who played bass like a cream dream. He had an easy-going nature that made him instantly likeable. Everybody knew he was the best bass player in Cardiff – Wales even. When I told my mates they just laughed that I would have the gall to ask someone as great as Pino to form a band. We met and discussed him bringing in his mate Kenny Driscoll, former frontman of local band Lone Star, who was also a brilliant guitarist. I already felt on the back foot, out of my league and tiny, but I said, 'OK'.

Pino got an offer to join Jools Holland's Big Band before we could even get in the studio. He came round one night, very apologetic for letting me down. It was the mark of a true gent. As I wished him the best of luck, I promised him we'd record together one day. He smiled, nodded and went off to become one of the finest and most in-demand bass players in the world.

The other bass player who almost stayed was Jake Bowie – another art school boy. The front room of the terraced house he lived in was a jungle of giant cheese plants and live exotic birds, which were allowed to fly freely. He played fretless like no other I'd ever heard before or have since: fast, sweet, pin-point accurate with a deliberate tone, like Flamenco stilettos on polished wood. Jake should've been playing with Weather Report but instead listened to the new wave of indie records while practising Charlie Parker solos amongst the chirping of his jungle birds.

Playing together, we sounded great – vibrant, erratic, fast; there was something special and different about this band. The music was angular: not Gang of Four, more Richie Havens thrown into a blender with speed-freak funk, XTC circa 'Statue of Liberty'. People who heard it got excited, we were on to something. So I was gutted and felt that cold fist in the pit of my stomach again when Jake told me his heart wasn't in it, and that was that.

Penarth, South Wales

Robert Johnson – 'I'll Be Waiting', 'Responsibility'; XTC – 'All Along the Watchtower'

RADIO RADIO

Ride the train to the Emerald City remembering not to sit on
the sunny side or you'll get fried. Breathe the dust of millions
gliding in the tube beneath the rhythm of their feet,
slipping out the hole on Oxford Street, cacophony and glorious
noise. Colours collide making music, shapes jump out of sounds,
and buildings generate words that fall close to the ear, whispering.
I'm attracted, nothing melancholy here.

J. J. Cale – 'Don't Go to Strangers'

The band back home (Talisman Wood) disintegrated amongst demijohns of homemade wine. The band with Ross died up in Tonypandy. The group with Jake didn't even get out of the recording studio, and the one with Pino didn't even get that far. I was left with a pile of gear and no one to make music with. Before moving to Penarth, I took a risk and blew my life savings on a reel-to-reel tape recorder, inspired in part by the memory of happier times back at home with Budgie's old Philips tape deck and three years experimenting with sound at art college. It turned out to be the first in a new era of 'best moves'; a period of *life after art*.

I went back to where we'd left off in the chair cupboard at school – experimenting with tape speeds, reversing the tape, learning how to make multi-track recordings, and all without an end result in mind: just enjoying the process and the sound. It was difficult to afford tapes on the £18 a week the social gave me, but if I stuck to tinned stew and bread it was just about possible. With the demise of that brilliant band that depended so heavily on Jake's bass playing, I returned to the tapes I'd recorded back in the rat-and-flea house.

The songs on them were 'odd', unlike anything in the charts, not current or trendy – more Wild Man Fischer than Elvis Costello.

I set about finding an 'odd' sounding band and for a while stuck to the plan, until I was seduced or worn down (or both) by the high-energy power pop on the radio and the reluctance of the musicians I met to cut loose. I'd never had to build a band from scratch before and felt completely alone, with no one to turn to for advice and no 'partner' to spark off. This new-found solitude did, however, mean I no longer had to accommodate anyone's opinions. It struck me that for the first time since I'd accepted the invitation to join my first band at eleven years old, I had nothing to lose. Whatever I chose to do was only limited by my imagination. I didn't have to conform to any genre or expectation, and for a fleeting second I didn't feel the need to have a picture in my mind of any kind of band at all. I was completely free to build a different kind of ensemble, its form directed purely by process. Sadly I let that thought go sailing past me like the ghost of a unicorn daydream.

I put an ad in the local paper. It got only one response. When I called round, the guy who opened the door seemed surprised to see me. He was fully dressed, with his dressing-gown on over the top. He impressed me with his knowledge of music, but freaked me out when he couldn't find his guitar. Eventually, as a last resort, he fished around behind the sofa, and pulled it out, covered in dust. It was a weird little nameless thing and I had to stifle a laugh as he proudly slung it over his shoulder using his dressing-gown cord as a strap. It was impossible to work out if this guy was off his rocker or a genius performance artist. The poor instrument was badly neglected, a copy of some thing that was never going to be good. The rust caked to the strings indicated it was both unloved and unplayed. As he fumbled to remember how to play he faked a chord and hacked at the strings with a plectrum he'd found imbedded in something sticky on the table.

I watched and waited for him to plug into an amp, to show me what he could really do, but noting my anticipation he apologised for not actually owning a guitar amp. Then, seeming to feel that this explanation was acceptable, he launched into his act, striding around the flat striking alarming poses as he hit the strings in wild spasms, his ostentatious dressing-gown flapping around his legs. I was really impressed by this madness and was fascinated to discover what quirk of genius had convinced him to answer my ad. He clearly didn't have a clue, but as I started to tell him he let it slip that he had access to a *private hall* where we could practise for free if I hired him. He was in! Then, just as I was leaving, the kid let it casually slip that he knew this guy at the Welsh College of Music and Drama called Alfie Thomas, who played bass. Intrigued and desperate enough to follow any lead, I asked him to set up a meeting.

Alf was a farmer's boy with ideas above his station and aspirations to escape small-town nowhere, to leave the farm, leave the country – a kindred spirit. He was a mature student who'd been in covers bands for years, taking a last shot at breaking free through studying drama, just like I'd escaped to art school. He had a light in his eyes, a gentle smile, an idiosyncratic dress sense, played a '62 P-Bass (the *real* thing!) and drove an old Morris Minor van (ex-Post Office) painted blue, which had an eight-track tape machine slotted under the seat. I liked him instantly, but the *van* was the clincher!

Seduced by seeing The Tubes performing 'White Punks on Dope' on the telly, I decided that any new band I was going to put together had to include a synthesiser player.

Synthesisers were the most exotic of instruments back then, and cripplingly expensive. Anyone who could afford such a fabulous thing was either in a band getting top whack and going places, or working at the steel works and not about to jeopardise their livelihood for a punt on a bunch of college kids with 'an idea'. It was all about the money. I needed to find musicians who didn't have any so they wouldn't miss it when it didn't come.

The New Moon Club sat on top of a broken thumb of decaying architecture marooned on bare earth at the end of St Mary Street. A vile little first-floor room for after-hours strays, perched above the lock-ups where market traders stored their barrows, it was *the* hangout for late-night drinkers, junkies, dealers and musicians *looking for more*, soundtracked by great live bands.

The walls were panelled in cheap laminated wood effect, and the only drinkable beer came in bottles. We were drawn like flies as soon as the pubs shut, packing it out, handing over anything left in our pockets for a bottle of warm Newcastle Brown. The dealers held the corner near the pay phone, watching the room, and cut you a look if you came too close – conversation was strictly business. I often wondered if, in exchange for a blind eye, they supplied security for the club, as it was the only room full of drunks high on music where I never saw a fight. An old colour television was always on, perched high up on the wall, sound off, except for the night of the Man farewell broadcast – that night the cherished sons of Wales were bequeathed the gift of sound *at the same time* as the house band.

At the top of a long narrow flight of stairs, a rotund man sat at a table taking money, greeting everyone with a wary nod. On the table beside him squatted a small greasy cabinet, where dubious pies were kept alive under lamps. The house band on weekends was an incredible three piece that included the legendary 'Tich' Gwilym on guitar and vocals. This was a band to make you drool – they made barroom standards cool, and had a sound that was so 'down' in its execution no sound engineer could do better. They put everything 'in the pocket', tight as a duck's, made you believe you too could be an axe god. Tich was one of the greatest guitarists ever to come out of Wales. Legend claims his playing used to be 'average' (impossible!) but that one summer he took his Strat and amp and a bag of weed off to a schoolroom in the valleys and practised until he emerged with a command of his instrument that stopped your breath.

The New Moon Club never let me down. On weekdays the house band was Eager Beaver, not as tight as the Saturday night guys, but with an attitude born out of a hunger to 'get out'. Eager Beaver had things I coveted: Dave, the wiry, cool-looking frontman with a shark's-tooth earring; a tour bus converted from an old charabanc; and 'a keyboard player'! Gary Bond worked at the tax office and had aspirations. He lived in Splott with his mom and dad, who welcomed me into their home with customary Welsh generosity, serving an endless supply of tea, biscuits and smiles when I called to tempt him to jump ship. He lit up when I asked and shook my hands eagerly. I had my keyboard player – now all we needed was a drummer.

    I went shopping at the best place in town to hear local bands who wanted to 'make it'. The Lion's Den, in the basement of the Railway pub, was accessed down a long flight of stairs which you had to brave to lug your gear down to a tiny stage at the end of a long, low, thin-arched ceilinged room that resembled Liverpool's Cavern Club. Zipper were the band 'most likely to', so I bypassed them. Their frontman was a mesmerising ball of attitude and had a great voice – I was jealous. They would crop up again in time to hurt and taunt me. The Spitfire Boys had a whole Velvet's thing going on, exuding a cool confidence that belonged in the Bowery. Then there was the Soft Centres. They had a great frontman – Stuart Kelling (built like a stick with skinny white jeans and diamond eyes). Like our former bass player in the Corsiars, Alex Burak, Stuart would go on to play a major role in the future of electronic dance music, but back then he had a drummer whose style I liked (sorry, Stuart). I had already worked with Steve Erwin on the session I did with Jake, but the last time we'd worked together he told me there was no way he would ever leave the Soft Centres. I couldn't resist asking one more time and made the call – he listened and shifted his allegiance. I had stolen myself a band.

Cardiff

J. J. Cale – 'Cocaine'; Man – 'C'mon'

THE SMELL OF TOUCHLINE

The raw of the grass, the rhythm of animated conversation under a sky of pale blue milk. Back on earth, shuffling foot-to-foot, front-row flasks of tea, bacon rolls with sauce – red or brown? Football.

Health – 'We Are Water'

I'M A MOLECULE HANGING IN THE WINDOW HISSING

The guest-list goes on, conflict resolution,
sensual space, a guide to stuff I purify myself with.
The strip, the freak, the light shines through at night between
the lines. Music and comedy get me through.

Chet Baker – 'You Are My Thrill'

DIAMOND TIME

Riding late night in the back of a taxi with lace-covered seats.
We spill out, laughing loud, rejoicing up Osaka alleyways.
The lights of the city shimmer, dripping off buildings, liquid
as rain. Perfect girls clutch themselves, delicately dressed and
cold on corners, chaperoned by sharp-suited Manga boys as we weave
between them, too much in love or lust to notice us.

Lonnie Holley – 'Mama's Little Baby'

Alfie came up with the name 'the Screen Gemz'. It suited that period's *zeitgeist* for bubble-gum and cheese. Alfie Thomas was gentle, dependable and loyal, with the kind of unquenchable enthusiasm that made me feel that I'd found the right man at last. Alf was a solid bass player, never shirked work, was always willing to stretch his playing, and had a rich ebullient voice that carried within it generations of South Wales farmers.

The band's first rehearsal studio was also its most luxurious (from which we went downhill). It was in a small village hall reserved exclusively for us in the grounds of a grand Victorian rectory on the outskirts of Cardiff. With no neighbours to disturb it was perfect until we kicked the owner's son out of the band. He did his best to keep up, but every week we waited a little longer for him to learn the songs, and every week his stress deepened as he fell a little further behind. I wouldn't have minded the dressing-gown guitar strap if only he could've played his bloody guitar. It was painful watching him struggle, knowing how much he wanted the gig. He was holding the band back and knew it. The kid saw it coming, took it graciously and squared it with his mom and dad for us to stay on. He had, however, done something extraordinary and life-changing by bringing along his mate, Alfie, a man whom I would come to love and admire and eventually release records with. The parents took it like most parents would. They put up with our noise till the end of summer, then politely asked us to leave.

Somewhere nice, outside Cardiff

The Knack – 'My Sharona'; Squeeze – 'Up the Junction'

WILDS CHOCOLATE

I found you late last night, dancing under spotlights
in the bowl of dreams, Van Gogh flames leaping from your feet
as you laughed, beckoning. Everybody lit up, eyes wide, twitching,
counting down in whispers to the unveiling of your creation.

Sister Rosetta Tharpe – 'Rock Me'

IMPRESSIONISTIC DOG

Took the bike out on the back roads of Essex in the early sun.
Birdsong, pheasant, crow, the hissing of hedgerows shimmering, the lazy hum of jets cruising high overhead.
The soundscape to this film hasn't changed since I lay in long grass as a summer boy.

James Brown – 'The Payback'

One guitarist down, we limped on for a week. Having previously broken up the Soft Centres by nicking their drummer, I went back on another raid and stole their singer. Stuart joined the Screen Gemz on guitar and vocals. He brought with him extreme attitude, skinny jeans, pointy shoes and a following of girls. And that's the way we stayed, becoming *the* band in Cardiff (for a minute).

Since leaving college all I'd done was sign on and write songs, giving me too much time to think about the 'image' of the band I was pulling together, and how best to utilise the newly acquired letters after my name. I took all that I'd learned in gaining my first class honours degree, gathered up the last of my precious canvas and painted a weedy little banner to hang behind the band. Then I painted my old Laney's pink and got the guys in the band to dye their clothes in bubblegum colours. I wanted us to look 'modern', like we knew what was going on up in London. It was important to send out the message that we were 'going places'. Through all our contacts we blagged enough gigs in local bars and college halls around town and built an enthusiastic following for what was really just a generic power pop outfit.

We recorded our songs, and when Radio 1 came to Cardiff to broadcast for a week I'd prepared a presentation pack full of press-shots to give them. I gave them cassettes of demos in boxes of shredded pink Latex, salvaged from my degree show – giving away the last of the crown jewels. The music didn't come close to the promise of the packaging. It was a second-rate reflection of what was already fading on the radio. Radio 1 never broadcast any of the music, though the *Breakfast Show* praised our 'packaging' live on air.

Cardiff

The Ruts – 'Something That I Said'; Tubeway Army – 'Are "Friends" Electric?'

CANVEY ISLAND

Canvey Island, home of Dr Feelgood, Thames Delta, Oil Town.
Counting tattoos in the sun – the cross of St John, bikini girls
in blue, Celtic runes up the arms, outstretched wings between the
shoulder blades, two crossed swords.

Momma feeds baby in an XL Beatles tee,T feeds baby, baby winces,
Momma feeds baby his first ice cream,
everybody rocks back laughing. Mine's a 99,
mine's a bucket 'n' spade,
two mugs o' tea darlin' and a Coke,
'Sausage Sandwich!'

Girls stagger to the shore cleaning cut toes in the river.
Down at the crabbing pool children stoop and peer into the water,
waiting like snipers, hearts scratched into the concrete curves
of the sea wall. Dogs pause at washing bowls laid down by kiosk owners
and drink as cargo ships cut lazy waves slipping upstream to London.

Across the other side, Kent is green and sunlit like a Miyazaki
dream, a single chimney towering surreal above the far horizon,
and were we to go over there and look back we'd find this island
floating mid-air, rooted in nothing but imagination.

The Conet Project – *Recordings of Shortwave Numbers Stations*

CONE ALONE

Today I practised turning off the head. It went so-so.
Nailing billboard shreds to the studio walls, waiting
for the dance of black marks to begin. Running the paper
through my head all day, watching orchestral forms
collide with sunlight and the sound of a single bee.

Miles Davis – *Dark Magus*

LONDON

Look around under your hat
A small felt halo
Different to all the others
Your bright white eyes find me
Rolling in time with my motion
Counting the angles of feet rooting strangers to the ground around us
Faces look down
Laugh out loud
Life is too serious
Perfumed to conceal its odour
Hold on tight
The others won't meet my eye
But you
Whites
Framed in midnight black
Hold connection

Powdered faces
Gold-banded diamond fingers
Pale and perfect lips
Ceremonial preparations
Coffee clutched
Wrapped in paper ribs
Above ground
Feet move fast with purpose
Stone expressions
As shop assistants check their hair and hems before opening
Rare groove pumping breakfast cafés
With exaggerated joy
You'll find me
In the corner
Featured in the healthy option
Dogboy

John Cage – *Diary: How to Improve the World (You Will Only Make Matters Worse)*

Our friend Alex Burak had moved to London to work in a small rehearsal-cum-recording studio in Victoria called the Point. He was one of the few musicians I knew who'd escaped Wales and made it across the border long enough to claim residency. Alex wanted to be an engineer, a producer, saw all too well the limitations of being a bass player in the valleys and was doing something about it.

Back then the Point was more of a rehearsal space, a room with brown carpeted walls that smelled of male BO. There was a tiny control room in the corner, with some basic gear if you wanted to record a demo, and a mirrored wall so you could check yourself out. From the street you wouldn't know the place existed, situated as it was behind the offices of Y Records, down a long and hazardous corridor at the back of a posh wine merchant's. Y Records at that time was home to The Pop Group – a proper indie label, serious about the music it put out, and, although everyone there greeted us with smiles and was nothing but amiable towards us, I found their commitment intimidating. Their office smelled of cardboard and vinyl, leagues above anything we had in Cardiff.

In the room above the studio stood the obligatory pool table – fat heavy wood and green abandoned beneath a tepid skylight, echoes of Van Gogh's *Potato Eaters*. A painting 'in progress' hung on the wall, there was the smell of oils and turpentine, and tubes and brushes arranged neatly on the floor. The games room doubled as a painting studio, the world I'd turned my back on was waiting for me, staring me down till I squirmed. The artist in residence lived in a tiny back room, bed on the floor (no luxury door on bricks). Related to the owner, she was friendly, beautiful, driven and unattainable, wary of musicians, all of which made her all the more attractive.

A band was rehearsing downstairs when we arrived so we rolled out our sleeping bags and went to a pub in a 'real London mews', like the kind Roger Moore lived in *The Saint*. High on adrenaline and London beer, we rolled home and settled back in the control room to watch and learn as the other band rehearsed.

Although we were huge fans of their album *Cut*, we never ended up meeting The Slits. That evening, we watched our own private gig through a sheet of glass, transfixed. John Peel had been championing them for ages, and we loved their jagged guitar style. They were teaching a new drummer how to play their signature grooves. He looked small and fragile as they towered over him (these were powerful and intimidating women, you didn't meet people like them in Cardiff), but when he started playing, this fantastic 'backwards beat' came out – a beat that we would reference on all our future recording sessions throughout the eighties. The small, fragile boy behind the kit would go on to leave that band and make that groove his own, becoming the master rhythm at the core of Siouxsie and the Banshees; known to the world then as Budgie.

Eccleston Street

The Slits – 'Typical Girls'

We cut two tracks at Point – 'I Can't Stand Cars' and 'Teenage Teenage', inspired by an obsession with Elvis Costello and the current *zeitgeist* for kitsch-cool.

I became a camp follower, deserting the rich path I'd found at art school for something generic, hunting a fast track into the VIP lounge of pop. We borrowed money from our then manager, local businessman John Dean, who came to us an enthusiastic fan, eager to help us build a career, and left disheartened, dragged down by our relentless youthful cruelty, as our frustrations grew along with a sense of our own importance. He was a good guy with a good heart, and I regret not having always treated him with the respect he deserved.

Having fled Penarth, I'd moved back to the bright lights and jumped several rungs up the evolutionary ladder. Now living on the poshest stretch of Cathedral Road, I set about designing the record sleeve in the nicest flat I'd had in years. Having abandoned Fine Art I started mimicking the current 'Memphis' trend in graphics and resurrected an old fascination for military imagery from my time on the foundation course. A book full of photographs of airforce dogfights, a bargain-bin purchase, was my current obsession over breakfast every morning. Tracings from the photographs became the basis of the cover art.

I was shallowing out, attracted to surface over substance, losing the rigour, the passion for exploration, becoming a third-rate imitator, sliding backwards with a swagger.

The A-side of the single got played on local radio. Radio 1 reviewed it, and even John Peel gave it a spin, but the music … the music was a sham: no heart, no identity, no risk. We flogged a few boxes to local record shops, and the rest went under the bed.

We carried on gigging around Cardiff, reaching our zenith one summer playing on the roof of the student union, with our stage set of broken TVs and a giant red and yellow polka-dot fridge that opened to disgorge party balloons into the audience. The police closed us down, but not before a young electronic engineering undergraduate – Rick Smith – had become temporarily smitten with the band.

The roof of the student union building, Cardiff

Elvis Costello – 'Less Than Zero'

STOLEN SUN

Newsflash! Sun no longer shines on Essex - police informed,
Birmingham suspected, panic ensues as suntans fade.

Steve Reich – Works, 1965–1995

SUN KIDNAPPED BY RAIN, BIRMINGHAM ACQUITTED

Essex lays back, succulent green under slate-grey sheets
of sky. Heavy rain punctuates spring's desire to liberate us all
from winter's dirge. Pre-Raphaelite rainbow and its sister shadow
raise arcs above the trees, spanning fields with biblical
promise as we call excitedly to one another, startled by royal
procession to clutch cameras, whispering, 'Wow!'
The sun was eventually discovered, handcuffed behind clouds,
and Birmingham rightfully exonerated,
apologies were dispatched from the south.

Bingo Gazingo – 'What a Life Some Sh*t'

There were excited rumours from the underground about this new band that had appeared out of nowhere, part of no scene, not connected with anyone we knew, didn't frequent our pubs or even share our taste in music – *something new*. The Grassroots Café on Charles Street wasn't on the live circuit, didn't even serve alcohol, and the gig was in the middle of the afternoon – weird and wrong and unsettling. These guys had either gone mad or …

We shuffled into the back of the café, found a table near the stage – a low-rise shelf too small for a band, but a sweet girl singer stepped up to the mic, backed by two skinny boys with sharp hair. Guitar and bass, no drums, just a cassette machine full of rhythms, these guys weren't even *trying*! We'd heard they were something special, but from their lack of serious gear the Young Marble Giants had a lot to learn. The audience sat in stunned silence as the gentle restrained music remained *gentle and restrained*, on and on and on, never breaking into anything more frantic than 'slight' for the whole of their (non-) performance, justifying our superior disdain.

We still laugh, remembering how Stuart ripped and shredded Coke cans in savage frustration, bored into aggression at their *self-restraint*. Halfway through we couldn't take any more – damn, it was too fucking sedate! We stood up and made a show of leaving in disgust. Years later every one of us admitted we'd felt threatened by what we'd witnessed. It was like they knew something we didn't, like they were privy to something we'd been excluded from. It was like they were looking down on us. We were the past and they were the future. We'd been *ambushed*.

The Marble Giants' music wasn't sexy enough for us. They were neither upbeat nor furious – not angry or joyous enough. It was nothing like us, or any music we were into. We thought it tedious and mind-numbing, but Rough Trade and the rest of the world didn't. We watched them become the first of our generation to 'make it' out of town, get a deal, become the new indie darlings and even tour America! We were left behind in their wake, making reproduction pop, dry as biscuits, plodding on. My response was to sneer, pull it to pieces and dismiss it – until John Peel championed them on his radio show and they made it onto the cover of the sacred *NME*.

Cardiff, 1978-79

Young Marble Giants – 'Colossal Youth'

We played more local gigs, and some were fun, but there was a growing sense of stagnation. We were losing our audience; you could see it in their eyes. Throughout our time together there had been two tribes within the band – the keyboard player and the rest of us. Gary was a good guy, enthusiastic about gigging, loved to be on stage. Maybe it was just down to musical tastes, but the time he didn't show for a rehearsal after a night on the lash, we took it as divine providence and asked him to leave. It may have seemed harsh the day Alf and I went round his house to give him the news, but within a week he was doing what he loved best with Eager Beaver.

With gigs booked there was a hole in our band that had to be filled quick. This gave us an opportunity to bring in someone on the same wavelength as the rest of us, though finding a keyboard player who could afford to own a synthesiser and who wasn't already earning good money with a 'big band' seemed impossible. Then Stuart remembered his best mate from school, an undergraduate electronic engineering student I'd first met when he'd 'fixed' an amp head abandoned by Wayne County. There are two things that I remember about that first encounter: what he said and what he wore.

Firstly: 'What bloody idiot filled this amp with knives and forks?', and, secondly: his was a fantastic overcoat!

At this time I was paying rent on the posh flat by working at the Lexington on Queen Street – an American-themed diner styled after the Hard Rock Café that gave refuge and employment to struggling musicians and ex-art students. As I had all the necessary credentials I was promoted to bun-cutter, dishwasher, salad preparer and dessert sculptor. With no requirement to engage my brain it was a perfect job. Rob, the owner, was an ex-musician himself, who gave us time off without hesitation if we had to travel away for gigs. He encouraged us to pursue our dreams, and wanted to hear all about it whenever we returned. Music was his passion, the burger trade wasn't, so he supported anyone who wanted to escape. One day, he came up to me with a photograph: 'See this lad, he used to work for me, a good guy. I really liked him. I think you'd like him too, we used to have a lot of laughs.'

I glanced at the picture. I didn't think much of his dungarees.

'It's a pity he's not working here now, you'd really get on. *He's* a musician too.'

'Oh, yeah! What's his name? Maybe I know him.'

'Rick Smith.'

Legend's shorthand recalls Stuart and me going over to Rick's flat on his twenty-first birthday, and how he'd sat in the bath drinking champagne as we talked. The most rock 'n' roll introduction to the least rock 'n' roll person I've had the privilege to spend most of my life with. Fully clothed, no water in the bath, yet clearly in high spirits, I still wonder if the booze impaired his common sense. Why else would he take the gig? All he had was a Fender Rhodes – no synth – but he was more willing than any other musician I knew, and the light in his eyes told me he was unlike any other.

Cardiff

M – 'Pop Muzik'; The Police – 'Roxanne'

Stuart was a talented guitarist, a brilliant history graduate, and always broke. He loved music, beer and good times, could pick up a tune in minutes and a girl in seconds. He didn't have a clue how to look after anything he owned, didn't even have much gear – he borrowed most of what the rest of us took as being essential. We bought him a vintage Fender Strat and he even managed to lose bits off *that*, as he moved bin bags full of clothes between borrowed flats, the soles of his pointy white winklepickers full of holes stuffed with cardboard. He wore a skimpy leather jacket from a charity shop (or borrowed from a girl) and came with a smile that opened hearts and doors. People loved him and he befriended every cool band that played the student's union.

His boundless charm and intellect allowed him access to all areas, to everyone's confidence, and their beds when they were out of town. He had a track record for never letting you down if you were looking for a good time. The Ramones would always seek him out when they were in Cardiff, demanding he take them for pints of 'Skull Attack' and breakfasting with him over recovery fry-ups at Ramon's Café on Salisbury Road. He knew them well. I was in awe.

Ramon's Café is still going strong. Stuart is a successful English language teacher running his own schools in northern Spain. The Ramones, tragically …

Cardiff

Ramones – *Rocket to Russia*

During the 'end times' of the Screen Gemz, in that final year when gigs were drying up and other bands were taking over, Dad got me a summer job packing carpets back at the factory. My partner for the whole of the summer was my old friend Cliff Yates, a boy I'd met when I was ten and he was fourteen, and we were both Red Cross cadets. He would turn up for the start of every 6-till-2 shift bright-eyed and full of beans. Every morning he would rise at 5 a.m. to practise his transcendental meditation, charging himself with good energy, while I was staggering into work after another heavy night on the lash, depressed and stinking of alcohol.

The killer blow came one day when Radio 1 put Virgin record's new signing Zipper on the 'A-list' with their single 'The Life of Riley'. The warehouse radio blasted it out all day, there was no escape. Everyone in Cardiff was havin' it large, except me. I was going nowhere and every hour that song would come round again on the radio and twist the knife.

Tomkinson's carpet factory – Kidderminster

The Comsat Angels – 'Independence Day'

The shiny new, yellow and blue InterCity 125 train became symbolic of an escape route for me during the trudging years. No deal, no hope, but every day the familiar sound of the 125s horn lit me up, promising to take me far away from Cardiff's depressing streets to the Emerald City across the border in the merry ole land of OZ.

Later than you think

TRINITY

Sanctified
Sweet liquor smile
The bride waits in the car
Barefoot
Tiny hands

Wolfman
Wrapped in black sheep's wool
Staring at a blind sky

All the crows
Vagabond scavengers
Kneeling between candles and lonely boys

The hand of God
Runs up alleys

Iron horses
Hug

Lakker – 'Herald'

SANCTUARY OF

Dressed in black
Waiting for the night
Look
Point
Into the light
Stick man
Stick people in the morning mist

Our beloved
Our redeemer
Feet wreathed in flowers
Swoons in shadow
In the sanctuary of your infinite love

Efterklang – *Tripper*

The last rehearsal studio was a disused grain bin in the roof of an old maltings warehouse in Cardiff docks. Now redundant, the building had been snapped up by a canny entrepreneur who divided it into units and leased them to small businesses. The old grain bins in the roof were useless to anyone, so they were rented to local bands, the only people desperate enough to pay to freeze in winter and fry in summer. To reach your allotted 'bin' you had to carry all your gear up flights of treacherous metal stairs, remembering where the holes in the floor were at night, so as not to fall through and die. The bands with the loudest gear could rehearse for as long as they wanted, all the others had to wait until those of us with 'bigger boxes' finished.

It was a joyless environment to work in, devoid of inspiration. Breathing in grain dust as we sang, it was no great surprise that in these conditions the Screen Gemz crumbled. My writing was mediocre at best, too besotted by this point with the Banshees and The Comsat Angels to try for anything original. It was as if I'd forgotten every sound installation, tape-loop experiment, synthesised signal path and quadraphonic composition I'd ever created at art school. I was infected with mediocrity, drowning in it, and taking the others down with me.

Worst of all, I'd become a tyrant, and everybody in the band was sick of it and rapidly losing faith. Rick saw the light and was the first to leave. Alf had endured months of my nagging and had trudged on through rehearsals with the demeanour of a beaten dog. When Rick left Alf followed and the band folded. I withdrew to the flat on Cathedral Road and found solace in 'art' again, spending every evening drawing late into the night, listening to Peel on the radio, soaking up everything he broadcast. One night my depression cleared and I realised I was *free again*.

I might have had no band, no direction and no career path, but I was no longer obsessed with copying other people. For the first time since leaving college I didn't want to make a *hit record* – I just wanted to *make sounds* and see what happened. I dug out my old reel-to-reel and started messing around. Rick and Alf had sold off their redundant live gear, bought a four-track Portastudio and had started recording in a back bedroom on the other side of town.

Cathedral Road and Tiger Bay

Is the War Over? – Cardiff compilation album

There's something about desperation that's never let me down. It brings clarity. With a tiny borrowed drum machine and a head full of art school, Lou Reed and Peel, I pressed 'record' and started cycling a droning riff. The next morning, before opening time at the Lexington, I tested the first iteration of 'Doot-Doot' on the house system for the waitresses. Although the title was borrowed from 'Walk on the Wild Side', when Rick heard it a few days later he asked in mild disbelief, 'Did you write that?' He seemed surprised that I'd written something that wasn't another imitation of somebody else's sound.

I was pleased he liked it. His leaving the band had shaken me. I realised, too late, that he could see stuff I couldn't. It was clear to me now that my future should have been spent working with him, but I'd blown it. There was no chance of us ever getting back together, but I had to ask. 'Doot-Doot' was an olive branch, all I had to indicate that 'maybe' I could write something half-decent and honest – something with its own sound that wasn't trying to be 'successful'. I talked a *lot* when I went round their house in Splott, and eventually (bless them both) Rick and Alf let me join their band. The rules had changed – this was to be on *their* terms: no power pop, no camp following, no acoustic drums, no rock guitars, no standard vocals; they wanted to experiment and see what happened. I was welcome as long as I played by *their* rules, and for a while I did, and it was great.

Rick was a gifted engineer and a natural producer, continually searching, exploring, questioning and surprising everyone with what he could get out of the modest equipment we had – I was lucky to be a part of his band. We evolved a sound out of machine beats and dub-inspired delays – a cultural fusion of the two forms of music we loved most. It quickly started to sound good – really good – and different to anything else. During evenings after we'd recorded, we'd sit in the front room and listen to dub, Kraftwerk and Bowie's *Low*.

More than anything of its era, *Low* transmitted seismic shockwaves. I felt like I was directly in their path. *Low* had a sound unlike anything I'd expected from *the* iconic frontman, the sheer ego-shedding *balls* he demonstrated with that one album still sets him apart from all other frontmen before or after – *what a genius move!* He stood back and let the molecules of electric Germany speak for him; Ziggy Stardust and the Thin White Duke were binned. When other frontmen would have clung to either for their entire careers, Bowie flushed them out, dispensed with their encumbrance, and let the soundscapes dance, unfettered by the crippling need to reduce them to yet another 'backing track' for another frontman. It went deep into the bone, stashed for later, ready to be recalled once dance music had rendered frontmen surplus to requirement yet I still craved to sing – that's when I'd follow precisely the direction of David Bowie's example, and put the groove in front of the voice, step back and let the music speak. Revel in taking the supporting role, make the voice subservient to the sound, and stop 'needing' to dominate it. Yeah, Bowie's *Low* inspired us – it reached far into the future and waited there for me to catch up.

For many months, we'd listen to Peel, Krautrock and a lot of Misty In Roots; we'd eat together in front of the telly, watch the *Whistle Test*, *Riverside* and *The Tube*; zone out to rented videos, buzzing, unable to sleep. Walking home from Rick and Alf's place in Splott through empty streets, the pubs and clubs having long since finished chucking out – solitary stagger-drunks lurched up Queen Street precinct, easy to spot, easy to swerve, too slow to do anything but puke – the city was mine after midnight: birdsong cacophony concealed in trees, everything green breathing oxygen back into the world, streets smelling sweet and clean. The city slept as I walked home, invisible boy, high on our new sound, adrenalised.

At the perfect time, Alex Burak reached out again. 'Did we want to come back to London and record for free?' Point studios had gone 24-track, totally upgraded with new equipment, painted, carpeted, everything new – and Alex wanted to test it out. Were we interested? We'd chucked our jobs at the Lexington after Rob sold it to some bloke we couldn't stand, so we had no money for cars. We borrowed a Nissan Sunny from Alf's cousin Del, loaded it with what little gear we had, and drove to London.

Over one night we re-recorded 'Doot-Doot' with a borrowed Strat, borrowed drum machine and Rick's mono synth to build a string section that sounded fabulous. Even now when I hear that song it still carries within it the silence of a sleeping city, the sound of its people dreaming as we worked against the clock to finish the track before dawn. No one slept, we stepped out into rush hour and drove back to Cardiff with Alf and Rick taking turns at the wheel, straining to keep their eyes open, but refusing to hand over to me – too scared I'd crash and kill them in their sleep.

'I hope you don't mind, but I've added some acoustic *drums*,' Alex announced on the phone a week later. 'The Thompson Twins are rehearsing here. I got their drummer to record an idea I had. It sounds great. Really hope you like it.'

'*Drums?!*'

Cardiff–London

The Cure – 'A Forest'

NEW HOME

Stood in the sun at 8 a.m. at the edge of a field feeling the warmth,
letting the quiet seep in.
Heard rubber on blacktop,
hidden approach from somewhere in the next town,
an engine struggling on an incline, changing gears, throaty.
Birds circle, rising on thermal currents, surfing the morning breeze.
Stooping to photograph a discarded Red Bull can I find stuff low
to the ground
thrown out of passing cars waiting to be reclaimed.
Plastic cigarette wrappers covered in dew, chocolate wrappers
overgrown,
juice cartons compressed into the mud
like tiny trapdoors into other worlds.

Curtis Mayfield – 'People Get Ready'

Rick slept in the back of a terraced house, in a bedroom painted entirely black. This was also *the studio* where we recorded our music, with a synth, a mic and guitar pedals for outboard effects. Voices were heavily processed, guitars only welcome if they agreed to be 'oscillators' – no rock, no pop, no 'twang-heads' admitted. Other musicians passing through the black room left their marks and opinions, some even sang, but none remained, only Alfie, Rick and me. Steered by Rick the three of us managed to swerve the temptation to fall into old habits or follow trends.

When we eventually agreed we had music worth hearing it was to John Peel that we sent cassettes concealed within boxes of cornflakes, along with copies of the magazine *Grunt*, which we created and printed ourselves. John was good to us, he played our music to the world, answered Rick's calls every time he rang, and gave us encouragement. His show was the only place anyone could hear us. We no longer performed live, so we were free to focus on writing and recording. Freed from the limitations of being a live band our sound was only limited by our imagination and what we could borrow. We'd signed on the dole to do this, but without gigs the money was really scarce.

The dole was never enough, so Alf signed up for a paid drugs trials at the Heath Hospital to help with the cost of batteries, strings and beans. On his 'guinea-pig' days, he'd leave on foot and arrive home in an ambulance, barely able to make it up the stairs to crawl into bed, and not reappear for twenty-four hours. The memory of how he looked after every hospital session – drained, ashen, a shadow man – disturbs me even now and yet, back then, I let him do it every week.

During this time, and perhaps because money was scarce, I cut down on the drinking, but the head was still off with the fairies – *reality* was a film on the telly in my head, a walk alone across the city after midnight, invisible to the world. *Actual reality* was something to be avoided. When it came to other bands that were hip and having it, the uniform was black or dour; the expressions bleak. They conveyed an image of a world without fun, months without sunlight, humourless. I couldn't stand the granite-and-slate-grey streets nor the breadline we'd been living on for years, and I couldn't stomach the idea of our clothes reflecting the depressing lifestyle we were trying to escape.

Besides that, what was the point in following the herd? I'd done that too many times and got nowhere. We needed something of our own, the opposite of all that long black overcoated hair – so we countered it with an explosion of colour. Plastics, brightly coloured furnishing fabrics, cheap jewellery, crimped hair and lip gloss – anything to get as far as possible away from life on the dole. You would think that, given our studio's proximity to the docks of Tiger Bay, we would have run into some hostility to the way we started dressing, but it never came. The worst we ever encountered was walking home one night in winter, past a gang of skinheads standing bollock-naked save for their wellies, knee-deep in snow outside a pub: 'Phworrr, come and get some of this, ladies!' they shouted, waving their willies in their hands as we passed. Cardiff has always nurtured eccentricity.

In Wales during the eighties, if you were in a band and short of funds, you could blag a gig on Welsh TV. They paid good money, as long as you sang in Welsh. Now languages aren't my forte, but we needed the cash, so I was more than happy to step aside for our old mate Stuart Kelling to take the mic when we landed slots on BBC and HTV Wales. Stuart has a brain the size of a planet, can turn his hand to anything, so we gave him free rein to dress as an acid Andy Pandy and stuck him out front to sing 'Doot-Doot' in the mother tongue. From experience we feared the TV engineers would screw up the mix, so we all plugged into the mixer on the Portastudio and let Rick use it to mix the band himself, handing the bemused engineers a simple stereo feed (and a blueprint for a future us). The only thing the engineers had to do when we appeared on the show was balance Stu's voice with the music, and they even found a way to cock that up by sticking a harmoniser on his vocal which put him out of tune with the band! At the back on drums, and for visual effect, we were joined by another former Screen Gem, Steve Erwin, for one night only.

The television slots paid us well, but the money soon ran out. We carried on like this – writing, experimenting, recording; with Alfie topping up the coffers donating his body to medicine – until Rick felt it was time to look for a deal. We needed a name. Brian Eno's studio 'philosophies' – the Oblique Strategies – intrigued us. They were games that helped free the head, swerve generic thinking, so we swerved and spent so long *not* coming up with a band name that on one fateful night, our final solution was to dump Rick with the responsibility of 'creating' it: 'Go into the studio, set up a mic, press "record", and the first thing that comes out of your mouth is the name of the band.'

I may have this wrong, but I seem to recall him leaving the room reluctantly. Twenty minutes later he returned: 'OK, it's done.'

Deep breath; press 'play'. The name of the band began with an 'F', followed by an almighty rolled 'R', and concluded with a sound like being sick with your tongue out.

'Fr-r-r-r-errr!'

Through Rick's (then) girlfriend, we'd met John Warwicker, a London-based graphic artist and multi-media PhD genius. We called him in the hope that he could connect us to good labels that might be interested in signing us. He did. There's a clip of us in the Spandau Ballet film, of the day we drove to London in the borrowed Nissan to meet Some Bizzare records. The old office is gone now, but it was up an alley in Soho that I'm still drawn to, a suite of tiny rooms above the old Trident recording studios, where thirteen years later we'd meet and collaborate with Goldie and his Metalheadz.

Back in 1981 we were meeting Rusty Egan, one of the faces of the New Romantic scene (Visage drummer, the man behind the legendary Blitz club) and his mate, the mythical indie label boss Stevo. We arrived high on self-belief, ready to take on the capital, a new generation of London Welsh. Alf came dressed in electric-blue tights, a short fake leopard fur jacket, *Alice in Wonderland* shoulder-length hair pulled back with a plastic hair band, lip gloss, eye shadow and little harem slip-ons. Rick had customised a sky-blue plastic tracksuit, puncturing it all over with fat blue plastic eyelets and embedding each one with short pieces of clear hosepipe. I wore bright green trousers made from stretch cushion covers, snug as tights, a mandarin-collared floral shirt and a 'shield-your-eyes-from-the-light' yellow plastic coat, black winklepickers, hair piled high in front, mullet at the back, cheeks flanked with Wolverine mutton chops.

Mid-meeting, in walked a Channel 4 camera crew headed up by Nicky Picasso. Nicky was the presenter of our favourite arts programme *Riverside*. Unbeknownst to us, our 'meeting' mysteriously coincided with a *Riverside* special on Rusty, Stevo and the Some Bizzare label. Watch the clip, witness the confusion. I still don't have a clue what went on, but I think we were meant to look like we were there to sign a deal. The 'scoop' that never was.

Soho, London

Soft Cell – 'Bedsitter'

THE FULL PACKAGE

You know what you're doing
Spreading thrills in trains
Even in the underground
Faces turn around
Disturbed in the wake of your passing
All their fantasy expressions
As you reanimate imagination
I watch them watch you
tapping rhythms in time with the wires in your ears
Acting like you don't know

Dane Terry – 'Eagles'

RIDING A DIRTY TRAIN

With beautiful stains

Male Gaze – 'Gale Maze'

Ian Curtis was found dead eight days after my twenty-third birthday, just as we were about to sign our first major record deal.

I never liked Joy Division – they were the soundtrack to the prison sentence of work in the kitchens of the Lexington. The cook was addicted to them; he drove us mad, playing them over and over all day. It brought me down, made the hours stretch as my salads grew limp and my desert creams congealed.

We took every opportunity to hide the cook's Joy Division tapes whenever he left the room, just to stop the endless doom and gloom. Even though King Peel was a massive supporter of the band, I just couldn't get into all that 'down'. That was, until 18 May 1980, when the news hit me like the death of Elvis.

Daytime radio started playing 'Love Will Tear Us Apart' like I was hearing it for the first time. Finally, the penny dropped.

The kitchen of the Lexington, Cardiff

Joy Division – 'Isolation'

Listening to as much dub and Kraftwerk as we did, it was inevitable that our sound would evolve into a fusion of both. We were three white kids obsessed with reggae and the electronic sounds emanating from Germany. Inspired to work with a dub-master, we took advice and sought out the great Dennis Bovell (who'd also produced The Slits album *Cut*). After hearing our music Dennis invited us to his Studio 80 complex on the southside of the Thames. A proper honour, we were levitating. He 'got' what we were about instantly and called friends on the phone to rave about us like he was one of the band.

Off the back of that first meeting he offered us his services and the use of his studio when we were ready. Now we knew we were on to something, but having lived on the dole for so long, the romance of the breadline was wearing thin. John Peel was playing us on the radio, Rough Trade were showing interest. Seeking out one of our other key influences, we sent a tape wrapped in pink rubber concealed within a soft fabric mutant clam to Brian Eno (we're still waiting to hear back, Brian).

We were walking our own path and it was *working*. People liked us! The last tape we sent out was to CBS. It was a long shot, with no real expectation of any positive response, but they really liked it and wanted to discuss a deal. CBS (later Sony) had released the first album I ever bought (Simon and Garfunkel's *Parsley, Sage, Rosemary and Thyme*) and were home to Santana (a band whose energy and groove had blown me away in the *Woodstock* movie). They were also the label who'd signed my guide and mentor Clifford T. Ward, Guru #1, the man who kick-started this whole journey. It felt like coming home.

CBS offered us money – loads – enough to eat more than beans and still be able to pay the rent. It was a huge sum by our meagre standards, but they wanted to make sure we were a *real band* who could actually play. All they'd seen was a TV clip of us playing 'Doot-Doot' on Welsh telly. They were so keen on what they saw in that clip that it took a lot to convince them that the vocals they liked so much in the demos were actually me, and not Stuart, who provided the Cymraeg. They wanted to see us live but we couldn't afford to transport our paltry pile of gear to London, and had no time to beg a gig in Cardiff, so we put the show on in Rick's bedroom. A&R men Dave Novik and Muff Winwood sat on the edge of Rick's bed as we plugged our instruments into the Portastudio (which ran out through a domestic stereo) and did our first gig as FREUR.

John Warwicker introduced us to two managers, both very different. One met us in a Park Lane hotel – sharp, professional, impressively short on time but with a disquieting self-assuredness in his eyes. The other – Simon Davis – operated out of a flat in Marylebone that he shared with the drummer from Ten Years After. He was a gentle man with a sweet smile that beamed out from beneath a mop of thick curly hair. At that time he was also looking after a guy called William Orbit and his Strange Cargo project. I don't remember what it was about him that convinced us he was the right man for the job, but Simon Davis got our signatures on his contract and we let him negotiate our first major record deal.

For a while, we were 'the band with no name' (because no one could pronounce it). The label persuaded us to create a symbol to represent the sound of it. They even had special printing blocks made so that publishers could print the 'squiggle' I came up with and John refined. If you look back at the *Music Week* charts in 1983 when 'Doot-Doot' was having its fifteen minutes, you'll find a funny little smudge thing where all the regular names of other bands were.

Eventually, CBS got us to soften up the pukey sound and write it with 'real letters' that could be printed and read. Little-by-little our rude outsider edges were tidied-up – some for better, some for worse. I was sniffing the pop-star carrot again, going back on my promises to Alf and Rick, desperate to do anything to avoid going back on the dole or end up in the factory talking about the time 'we came *this* close'.

1982, Southwark–Splott–Marylebone–Soho

Steve Miller Band – 'Abracadabra'

FOR YOUR FINGERS

Another man
Back page
Naked
Toy shark
Tiger man
Costume
Poser
Staring at the camera
Laughing

Hits the ball with a wild stick
In the street
Widow on the corner
Watching Cadillacs
Dancing at the crossroads

Empty chairs
Watch a painting of an empty road
Empty buses
Parked
Beneath an empty sky

Sleater-Kinney – 'No Cities to Love'

It was perhaps inevitable that a major label would never let a bunch of unknowns loose with a pile of money to produce their own music. There would have to be a grown-up holding our hand, someone they could trust to deliver, even though we knew the job we'd done on 'Doot-Doot' warranted their faith in us producing ourselves.

'We have a producer in mind for you,' they announced. We dropped our heads and growled, but they offered us no choice. Remembering the beans, we complied.

Autumn 1981, contracts signed, cheques banked (but not for long!), we filed into a triple-brown chocolate bedroom in a tired executive hotel out at Heathrow Airport. There, in the corner, midday curtains drawn, table lamps sucking light out of the room, sat a giant, a legend, a shadow man with a fat silver beatbox across his legs. With all the respect due to such a genius, our A&R man announced, 'Lads, meet Conny Plank.'

We grinned, levitated. This man was the reason we loved German electronic music, why we had gone in deep. It was in our blood, our bones, core to our groove. His sense of rhythm, space and pursuit of what was unique in contemporary music had driven us, kept us going when we were queuing down the dole office. Countless nights we had watched the sun come up over the streets of Splott listening to the records he'd produced. Outside of Brian Eno, this visionary man, squeezed into a tiny chair, was the most important producer in our record collections.

Heathrow Airport hotel

Kowalski – 'Ultradeterminanten'

Soon after the advance was banked, Rick and Alf bought a piece of jacked-up American rolling junk. A massive Chevy Blazer with kangaroo bars and detachable roof, it came with fat tyres and fatter fuel bills. Coming straight off the dole, it was an insane thing to buy. I had no idea that I was 'co-owner' of the beast until they picked me up in it and told me.

The rest of the money went on a synth, and a first-generation sampler that measured its memory in seconds and died in an office fire a few years later. It ended its days nailed to the wall of a south London council flat as a comedy trophy.

We drove to the dole office in the big American truck, signed on, then booked flights to Germany.

We decided to look for a drummer – a real one – to augment our sound. There was nothing wrong or missing from the beautiful, dependable, infectious, relentless, metronymic beat of our machines, but a drummer seemed like a good idea. We were looking for something unexpected, someone wild and unleashed – a counterbalance to the wonderfully predictable rhythm of a drum machine. If Keith Moon had been alive we would have asked him. He would've been the perfect foil to three outsiders from Cardiff dressed in plastic, pearls and poodle-crimped fountains of hair.

'I know this guy who drums with the Fabulous Poodles,' the gentle manager with the sweet smile offered. 'He's really crazy.'

'How crazy?''

'Oh, *really* crazy, believe me!'

'Sounds great. Does he smash stuff up?'

'Yeah.'

'Brilliant. Get his number!'

Bryn Burrows was a proper musician. A veteran of several American tours, he was rock steady and small and wilder than ten men twice his size. The look in his eyes assured you he'd give 200 per cent if you gave him the gig. He arrived with a skinhead cut, in a biker jacket, black T, skinny black jeans and Docs. He looked us up and down and chuckled, 'I liked your demo tape.'

He was funny, surprisingly amiable, and possessed a promising undercurrent of unpredictability – he was a man who looked ready to get the job done to exacting standards; a drummer who would headbutt cymbals if the mood took him (and the mood often took him). Bryn was perfect and The Who weren't about to recall him. Now we had a *proper band*. CBS was thrilled.

Cardiff–London

Fabulous Poodles – 'Mirror Star'

I flew in an aeroplane for the first time at the age of twenty-five – London to Cologne, through an electric storm so rough the plane bucked, rocked, slid and dropped out of the sky until we screamed then howled with laughter. I thought that fantastic fairground ride was normal until we reached Germany and saw Bryn (a veteran flyer) had turned white. He shook as he explained just how close to death we'd come.

At the airport we were greeted by a bunch of techno hippies in woolly jumpers and beards, who collected us in a giant World War II troop-carrier painted banana yellow. They eyed us with caution as we exploded onto the street, dressed in Day-Glo plastics: 'He-llo … are you … Fr-e-u-r?'

There were campfire stories and legends rehashed in the years following that week at Conny's place – about the pinball machines that commiserated in German ('*Shaaad!*'), and the football team which met nightly in the bar at the B&B where we slept, their beer-fuelled, testosterone-induced drinking games trotted out to impress the weird boys from England. They harassed Bryn, forced him to sit on a chair which they then took in turns to lift one-handed, roaring with laughter at the shock on his face. They thought we were freaks, but regarded us as 'all right' because we'd drink with them all night.

Holger Czukay from Can called by the studio unexpectedly one day and bestowed gentle wisdom (a ride cymbal brushed 'veeery, veeery lightly' in time with the track would cure its ills). Around the dinner table every night Conny told stories about his wayward youth, his passions, Kraftwerk, and the morning his son Stephan woke Brian Eno by beating him over the head with a piece of 2x4. Connie taught Bryn how to 'backwards drum', how to leave 'spaces', to think 'not drum' more than 'drum'. It reminded me of watching The Slits teach Budgie. Conny programmed Bryn's Simmons kit (the latest in electronic drum kits, purchased with a renegotiated advance from the record company) with unexpected sounds he was encouraged to embrace. And he encouraged him to record his first-take reactions to whatever he was given. Bryn became great at this, and turned it into one of the 'signature things' we did whenever we recorded drums.

In return, Bryn reciprocated Conny's love of Prince, as they talked for hours about the phenomenon of the genius from Minneapolis, an artist I just didn't get. Prince's sound was too 'thin' for me, I was still stuck on the *implied scale* of rock music, my ears were closed to anything that didn't sound 'beefy'.

If the 'studio' was Conny's concert hall, then the Eventide Harmoniser was his Stradivarius. He was a master of the dial, ripping the sound of anything that passed through it into shuddering, exhilarating shreds; spitting it back out transformed into something worthy of your attention.

The studio loaned us an old car to get around in, but forgot to register the fact with the local police. They stopped us one night crossing the river into town and marched our manager away at machine-gun point under suspicion of car theft. They told us to sit and wait and didn't flinch for a second at the way we dressed, but as they marched him off to an armoured car, ashen-faced, we howled with tears of laughter at the fear in his eyes – dark humour was a comfort to us.

'I gave you a cassette of a new band I just made an album with,' Connie announced one day, as we piled into the studio car. 'They used to be called the Tourists, but they've changed to Eurythmics. Let me know what you think.'

It was simple, stripped-down electronic soul with a dark twist. 'It's good! Really good!' By the end of the decade, on the eve of our second implosion, we'd be opening for them on their farewell victory lap of America.

Cologne, West Germany

Eurythmics – 'Never Gonna Cry Again'

CHILL

A bitter fog to start the day, cold and thick grey soup that clings to glass and metal, permeating everything with holes. A cold wait on the platform, another delay on the rails. The magic of a carriage cold above the waste and freezing below again, sliding into the city with closed eyes meditating. It started dark and caged and found the light mid-morning, talking to the man who came to collect a drum kit whose life was saved by paramedics back in April as he lay twitching on the Tarmac outside a north London rehearsal studio.

I asked him, 'What went through your mind?'
He said, 'That I was too young and I'd been short short-changed.'

Patti Smith – 'Piss Factory'

Back in England, CBS preferred our original version of 'Doot-Doot' to the one we recorded with Conny. They put us in Mayfair Studios, a hugely expensive facility in Primrose Hill, with John Hudson, a brilliant engineer with a long track record of hits, to guide us. John had reworked the latest and most successful Ultravox album that Conny had recorded, and the label's logic (though transparent) worked for us.

We spent tens of thousands of pounds on that record. We were let loose to experiment with one of the finest studio engineers in the business. We were moving with a whole new crowd now who wore the sweet perfume of 'success'; running with the platinum pack, spraying money around like water – no clue about restraint, hungry to explore everything on offer in one of the best studios in the country, no matter what the cost. Anything to make our music great.

The funds rolled in and we kept spending. We accrued huge studio bills. Rick and John became co-producers, working into the early hours every night. I built towering sculptures out of masking tape, and inadvertently changed the sound of the control room by hanging art all over the wall. I'd regularly fall asleep under the mixing desk, exhausted on curry and beer.

When 'Doot-Doot' was released in 1983, it went to number one in Italy. We took full advantage of our short-lived 'stardom' there and played huge televised festivals in ancient Roman arenas all over the country. We flew luxury class weekly, heading direct from a terraced house in Cardiff docks to a five-star hotel in Milan. There, the walls were covered in hand-stitched suede, and a one-eyed doorman greeted us as prodigal sons. I remember us all standing on the street one day, waiting for taxis, dressed in vibrant plastic skins, crimped hair, strings of fake pearls, paste diamonds, pointy boots, mascara and lip gloss. Turning around and looking back I saw Charles Aznavour, lounging up against a wall – classic Mackintosh, cigarette in mouth, he was watching us intently. I was thinking, he's thinking, 'How long will *that lot* last?!'

Across the street there was a beautiful blonde leaning on a white '56 T-bird straight out of *American Graffiti*. She waved to us, we waved back, a car pulled up alongside her and a guy wound down the window, then pulled away. She started her car and followed. Thirty minutes later she was back at the curbside, leaning against her sleek white convertible. We were living in a Hollywood film.

We had bodyguards and ate in the finest restaurants Milan and Rome could offer; we were invited into the cockpit of Alitalia flights alongside some Italian football stars. Every night I would be found, wandering the romantic streets of Italian cities, pissed and alone, chanting, 'Take me now, Lord.' We racked up massive debt; a fortune in airport breakfasts. Life was amazing. Living the dream, we had finally *made it*. Famous musicians nodded in recognition when we walked in, we were the new kids on the block. The label was getting great feedback from the press.

All the years we'd been trying to have a career back in Cardiff, we'd been beholden to the music papers, genuinely consumed by who was hot and who was not, who was this week's darling and last week's forgotten. As outsiders looking in we'd grown tired of being fed the flavour of the month, were numb to the same old set of claims made by yet another new face saying nothing different from the old face. We wanted to do it different, not stick more noise on the newsstands. So, when the CBS press department enthusiastically showed us what they'd lined up for us, we turned it all down and refused to do any press at all.

And that, basically, was the end of a beautiful relationship.

I tried to woo them back, but the damage was done. We'd shot ourselves in both feet. We'd never walk again.

'Doot-Doot' was climbing fast towards the UK top ten, and we'd secured a residency at London's Marquee Club, a black box off Wardour Street with a coffin-like dressing room that was tattooed with the scrawl of ten thousand bands. The gigs went out on the telly show *Live From London* to the whole of Europe: Bryn on drums, Alf on guitar and vocals, Rick on synthesisers and vocals, me on voice and guitar, and John Warwicker live-jamming video tapes on one of those massive pub TV projector screens. Images of bees in flight blurred into screwed up images of TV interference. The label had made him sign as a 'keyboard player' because nobody could get their head around the idea that video decks were instruments and very few (if any) saw the prophecy in what John was doing right there on stage in 1983.

We flew into Bologna for an open-air festival in the town square. During the show something went wrong as we were going through our customary smashing up of gear: a piece of Rick's instrument flew off stage and into the crowd. We looked around to make sure no one was hurt – everyone was OK, there was big applause, screams even. We waved, smiled and headed back to the dressing room shared with two other artists on the bill – Peter Gabriel and Richie Havens! I was a schoolboy again as I shuffled up to him, shyly extending a hand: 'Mr Havens, I just wanted to say, "Thank you".'

I don't remember if he said anything. I have a vague recollection of a rich deep tone, but a strong memory of a massive hand that extended back towards me – the softest, gentlest giant's hand I've ever held – and of eyes that were calm and unfazed, ready for action, full of compassion. Then the chief of police burst in, dressed all in white, flanked by men in black: 'Everyone get out! No, not you!'

We were told the piece of broken gear flew into the crowd and hit a *mother and child*. We were done for. Apologies were useless. 'Something has to be done. An example must be set!'

Glancing down at my fingers, I counted them and whispered, 'Goodbye.' Our interpreter spoke fast, words were exchanged in Italian, curses, sighs. Resigned expressions, we did what was asked (our signatures on promo records). Respect was restored, we walked out of there with all our body parts and straight into a crowd of angry protesters. I smiled and waved, making the universal sign for 'Autograph?'

'Come away, fast,' said the interpreter. 'You don't want to know what they're shouting!'

The record was everywhere, we sold out every night at the Marquee. Everything was going great, until an enthusiastic 'friend', in a misguided attempt to express loyalty to us, was caught buying more than one copy of our single. The hammer came down on us, swift and hard. We could choose to be removed from the charts altogether, or lose all our sales for that week (our best week). We chose the latter.

The single appeared to falter. It stuttered and stopped climbing (when in fact it was selling more than ever). Radio took instant action and we were eased quietly from the playlist. 'Doot-Doot' dropped off the planet. Nothing could compensate for that sudden disappearance from the charts – neither the subsequent album nor the UK tour with Annie Nightingale opening for us (not even Radio 1 reporting daily from where Annie and the 'band with a squiggle for a name' were playing). The campaign was over. CBS switched their attention to Prefab Sprout.

Although in the following summer we played our first Glastonbury, in a small wedding marquee, we were unable to regain our former momentum. When our star had been in the ascent, we'd decided to leave the mean streets of Cardiff and head to a genteel little house nestled amongst the tearooms and retiring pensioners on the seafront at Bexhill-on-Sea. When that star went into freefall, that fairytale idyll was where we withdrew to in our jacked-up Chevy and freaked-out clothes to write the follow-up and lick our wounds.

The follow-up, *Get Us Out of Here*, was recorded in a low-budget studio in Eastbourne. Every day at 4 p.m., the session had to pause to let the school across the road put the kettle on because if we didn't, the studio speakers would go 'BANG!' The music for this album was very different from the first. I'd written a bunch of songs influenced by moving to the seaside, soaking up local traditions, shanties – folk music! To augment the band, my mate Jake Bowie had been drafted in on bass. His flighty, staccato style was something we thought might be good for our new sound.

I'd stopped listening to radio altogether and wasn't interested in anything contemporary; I was immersed in old books on local rituals. I got all connected to the land – heynonny-no – and disappeared off on some electric gypsy trip, bought the hat, the billowing shirt, the works. We took the finished recordings back to London and delivered them to John Hudson at Mayfair, and together he and Rick tried to turn them into a record.

The most physically painful of photo-sessions then followed, with photographer Simon Fowler, whose signature style required us to stand rock-still in total darkness while he 'painted us in' with torches. One winter's night, we suffered for art under the cliffs at Beachy Head in a freezing wind, standing still for hours while Simon worked – shirts the pictures but not the music, pressed up a few copies and stuck them in the back of open to the waist, billowing romantically beneath artfully stubbled chins. The label liked the pictures but not the music, pressed up a few copies and stuck them in the back of a cupboard at their London HQ, where they languished until I discovered them there.

With the support of the head of international (who probably knew what was coming), the record got a minor release in Holland but nowhere else. We were dropped.

A band abandoned, we frequented a seaside dole office in a town renowned as the place where the elderly moved for the last time. I wanted to be in the music business, not out, and I craved contact with it at any price. It hurt so much to be an outsider I pulled a favour from a mate back at CBS and got a day as an extra in Alison Moyet's 'Invisible' video. Even the other extras didn't want me there, they were pissed off that I didn't know how to fake 'making conversation for the camera'. They recoiled every time I talked to them and kept asking me, 'Why are you here?'

Jake left the band again – he couldn't stand posing for pictures, nor the funny clothes. He was replaced by Chris Bell, who remained with us long enough to do a two-month residency at London's Hippodrome. The club's owner, Peter Stringfellow, was courting us for his new label he was trying to set up around the singer Edwin Starr of 'War' fame. One of those nights, parked up in Soho, the Chevy got rammed in a five car pile-up but didn't show the slightest scratch. It spat glass out of its twin exhausts when the police asked us to start it up, sending them into fits of laughter.

A couple of weeks later we discovered the crash had twisted our truck's chassis, rendering it a write-off. When the engine started to go we didn't have the money to fix it. Rick put an ad in the trade papers and secured us a straight swap for a BMW Series 7. I guess because of the way we dressed it never looked like we could afford a car like that legally, so we used to get pulled over all the time. Once, on a shitty European tour, West German police found a map Rick had 'modified' into a work of art by cutting out their country and sticking it in Russia.

Another time, we drove to Paris to rescue my girlfriend. When we got there the girlfriend had left. French customs couldn't believe two twentysomethings dressed in cushion covers could afford a BMW Series 7 so they ripped the car to bits, ecstatic to be gifted a guaranteed bust. They were bummed to discover we were clean and the legal owners of a top-end Beamer. On the other hand, we'd been listening to Burl Ives and Marty Robbins tapes non-stop since leaving England. Awake for twenty-four hours, they gave us back our car but I'd already lost it. I found myself insisting that they remove every panel left on the car (while helping them to do so), howling, *'C'mon, here's another one you've missed!'* The heater matrix finally blew during a bitter winter and we had to drive around wrapped in blankets with the windows open to keep the windscreen from fogging. Living the dream, beyond our means.

That same winter, the gas was cut off because we couldn't pay the bill, so we all huddled round a portable gas heater in one room to stay warm. Dinners were prepared in a slow cooker that took all day, courtesy of Alf, who got it as a free gift for signing up to a mail-order catalogue. I hit bottom, lost it. Dark, dark, depression. Couldn't move, didn't want to live, had nothing left to give – no vision, total shutdown, stared into space all day. Alf pulled me out. It was the most oblique of cures: he wheeled me into his room, sat me in front of a telly, wrapped a blanket round my shoulders, slipped in a video and made me watch a bad bootleg copy of *U2 Live at Red Rocks, Under a Blood Red Sky*.

The energy coming off them that night in that setting – the polyrhythms, the glances, one to another, the joy on the faces of the crowd – transmitted, touched, electrified. It lifted me, plugged me into something beyond myself, 240 volts direct. It made me want to stand up and dance. Maybe I still had something to say. OK, let's give it another go.

I wrote in the studio every night till sunrise, not a clue where I was going but enthused again to make music. Rick set up experiments in the front room overlooking the ocean, circular piles of equipment plugged into an eight-track reel-to-reel.

On weekends, Rick, Alf, Bryn, Chris and I would huddle around the circle of gear, playing on whatever was in front of us, recording whatever came out of us, then rotating on to the next instrument. Sometimes you got a synth, sometimes drums, a guitar, a bass, or a mic. Sometimes Rick would put on videos – films with the sound off (*The Terminator* was a favourite) – and we would create new scores for them, watching and recording as we went. The results were stronger than anything we'd written in years. We were finding a sound again, based on electronics again – the sound we were always drawn to whenever we weren't trying to write 'hits'. That was a productive period for us. Poor, scarce of food, the five-star hotels a fading memory, but with the music finally going somewhere.

During this time, I stayed in touch with Annie Nightingale. We'd had a good time on tour together in '83 and had become friends. She'd impressed upon us to never lose touch. Annie was our only connection with a world I wanted to be a part of. She was kind to us and took my calls whenever I was down; would talk for hours if I needed to, and was always encouraging, always pleased to hear from us. To this day, whenever we meet, she gives me an ear-full for not telling her we were on our arses back then: 'If you'd told me how bad things were I would've had you round my house and cooked for you every night!'

That kindness will never be forgotten.

Bexhill-on-Sea, East Sussex

ON THE OTHER SIDE OF THE WORLD

The body craves sleep in the back of taxis listening to stories of drivers a long way from home. Families scattered around the globe in the eternal search for work and a better life. Software programmers driving cabs for rent, fresh out of universities in San Diego. Drunk, happy laughter in the corridor outside my hotel room sings me off to sleep, to heal, dripping with Technicolor dreams of all tomorrow's music.

ON THE LOOSE IN SYDNEY

Slept all the way from Melbourne to touchdown in sweet
spring heat, balmy even. Strolling through Sydney with
the band, taking time, coffee and Italian cuisine in the
bay, feeding on sunlight laughter.

Street artists and techno didgeridoo jammers sell $10 CDs to tourists
as an old ghost with a trumpet tips his hat to no one,
drifting through the holiday crowds.
Another Charlie Chaplin hangs off another lamppost,
mannequin simulations for weekend snappers
whose children jump and squeal when he suddenly moves.

The markets are piled high with bright things,
handmade artefacts under canvas. Bar bands beat out
precision rhythms, mimicking past genres for the nostalgic,
while romantics gather in ex-pat bars swaying to songs
from the old country.
The puppet shop has gone the way of the fruit bats we
seek, but parrots still infest the evening trees
with the celebration of their cacophony as we drift
into the night like lovers, tired and lagged, catch each other's eye
and smile to find a light that only gratitude could ignite.

POST-SHOW POTATO CHIPS

Honey-dipped and salty to accompany gummy bears, pears and 70 per
cent chocolate in the after-show euphoria backstage at Sydney Opera.
We dance and sweat, breathing each other's breath until the salt
runs down our backs. Upminster Dave comes back for a beer,
hasn't changed in all these years.

Cheese and ham, tomatoes and salad cream on a dry brown slice,
washed down with Throat Coat in the half-light of a dressing room.
I dropped bum notes in the shadows up on stage tonight,
but the train kept rolling. We smiled and laughed
and for an hour and a half transcend jet-lag.

A long black car takes the crew to a hotel room –
beer, tea, Kettle Chips and chocolate –
as I glide across the bridge in an anonymous taxi
listening to Ziggy, Sly, and The Doors.

Efterklang – Tripper

Just couldn't get into Prince until he was fed to me through sweet-tuned speakers and fat subs. We'd struck up a relationship with the boys at Turbosound, the cutting-edge PA company whose equipment we'd fallen in love with. They called us round to their workshop in the grounds of Ridge Farm Studios – where we'd recorded 'Matters of the Heart' back when Freur was on the rise – to convert us to what had become their latest obsession. Rick, Alf and I sat in respectful silence clutching mugs of tea.

'I Wanna Be Your Lover', off Prince's eponymous first album, was a groove and a sound the like of which I'd never heard, never bothered to track down. Up close, it was seductively dirty. It hit home, straight to the bone, the motherlode connection.

That day completely changed my thinking. At a time when we were label-less, penniless and drifting, Prince became an earworm, an obsession affecting everything I wrote and thought about for what became Underworld MKI. I was off copying someone else's thing again, *following* instead of searching, trying too hard to be let *in* when I could've been happy to be *out*. I was back checking my reflection, making sure I looked the part.

Prince, Prince, Prince. The last words I'd hear Miles Davis say, years in the future.

Turbosound HQ, Surrey – England

HORNS IN THE FOG

Walking back across Sydney Harbour Bridge at 8 a.m., boats call
to one another like love-sick bulls. Joggers cut a line beneath
a tunnel of razor wire that guides us safely home. Everything
is black and white and simple, beautiful, rhythmic poetry, the bones
of a giant beast cooling itself in the morning fog.
My brothers and sisters fly home today, only crazy Peter and me left
behind. He's lying face down in a brandy and mayonnaise stupor,
I'm clean, heading back out to the streets, cruising for conversations
as Sydney slips off its gossamer mantle and lays back on the shore,
inviting sunlight.

CBS gave us a parting gift as they dropped us, offering us the soundtrack for a Clive Barker horror film called *Underworld*. This was a chance to show what we'd learned from years of watching late-night movies together, enthralled with the scores, absorbing it into our band's sound. This was a chance to bring our music to the screen where it belonged.

We separated from our management, went back on the dole and part exchanged the Series 7 for an orange Ford Cortina – a rough-looker, but easy on the purse. It bought us time to regroup and write new songs. Rick's new experiments were taking place in the front room of our sweet, little-old-lady seaside home, while the band free-formed to rented videos. It was a momentary high point, a pause on the road of recurring failure. Cut loose from 'chart thinking' and with enough money to eat and pay the rent, we returned to the roots of our sound – electronics, dub and film scores.

We found a new manager – Rupert Merton. He had published 'Doot-Doot' back when we first recorded it at his studio in Victoria. After that, he went on to co-manage the meteoric ascent of the Thompson Twins' career. They'd parted company, and we'd twisted his arm to give management one more shot, and advance us enough to get the gas reconnected. After that, I stopped cutting loose, listened to Prince exclusively, and told the band I'd had a *vision*. God knows how but I persuaded them that we should reinvent ourselves as a sub-funk pop group. Chart lust was on me again.

Rupert was very clear that we had to change the name of the band, and suggested we use the name of the film we'd just scored.

Paths were converging, something felt right, yet at the same time wrong. We were going out of sync with our intuitive direction. I was going snow-blind again, chasing fame. Art school was forgotten. I was determined to shake the fear of returning to the Midlands with my tail between my legs.

Underworld finally became a proper band when we found Baz Allen, a young drummer-turned-bass player who we'd first met as a trainee tape-op at Mayfair Studios. He had all the required credentials. He'd left the studio to become a Rare Groove DJ; he loved James Brown and could power a small town on his love of funk. We cut demos in the front room at Bexhill then booked a cheap rehearsal studio out in the country and invited labels down. They all passed. Our sound got tighter, funkier; we moved into our manager's studio and invited Seymour Stein (head of Sire Records) to come see us play. At the end of our 'gig for one' in a tiny room opposite Wandsworth Prison, we handed Seymour the cassette on which we'd just recorded it all and said, 'There's our demo, hope you like it.'

It worked. We got our deal. We were 'back in the business'. Paths were converging again.

I'd accepted a long time ago that we would never get to America, so it was surreal to actually step off the plane at JFK and take our first yellow cab ride into Manhattan. It was Super Bowl weekend, bitterly cold, and we were back in black (and white), living the dream – three blokes from Cardiff in town for a week, crashing on the floor of a tiny flat in Chelsea with a woman we'd never met before. We'd ditched the plastic colours and turned monochrome. Rick and Alf's rich Welsh accents lit people up. Everyone we met smiled, shook our hands, told us they were thrilled to meet us.

Madonna, Ramones and Talking Heads walked the corridors of Sire – fantastic things happened here. Seymour wanted to hear new material, so we performed it live for him in his office, recorded it for him there and then and handed over the tape. We climbed the Empire State Building, breakfasted in real American diners, and learned to treat every waitress with respect. We saw *Platoon* the week it came out: three weird boys head to toe in black and white in a theatre full of Vietnam vets, audible gasps of recognition before every ambush up on the screen. I found the whole experience disturbing, like we were gate-crashing someone else's funeral.

Everything about New York was like being in a film. We'd grown up with it all on TV since we were kids, so the streets of Manhattan were practically second nature to us, yet the reality of them (the smell, the up-close-in-your-face-ness) gradually overwhelmed me. I started to oscillate, vibrate and shake. I was overdosing on the *reality of the city*. On Wooster Street we huddled together in a theatre no bigger than a large apartment to watch The Wooster Group perform. There on stage Willem Dafoe in the flesh, no more than a couple of feet away from me. The jet-lag and the violence of the sounds the actors made transmitted shockwaves that snapped me, smashed me up, left me shaking in a silent 'fit' by the halftime break. 'Yeah, some people get sensory overload when they come to New York for the first time,' our manager chuckled reassuringly. I kept rocking and chanting, 'I need to sit in an English field …'

I got over it by getting drunk. At the end of the week, a party was thrown for us in a swanky loft on Bleecker Street owned by a film star. Robert Woodruff turned up and we were pushed into performing the new songs. Moki and Don Cherry were there in the 'audience' too. Afterwards, we videoed Don teaching us grooves by singing them to us. That video is lost amongst scores of tapes that we made on that and subsequent tours. Every few years we look for it but it's never shown up.

As the party rolled through the night I got progressively more wasted before slipping off (as was my style) to look out at the city, tucked under a thick blanket of snow. Everything glowed orange under streetlights. I cooled my head against a window. It felt good – *really good* – I was blissed out. Everything had fallen into place. I was savouring the taste of a perfect place, the moment in the moment. Unlike that time in the back of a car, this time I didn't want to die, even though I knew this was as good as it was going to get. We still didn't have that magic to take us beyond ourselves. This was a temporary bliss. For one night at least I was happy.

The *Underneath the Radar* album was recorded live at Farmyard Studios in the Cotswolds, with Rupert Hine producing. We were back spending big money, enjoying every amenity of a luxurious residential studio. Rupert was a good listener and guide. His partner in the business was the uniquely gifted Trevor Morais, then in demand as one of the hottest session drummers in the business. When not on the road, Trevor could be found in the Farmyard, stripped to the waste, smoking in the sun on the kitchen step and administering wisdom.

The reality was, Underworld MKI was a junkyard car. A misfit of parts, a vehicle cobbled together (in my head) to carry us as far from the dole queue as possible. Similarly, the music was a sub-generic clatter of discarded sweepings from the floors of hit factories, glued together with blatant dishonesty in order to do a job that it never delivered on. For me, bar a couple of happy accidents, that band will forever have a bad whiff about it.

One minor hit with the track 'Underneath the Radar' didn't even buy a plate of beans, let alone secure us a career. Always image conscious and with my blinkered sights fixed on end results, I sweet-talked and enlisted the support of loyal friends, then herded them over the precipice.

I have hours of filmed concerts from that era – German TV broadcasts, videos shot at ridiculous expense in Spanish deserts, and archive footage of our flamboyantly costumed younger selves (an *exotic* period in our lives) when we were engaged again by Peter Stringfellow for a residency at the club he owned at the time, the Hippodrome Theatre in Leicester Square. The rest of it remains an embarrassment of necessities to help us escape the eighties. In hindsight, the best thing about MKI was ensuring that the stupid mistakes we made wouldn't have to be repeated in the future.

Farmyard Studios

Sometime in 1988, around *Underneath the Radar*, we were contacted by a 'happening' American DJ/producer who was chomping at the bit to remix a track of ours called 'Shock the Doctor' for the dance clubs of New York.

Rick, Alf and our management were keen, thought it was a really cool idea, a no-brainer, a way to reach a whole other audience. So they thought I was mad when, in one of my infinitely blinkered tirades, I refused, arguing that I didn't want people to think we were *a dance band!* Rick intuitively felt we should let this guy do his thing, but I dug my heels in.

I can see now how frustrating this must have been for him, and how it would have tested a saint's patience to have worked with me. I was too wrapped up in my parochial musical tastes to see a good thing, even when it was offered on a plate, but I agreed to meet the producer with Rick and Alf anyway (to give one of my vintage speeches!) over at Good Earth Studios in Soho, just a few yards from the music shop on Shaftesbury Avenue where I didn't buy that vintage Gibson, because of another knee-jerk of emotions.

Fifteen years on, same streets. Nothing had changed.

Soho, London

Talk Talk – *Spirit of Eden*

Two nights and a day in the Sahara Desert. A unique silence, so quiet I was deafened by the noise in my head.

North Africa

Ali Farka Touré – *Ali Farka Touré*

We toured America in our first ever tour bus, driven by a guy who was the spitting image of Kenny Rogers. He drank Mountain Dew to stay awake on long hauls, listened non-stop to country music, and kept a loaded Magnum under his seat. I'd sit upfront with him during the day, connecting over the classic hits of the Marshall Tucker Band, listening to him talk about life on the road, his precious car and boat back home in the South, and his deep-seated hatred of rap music.

Thanks to Sire's persistence, we played places where they knew us, and places where we barely scraped an audience. We bought tie-dyed T's from Deadheads in Atlantic City, played First Avenue in Minneapolis, where Prince filmed *Purple Rain*, had a private tour around Graceland, walked to the Mississippi under a fever-yellow Memphis sky ignoring smog warnings, drove through snow and rain and the heat of the Southern States (when the bus air conditioning broke), shook hands with Bill Graham and re-recorded our album in front of live audiences all over the US. We gave each session's tape away to the audience every night, left radio stations happy everywhere we made personal appearances, shook every hand, answered every question, signed every autograph and left not even the slightest impression on a country so vast the only way we could've made a mark would have been to relocate and tour non-stop. Bands did that back then, but not us.

Six weeks was long enough. It still remains the longest tour we've ever done. Weird stuff happens to your head when you're touring with a band that long – people turn in on themselves and come out swinging. One night, in Charlotte, North Carolina, in heat so close it could boil thoughts, Bryn came to the end of his road. It was his birthday, too far from home and fuelled on Jack, he lost it. We limped back to the UK, Rick relocated to Romford and we moved our base there, making it harder for Bryn to get to rehearsals. I was living miles away from anyone in a tiny low-rent flat on Kensington Church Street, in the roof of a building that rocked when tube trains passed underneath. Just before the first Australian tour I got the call: 'I can't do it any more, I'm sorry.'

That familiar punch to the guts, same as the night my band broke up back home. Beyond comprehension, a world upside down. Weeks before we were about to fly to Australia, a country he'd always wanted to tour, Bryn bailed. Years later he confided, 'I left before you kicked me out.'

We were rehearsing in an industrial unit Rick had found us on a farm on the outskirts of Romford. All the other businesses complained about the noise, so we had to do something or be forced out. Places like that don't come along every day, so we persuaded Sire to give us the money to build a studio of our own. It was an unusual request, but Sire was no ordinary label, and they said, 'Yes.' From the outside it looked like exactly the same industrial unit it always was, but when the huge double doors were slid back another building was revealed inside. A house within a house, a shed within a shed, like walking onto the set of *Dr Who*.

We asked Baz, 'If you could play with any drummer in London who would that be?' We got his dream drummer's phone number and he joined – just like that. Pascal Console laid an easy funk groove that made everyone nod. Our rhythm section sounded fantastic, but something was out of sync again.

For months we'd been tuning into the east London pirate stations. Pirate broadcasts were important again, and all of them were playing acid house – a sublime, electric thrill that reminded me of music from my youth – Kraftwerk, Hawkwind, Tangerine Dream and the sound of electric Germany, all glued together for an outsider generation who no longer needed a music industry to give it what it wanted. Tens of thousands of people were dancing all night in secret locations, surfing on the vibrations of makeshift sound systems. Records were being made in bedrooms – the new generation of studio. Records were pressed on the cheap and sold from the backs of cars direct to record shops all over the country.

It was a revolution, the one punk rock had stopped short of delivering. Musicians, DJs and composers were directly injecting their music into the night to a rapidly expanding audience of willing takers ready to buy and hungry for more. The pirate stations were direct descendants of the offshore broadcasters from the sixties that I grew up on. Both were the voice of a generation playing music ignored by national radio. The revolution was happening without us, and we were rehearsing a tired old funk rock sound to tour Australia. It was all so familiar. A smiley face, stencilled on a sun-bleached wall in Perth, grinned at us. It seemed to be saying, 'The boat's leaving, boys, and you're not on it.'

Change the Weather, our second album as Underworld, was demoed entirely by Rick on his brand new computer. I added voice and guitar, expecting us to call the band in and record it 'properly'. The few people who heard those recordings told us, 'Leave it exactly like it is. It's the best thing you've ever done.' I just couldn't hear it – dumb, so dumb; no faith. I was still too screwed up by cousin Ian's comments to believe in the sound of my own voice, and I couldn't let go of the rock-thing. That fear extended into everything else. I didn't think I had anything worth saying; I was always chasing somebody else's dream, following on behind. I had ideas in my head that I could almost – but never quite – grasp. I never gave them time to form on their own. I was always too afraid of being sent back to the factory. Rick humoured me, suffered me one last time by reluctantly going along with my myopic insistence that we had to get a 'real band' on the record, and replace the machines.

This was the end. And with it, the real beginning.

Abridge, Essex

Soul II Soul – 'Back to Life'; Public Enemy – 'Fight the Power';
A Guy Called Gerald – 'Voodoo Ray'; Frankie Knuckles presents Satoshi Tomiie – 'Tears';
Lil Louis – 'French Kiss'; Technotronic feat. Felly – 'Pump Up the Jam'

A rare night in London at the Town and Country Club to hear the On-U Sound System – Keith LeBlanc and Tackhead performing but, most importantly, most impressively, Adrian Sherwood at the controls. The mixing desk as an instrument, using the sound system in a way I'd never experienced before. Realising the gig had started since the second the power had been switched on and the doors opened, it was a totally immersive experience, completely unlike the standard approach of every gig I'd ever been to. Although reggae systems had been doing this forever, this was our introduction. We were hooked, couldn't stop talking about it for days.

Kentish Town, London

Keith LeBlanc – 'But Whitey', 'Einstein'

The most beautiful music I ever heard was the sound of the New York rush hour.

Lying in bed, uptown

John Cage – *Empty Words* 'Part II'

Lola was a radio DJ in Hamburg. I had been interviewed by her on air many times over the years and we had become friends through our mutual love of music.

'Have you heard the *New York* album?' she asked, as we left the studio one day. 'You'll love it.'

'I'm not really that big a Lou Reed fan.'

'Oh, but this album is different. It's fantastic.' She gave me her personal copy. 'You're going to love it.'

I refused to listen to it straight away, but Lola was a dear friend so I accepted her gift and filed it under 'one day maybe but probably not'. I procrastinated for ages, then there it was in the CD player, with my finger pressing play.

The simple synopsis of what happened next could be that Lou Reed's *New York* album changed my life, inspired me to radically alter the way I gathered words and wrote lyrics. Imagining how Lou might have collected his words, straight off the streets of New York, I started concealing myself in public places, writing down overheard conversations and documenting my nocturnal journeys through cities.

Norman Cook once told me that when he heard 'Cowgirl' a penny dropped for him. For me it was Lou Reed's 'Last Great American Whale'.

Hamburg

OK, so I've been emailing and asking around, and nobody admits they turned me on to it, so maybe it was me that went out and bought Sam Shepard's *Motel Chronicles* unprompted. I find it hard to believe I'd do something that smart – perhaps it was a mistake? – but there it was in my hand, a book of bits by my favourite playwright, a man I could never aspire to be a tenth as good as, who told stories of such rich intensity you could taste them, smell them coming across the fields, and breathe in the dust kicked up by their boots.

I could never write stories with beginnings, middles and ends. *Motel Chronicles* is a collection of 'middles' – fabulous shiny things, vignettes, snapshots of half-remembered memories, photographs clicked from the hip. I could do that; I could *try* to do that, at least.

I already carried a notebook and pen for collecting scraps off the street, out of the windows of cars, from the tables of bars. I didn't know what I was writing them for, but I liked the sensation. I was always running out of words for lyrics that Rick was forever waiting for me to write, so maybe this new process could provide a steady stream. I was always searching for something great, something that would surprise Rick, delight him, something to replace the vocal mumblings I'd record to hold place on the songs I wrote. Every time I replaced those noises that sounded so good, I did it with words that were limp and contrived, which beat the joy out of the songs before throwing them lifeless to the ground.

Motel Chronicles became my bible. It travelled everywhere with me. I read it from cover to cover and back again, month after month, soaking up the rhythm of Shepard's words until they were second nature, a world of scattered fragments. All I had to do was open my notebook and let them fall in.

A light goes on

LONELY

A strange feeling after so much time in the company of
friends and dancing in the euphoria of electric pure joy faces.

Last night, at the end of a week connected to all that's good,
I returned to an empty hotel room where my dog was waiting.

That familiar voice of hopeless desolation keen to pick up
the conversation. Had to laugh, a patient and dedicated companion,
never disappoints. I should've known he'd stow away - the baggage
of the past comes out to play when I'm alone.

Laughter is the antidote as, even in the rain, we find joy - my dog
and me.

Yesterday's fog stopped the band going home - no planes flying.
I spent the day in radio stations, doing what I love, broadcasting,
spending time with people who relish spreading their passion for music.

Radio stations smell great, look great, and everyone I met yesterday
reminded me why I'm on this road. Found a poster of Bob and the
Boomtown Rats
in a back corridor, carried a purple key on an elastic band tied to
a bulldog clip to a private toilet, a sanctuary with a lock on the
door, quiet time.

Heard music that made me want to make more, found connections to
Jagwar Ma,
a sign I was on the right road. Found a man, eyes full of light,
who turned me on to lost John Martyn recordings, and I made a phone
call from the floor below to a girl going live to air who talked
excitedly about
the legend of a dog whose name became a drinking anthem.

And then we met in the harbour, you were pulling a case on wheels.
We drank coffee in the sun and smiled, one to the other,
remembering how far we've come and how lucky.

We'd been there at their inception back in Conny's studio, and now we were travelling around America at the end of the Eurythmics' journey. Securing such a coveted support slot on their farewell tour was in no small part down to my dad. There's this thing he's always said to me every since I can remember: 'If you don't ask, you don't get.'

Underworld MKI were on another scrappy little tour around northern Europe when I saw an interview with Dave Stewart and Annie Lennox talking about heading off to America one last time. Dad's words were loud and clear when I had the ridiculous idea that *if we just asked them* they might invite us to tour with them, and so I called our manager Rupert Merton, persuading him that it was at least worth a shot. Rupert asked and the Eurythmics said, 'Yes.' (Thanks, Dad.)

On the tour, they were bowing out by playing arenas and we were falling apart in support. Our buses parked side-by-side indoors, backstage; 15,000 people a night, a dream come true and yet, by increments, we hated it. Not the Eurythmics – they treated us with respect and gave us all we needed to hang ourselves. It was the arriving at a place we'd believed we belonged, only to discover it wasn't our place at all. Every night was a grind, the music like lead in our veins. I gritted my teeth and faked it, chanting the same words again, going through the motions.

In Kansas City Rick twisted his ankle badly on stage and spent the rest of the tour on crutches. I didn't know how to be a mate. Alf sat with him for hours in A&E, I went back to my hotel room, couldn't do the right thing so got drunk instead. Then got drunk again after the gig in Houston, disappeared and found myself in a park with a giant cake floating on a midnight lake. We got food poisoning in a vegan restaurant, played Radio City Music Hall, learned to pay respect to the unions, saw the fall of the Berlin Wall as we drove through the back streets of Philadelphia listening to Wagner, ate our first Philly-dogs, met Fat Dawg at Subway Guitars in Berkeley, signed up for his Rock Against Racism bulletins, embarrassed myself meeting Jack Nicholson and k. d. lang at an aftershow party, and finished our career playing two nights at Universal Amphitheatre in Los Angeles.

Thanksgiving 1989, Underworld gathered for a last supper at our American manager's house. Pumpkin pie as dessert for the final act. One by one, taxis drew up outside to collect Baz and Pascal, then Rick and Alf, until I was left alone with that cold-knotted fist in the pit of my stomach again.

Los Angeles

Eurythmics – 'Here Comes the Rain Again'

Through Underworld's then publisher, Warner Chappell, Rick and I were introduced to Terri Nunn, with the idea that we try co-writing songs for her. I knew very little about Terri other than she'd had a massive global hit with a song called 'Take My Breath Away'. It had been on *Top of the Pops* every week for longer than I could remember – even longer than The Archies' 'Sugar, Sugar' – and though I couldn't stand it, I had to admit I was unlikely to ever forget it. Written and produced by Giorgio Moroder, a man I'd previously held in high regard for his peerless 'I Feel Love' (with the fabulous Donna Summer singing that joyous refrain), a track that redefined pop and liberated electronic music from dance-club obscurity with a force that slapped it straight onto the A list of every pop radio station in the world. 'Take My Breath Away', on the other hand, was the signature track of the huge Hollywood blockbuster *Top Gun*, a film I had no interest in. To me it was just another irritating MOR track clogging up the radio waves. Terri had previously enjoyed notable success fronting the cult American new wave band Berlin, and over time she convinced me that her heart was set on a return to a sound she saw as being more credible, citing The Sisters of Mercy as inspiration. I liked her energy and drive. There was something so wonderfully positive and unstoppable about her, and I was excited to start working with her.

Co-writing was something new for me – a challenge, an opportunity to write for someone else and expand Underworld's reach – so Rick and I agreed to an exploratory writing session. We began at our studio out in Abridge, recording together through one of the bitterest Essex winters I can recall, and for a week, one of the most famous pop singers of the eighties, resident of the sunshine state of California, rented a freezing little box room in a terraced house in Romford, and commuted every day to an industrial barn at the end of a muddy farm track, where our studio was concealed, to see if we could help her realise her vision. Though she was very persuasive in convincing me of her determination to shake off the global image she had acquired through 'Take My Breath Away' I knew it could be a long road back for her, even if we managed to perfectly deliver everything she hoped for. For some reason, though Terri included the track Rick and I wrote with her on her album, she decided to continue writing with me alone, and thus began a dark, disturbing and lonely journey.

A lot of what I learned from this (and the sessions that followed) brought me face to face with some of the harsher realities of the music business as it was in LA circa 1989–90. Throughout it all, I tried as best I could to give her the sound she wanted, even though it became evident her record label saw her potential as a huge pop star with a string of hit records, repeating the success of that first massive hit. Soon, 'friends' and managers would fade away. Carrots that were dangled would disappear, and doors that had once been open would be slammed shut. I would become just another Brit couch-surfing the California scrap heap, no longer the new kid in town but facing the cold reality of having no income and losing the home my girlfriend and I had mortgaged our lives to buy if I didn't go the distance with this project and bring home the bacon.

The taxi dropped me at a hotel off Sunset. Round the corner was Barney's Beanery, a bar that inspired a famous art installation by Ed Kienholz that I'd seen in a gallery in Amsterdam backpacking with my girlfriend. Here in LA they had the real thing – a place to numb the pain with booze and fries and late-night pool to *make it all go away*. I had no band and no tribe, but at least I had a job to go to playing guitar, an obligation that got me out of bed, kept a roof over my head back in Romford.

Now I was trying to help fellow singer Terri find herself. It meant a lot to me that someone believed I had the answer to their question, and I clung on to that like a life raft. Throughout the whole of this LA period I genuinely tried to give everything Terri asked me for, all the while suspecting it wasn't what her record company wanted.

My new songs were different from anything Underworld had recorded. We demoed them late into the night at a backstreet studio, surviving on macrobiotic takeaways from the Source, which were delivered by scary pseudo-mystical women identically dressed in white. We drove up into the hills, the air fiercely hot while we waded knee-deep in snow, cruised the strip outside Edwards Air Force Base, saw the graveyard of planes made famous in the 'Take My Breath Away' video, and watched stunt kites in tight formation dance above the beach on the lips of the Pacific Ocean. This was as close to living the rock-star life as I'd ever get. It was all that I had imagined, and yet so much less, particularly the money and job security.

Terri liked my songs and genuinely believed that 'together' we could find her sound, connect her to the person she wanted to be. Even though her label had their own idea about the path she should take, they let us loose to do our own thing for a couple of weeks. The first time we worked together was fun; the second was cold steel. I was unwanted by the new producer, the label and the cartoon-Californian silver-tip-booted rock-god of a keyboard player, who was actually English and who eyed me with disdain at our first rehearsal. Standing behind his keyboards at our first rehearsal he flicked back his cascading mane and talked down to me with the most exaggerated English accent I have ever heard.

Him and his buddy the producer (another Englishman) wanted me out of the band. They made me play things they knew were hard for me, things I'd never had to play in my life. They were on my back every day, critical of everything I did. Nothing was right, nothing was good enough – they hated my sound, my style, my inability to instantly copy styles to order. Worst of all, they were stuck with me. I met Sharona of 'My Sharona' fame (one of Terri's closest mates and a real estate agent) and when the label turned down most of my songs, Terri and I went to meet with the big-name songwriters, who were generating millions for labels in the US charts, to ask for their help.

We met Ric Ocasek from The Cars at the Hotel California, and asked him for a song. I then reunited Terri with Giorgio Moroder in the hope that together they would record the hit I believed she deserved. We sat with one of the most important electronic producers of all time, trying to add his magic to some Banshees-lite rock songs written by a boy from Bewdley.

We hawked around LA meeting and greeting American songwriting royalty in an attempt to get them interested in writing for the project. The band assembled for Terri moved from the rehearsal studio to Ocean Way on Sunset Boulevard. Palm trees, Denny's diner, the Capitol Records tower, Terri's white Jeep in the parking lot. White heat, scorched blacktop. Every morning we outrode earthquakes together, all the way into town from Playa del Rey, to set up our gear on the rich patina of classic studio parquet. The sound of the Beach Boys and the historic lineage of Californian music came out of this place, and I came within seconds of being sacked from the session.

Randy Castillo - Terri's drummer, direct from Ozzy Osbourne's band - was a gentleman I warmed to instantly. He welcomed me in and seemed to like me; he picked me up when the keyboard player and the producer Steve Brown were on my back. The session started with Randy laying all his drum tracks down then leaving for another session across town. Alone again, I found myself exposed to the displeasure I roused in my fellow Brits. 'OK, your turn,' the producer sighed. I tried, but I couldn't lock onto the drums, the groove kept slipping away from me, slowing and speeding in tiny increments. Back in England I was used to jamming along to drum machines, getting locked to their groove, moving across them in fractions to produce oscillations that only being tight could create, and yet here I was unable to stay in time with the drums. I was sunk.

'OK, thanks, Karl, take a break. We just want to have a think.'

'I think the drums are going out of time,' I offered.

'Sorry, mate, not likely. Take a walk, maybe - get some air. Let us think what we should do.'

I knew what was coming, so I thought I'd use what little time I had left to let off steam, play the way I knew best. I asked the tape-op to set up a drum machine for me so I could mess around, relax. With a machine groove to ride I started looping funk riffs, losing myself in music that I loved. Man/machine, trancing.

'Could you come in here a minute, Karl?'

Here we go.

'Er, I didn't know you could play like that!'

'Yeah, I do it a lot.'

'It looks like you were right, the drums are going out of time. Got any ideas?'

'Now I know it's the tempo that's changing, I can ride his groove.'

'You can do that?'

'Yeah.'

After that, me and Steve, the producer, never crossed words again. We got on, laughed, joked, became drinking buddies until the day he left the project. The plum-voiced keyboard player with the Californian hairdo was called 'Flashman' (truth). He seemed to do a 180 degree turn in his opinion of me, gave me his sofa when I was homeless, introduced me to the ex-pat community and took me drinking in their bars around LA. We became and remain the closest of friends, regardless of any physical distance between us – a friendship as deep as bone. Something clicked.

This friendship would be crucial when we were recalled for the third session. A new band was assembled out of LA and New York session players, all gathered together for an extraordinary journey through a Minnesota winter at Prince's Paisley Park Studios.

Los Angeles

Terri Nunn – 'Confession Time'

A recommendation from our friend Rupert Hine led to us forming one of the most rewarding relationships of our musical career (and in turn, our lives). A beautifully uncynical veteran of several decades in the industry, Geoff Jukes had been responsible for some of the legendary Happenings at the Roundhouse in the late sixties – forerunners for the acid house parties that would inspire us years later. At the time we met, he was managing Penguin Café Orchestra, renting office space to Brian Eno's Opal Records and working closely with the Dalai Lama. The best and fairest negotiator of the many who had looked after us over the years, Geoff was the first person to offer to find me help beyond what I'd found in a bottle.

Playa del Rey. A two-room apartment set back from the road. Short lease, no garden, Tarmac out front. Only terrestrial channels on a borrowed TV. A four-track tape recorder, a microphone, a guitar, a drum machine, a bunch of effects pedals. Bed, sofa, kitchenette. The convenience store next door smells of cinnamon and stewed coffee. The owner says, 'Hi!' every morning like he knows me.

Playa del Rey, California

When most of the songs I'd written with Terri were turned down by her label, I returned to the little ground-floor flat I shared with my girlfriend in Romford. The first time I got back together with Rick, he played me 'Fools Gold' by The Stone Roses, an infectious groove with a haunting vocal attitude floating unfettered across the top of it. He then sat me down and played me '"B" Movie' by Gil Scott-Heron and told me, 'Listen!' He spoke about how a song could be if it was free of radio butchery, and what could happen if you let it loose to go on a journey. For the first time, I listened to what he said. I let him teach me, prime me and load me. Then I got the recall and flew back to the USA.

Maybe our accents had swung it – only myself and Flashman being retained. The roll call of British musicians who have made this pilgrimage only to hang up their spurs is long. At night we drank in bars, pooling our dollars to get the rounds in, reliant on anyone with a car to get around. I was marooned – a freak on foot, walking for miles across the city from home to studio, attracting disapproving stares from passing motorists, pulled over by cops who enquired, 'What are you doing?'

Underworld's American manager stopped taking my calls. It got dark and lonely. The only comforts were a couch and a mate with silver-tipped boots who ferried me to parties. He kept me afloat when the wind was dying in the sails, and there was no way of paying a mortgage back in Romford. The Black Dog lay down with me every night, whispering in my ear. These lyrics are from a notebook of that period:

I will not be confused, you left me confused,
I will not be confused with another man
... the pressure of opinions!

One violently sunny LA morning, a shocking-pink Cadillac, a 1960s vintage with the top down, pulled up outside the Flashman B&B. Chaz Jankel at the wheel, honked the horn. I don't remember how it came about – maybe one of those typical LA connections, someone knew someone, someone had a mad idea at a party – but here we were, the boy from Romford and the guitarist from the Blockheads, driving to the cheaper side of town to write a song. A tiny domestic studio in the back of a suburban low-rise – a bedroom with some tech injection – signalled the future. A young Hispanic kid at the controls, Chaz and him and me recording a song for Terri that I felt nothing for. I was clutching at straws. I'd leave the room to rinse my brain in front of a gargantuan TV in the next room. Twenty-four-hour MTV, with the colours cranked until they stabbed your eyes with violent pixel knives. It was colour to make you crave black and white, but then a sound ... familiar, home, calling me.

'Guys, you got to come and hear this, it's fantastic!'

Chaz and Boy-Studio sloped in. After ten beats, they grunted, turned and left.

'But it's beautiful – listen!'

The studio door shut. Me on the outside – a metaphor, a path, some are called, few get up. The Stone Roses were playing 'Fools Gold' on MTV and no one could hear it but me. A light turned on, a memory of that 12-inch Rick had played me back home – a groove in its bone, a sound in my head. This was 'European' music, my music, the sound of my tribe, the people I belonged with – not here, not in this city of lost angels.

Rick was calling me back to Romford, where I should've been all along. 'Click.' With the last of my money I caught a taxi to LAX and flew home to Essex.

Los Angeles

The Stone Roses – 'Fools Gold'; Happy Mondays – 'Hallelujah'

KARL HYDE

FOR COLLECTION 28th MAY

Do not touch

HOME

Essex in the rain looks more beautiful than ever.
Jet-lagged on the M25, a thin piece of wire pulled through
the head, feel sick and phasing in and out of sleep.
Things go too fast and emails come in torrents.
Ha, ha, ha, everything is green and beautiful.

Allan Kaprow – *How to Make a Happening*

RETURN OF THE YELLOW STUFF

There's a discernible taste to the air, breathing isn't
so much fun. The season of the Yellow Stuff returns and
with it the subtle beauty of hawthorn blooms. Hedgerows
and verges explode with delicate shades of white, the last
blossom of the season, promising gentle summer walks
at sunrise and long balmy evenings punctuated with the
sound of laughter and alfresco dining.

Yesterday I drove to a café, returning to the joy
of notating loud conversation, parked up in the sun and
sat quiet with clear thoughts about the work to come.
In late afternoon we rescued blue-tit chicks fallen from
the nest, between sessions in the studio enjoying
the return to making music,
watching the sun sink slow into the trees
passing a calming hand over Essex.

Part Chimp – *Chart Pimp*

Essex was the first place I felt like I belonged, the only place I belong.

My girlfriend and I bought a little ground-floor flat opposite the bus garage – 179 North Street, where the buses idled, engines running, making the whole house shake. After-hour drunks on their way home would piss up our bedroom window and steal our hubcaps, but we were welcomed into the community by Romford families as if we were one of their own. Homes were opened to us, and we were made to feel part of every family.

South Essex, and in particular Romford, has always had an energy about it that's very different to where I'm from. Back in the West Midlands, it used to feel like we were living under a perpetual cloud, dreams were stillborn. Here in Romford anything was possible, all you needed was 'drive', and Essex has more of that than anywhere I've lived – an aspirational positivity that's infectious even to a dour Midlander like me, something I could never drag down or beat. I caught the bug and fell in love.

Essex is a state of mind, the Yin to my Yang, the light to my dark. It offers hope when there is none; it was the place that welcomed me in off the street when I admitted the drink was killing me. Whenever I've asked for help, Essex has never turned its back: 'Get the kettle on, everything's gonna be all right. I know a bloke with a van!'

Romford

Back from LA and with no other income available, I took a job with a mate's temping agency, working for Coopers and Lybrand Deloitte – a multinational accountancy firm. It was the first 'proper job' I'd ever had. I wore a suit, shined my shoes and combed my hair. I toed the line and felt like an utter failure. I was a sell-out in a suit, the lowest of the low, riding grey commuter trains in and out of the City surrounded by tired faces, long staring eyes, gagging on the smell of soap and aftershave. The knots of ties like hangman's nooses crowded round as I wrote it all down in the notebook I carried with me to keep me sane, fantasising I was an undercover writer.

'What's your real profession?' people in the office asked.

'Oh, er, well, I'm actually a travel writer.'

I clocked on, did what they wanted me to, did it well and a little more. They asked me to stay on, increased my responsibilities and wages. I thought, 'Wow, this is easy. You turn up, do your job, and get paid! How come I spent so much time knocking myself out in bands when there's an easier route right here?' It all seemed so simple and I started to enjoy myself, met people who were far more interesting than most I'd met in the music business – real people, nice people, people who had your back if you needed help. I liked their stories, liked the way they thought, talked, drank … Every lunch time we'd go to the pub together. I was expert at this bit, the etiquette, and even how not to drink too much (at first).

'You're *all right*,' they'd say.

I was happy, took myself off to the riverbank after lunch at the pub, and talked to the notebook. I took it home every night to Rick, who'd been hard at it in his studio all day, dog-tired, in need of a rest.

'OK if I come round and record with you tonight, Rick?'

I pushed him beyond tired most nights of the week, selfish and hungry to balance my day by spending at least some of it playing at being a musician. Rick wasn't playing at anything. He was doing it – music all day, every day, the real deal. He never threw the towel in once, never 'got a job', stuck to what he did best, and had faith. I knew that with him was where I was meant to be, but I didn't have his courage or drive or skills. The best I can say is I stuck around. Rick was writing with other artists now, finding his voice and sounding great. I was jealous. That jealousy was probably what made me want it again when the boss called me into his office and said, 'We like the way you work. I'm sending you on a management course.'

I thanked him, shook his hand, and asked if he would mind if I took a couple of days to think about it. Counting my savings I calculated there was enough for three months' mortgage. Everyone in the office was shocked when I handed in my notice. I was surprised too. It was the best and easiest money I'd ever made – life was simple, no worries. Work the system, fall in line, and drink with the right people. Give more than you were asked and the rewards were sweet; the easy life, and yet ... that talk of a 'management' course shook me, made me realise how much I still loved being a musician. I wanted to work with Rick, and knew I wasn't finished yet.

Within a week, I quit the job and told myself I'd give music three months.

With it looking like my partnership with Rick would continue, his wife took me to one side.

'If you two want to carry on together, you are going to need to do something different. You're going to have to find something special.'

For once I actually listened and, taking her advice seriously, instantly recalled the time I used alcohol at art school to liberate me from my naturally timid self. It had *enabled me* to experience the world unfettered by my fears and *delivered me* that first class honours degree (or so I thought). It had also been a fantastic adventure.

Now I had a plan!

The way ahead was clear and simple. I made a pact with myself right then to become *two people*. At night, I'd be the drunk, trawling streets, notebook and pen in hand, painstakingly, voyeuristically documenting every encounter and emotion. In the morning, the sober me would come round to discover pages full of words. Those words – documented unawares and poured raw into the lines of countless notebooks – would be shaped to form lyrics way beyond my sober capabilities. The conscious mind had become an encumbrance, I had to liberate my unconscious and allow it free rein. Alcohol would be my best friend and muse.

City of London, early 1990

Adamski Feat. Seal – 'Killer'; the B-52's – 'Roam'; LFO – 'LFO'; Happy Mondays – 'Kinky Afro'

Early 1990, still winter, snow covering the prairies. Minnesota, the state of 10,000 lakes, ice so thick you could drive trucks across it, erect wooden buildings on it, cut holes in it to fish. No one was more shocked than me that I was back for a three-month 'trial period' to work on Terri's album. It had been cool of her to fight for me, but the label still didn't like me or my sound. I woke up as we were coming into land, looked out of the window and didn't have a clue what I was seeing: bomb craters for miles, a landscape ravaged by war; mud, rock and tank tracks … I tried to work out how we'd been redirected into this nightmare. Then I remembered, we were coming into land in Minneapolis. What the hell were all these craters?

The album sessions reconvened at Prince's Paisley Park Studios under the guidance of producer David Z (whose brother Bobby drummed with Prince's Revolution). David was riding high on his success with the Fine Young Cannibals' 'She Drives Me Crazy'. He had a 'sound', and a natural touch with a groove. He programmed his LinnDrum machine in that Minnesota zone between rock and hip hop that was taking over the world. I liked David and he seemed to like me enough. The band for the session was put together with people he knew from LA, New York and right there in the prairies. These were serious musicians, who scared the shit out of me at first. I knew they could see right through me, I felt one inch tall. But they turned out to be human: not one of them put me down, instead they all rallied round and gave me support and encouragement, even threatened strike action when my pay cheque was overdue. These strangers quickly became friends, and along with my old saviour Andrew Flashman, they became my tribe.

One night, in the spring of 1990, I lay awake in my room – a bed in a box decorated in Laura Ashley chintz – fly-screen windows wide open, listening to the approach of another storm. Every week they tested the tornado sirens on the edge of town, the prairie country on the banks of the Mississippi. We were billeted in a half-built hotel in a one-street town, with a dinner theatre, a bar, a few local shops and a drive-through bank. Every morning, the cops would call in for coffee and donuts, to rest up and talk to the owner while monitoring their radios. 'Thunderheads are coming in,' said the owner. That night, as I lay awake in my room, listening to another storm approaching, I reached for my notebook:

'Thunder, Thunder, Lightning ahead.'

Chanhassen, Minnesota

Prince – 'Get Off'

Dr. Mambo's Combo were the resident band at Bunker's Music Bar & Grill on the night we piled into a white Ford Probe and drove into Minneapolis. Wikipedia says they've been resident there since '87, but it was the first and only time I ever saw them, reinforcing a long-held belief that American bar bands are leagues ahead of pub bands in the UK. Until we got there I'd always thought 'uptown' was just a cool line in a Prince song, but here it was, wrapped around us, everthing on show and beggin' for it, vibrant, luminous and hungry.

I was out with Flashman, and drummer Billy Ward and bass player Mark Leonard came with us that night as we squeezed through a packed house to find a booth at the back, from where it was impossible to see the band. It was equally impossible to feel anything but physically connected to their groove – they were totally *in the pocket*. Michael Bland (who Prince had discovered drumming with the Combo) was holding down the coolest beat, smiling and nodding as we walked in.

We'd met up at Paisley Park and watched him rehearsing with Prince for his latest band, the New Power Generation. Here, live and direct from super-league rehearsals, he was sitting in with his old bar-band buddies. These guys *loved* playing; Dr. Mambo's Combo were tight and funky. The presence of Prince's groove was evident in the city – combine that with the production and feel of local producers Jam and Lewis, and the Minneapolis streets were laying down their marker as the home of funk. We were talking fast, drinking loose, on a rare night off from the studio, getting deep into cross-fire stories, letting our guard down and becoming a unit (important on a session so far from home).

Suddenly, the vibe in the room changed, tilted, twisted on an invisible axis, stopped the conversation dead. The noise in the bar filtered, focused; everyone looked in one direction. 'What the hell? What happened?' Billy climbed up on top of the booth and yelled, 'You gotta see this!'

Something fantastic was happening on the other side of the crowd. We stood up on our seats to glimpse an incongruous figure in white, almost hidden behind the kit, beautiful and wild, laying down a scary groove. It filled the room with a vibe the like of which I've only heard one other time – watching Prince at Birmingham NEC arena with that same drummer. Without dropping a single beat, Michael had slipped out from behind his kit and handed over to Sheila E! The whole groove in the room shifted. It became tighter, funkier, sexier. An already rammed dancefloor became an electrified frenzy, like someone had flicked on a turbo switch. And the beer – even the light stuff – tasted so much sweeter.

Bunker's, Minneapolis

Prince – 'Uptown'

ON THE POETRY OF LAST TRAINS

Drunk boys ask violently who they are, swaggering in shirt sleeves for a place on the last train, fists like first class honours degrees, knuckles as white as the drunk woman, holding court on the train, brandishing profanities like an honorary membership to the gutter.
'Inside I feel 19!' She shouts perhaps in compensation for how she feels about her appearance. Hair in pigtails, clothes too tight, too loud, a story without a punch line. We pause on our journey home to witness grinning boys with arms of tattooed stars herd wide eyed girls into the dark, out towards their promised lands.

New Buffalo – 'About Last Night'

There have been times in my life when I wished for the end, usually when I was blissed out and bumping along the bottom. All of them involved drink. That first time was in the backseat of Haggis's dark blue Ford. Seventeen years later, I'm riding out of Minneapolis in the back of another Ford after a late-night session at David Z's house – a party where I heard Prince's demo for 'Kiss' (genius) and cleared the house out of vodka, *twice*.

'I gotta throw up, pull over!'

The car swerved to the side of the road. I leapt out and hacked across fields of snow, thigh-deep. I disappeared into a storm, looking for somewhere out of sight to chuck-up – an attempt to find a little dignity in the dirt. I peeled off my clothes, dropped 'em as I walked on, so as not to get puke down them, and kept walking into the storm until I reached a chain-link fence and just hung there, feeling nothing. No cold, just calm. Still, at peace.

'This is a good place to die,' I thought, falling asleep, hanging on the wire.

'Hey! Karl! What you doing, brother? We thought we'd lost you. I followed your trail, you got barely anything on! You'll catch your death out here!'

Flashman, heavy-coated, his furious hair a long black flag flailing 90 degrees in the wind. All my clothes bundled in his arms. The most English voice I'd ever heard, talking low and gentle to me now, 'Come on, we got to get you inside, it'll be all right …'

Snowstorm, Minnesota

The six weeks spent at Paisley Park were weird and great.

I met a lot of generous and talented musicians, who were patient and professional and always treated me like one of their own. Had it not been for them and the studio staff, who pretty much adopted me, it would have been too painful a time, too much flux and dark uncertainty.

Paisley Park is one of the most beautiful studio complexes I've recorded in. Everything about it, from the staff to Prince's Purple Cops and the huge film stage out back, set it apart from all the other studios I've worked in. The half-finished hotel, outside the city in Chanhassen, was run by an ex-submarine captain who, though friendly to everyone, gave special attention to anyone on an extended mission a long way from home.

Though it was within walking distance, we usually drove the courtesy white Ford to the session every day. As the sessions began to start progressively later, Flashman and I would get up early, breakfast with the cops, and take off for hours across the prairies. There were a lot of ex-Northern European tribes out there, towns with German street names, full of flaxen-haired people with Scandinavian features and dartboards in their bars. We bought maps to follow the curves of the Mississippi, pinpointing places that looked weird enough to explore.

Winter turned into spring as Ski-Doo runs melted, making way for the gentle rhythm of breeze-blown prairie grasses. Trucks that had been parked all winter on feet-thick lake-ice were removed. Fishermen's huts were hauled away for another year as ice-holes melted, making way for speedboats and sleek white cruisers to ferry barbecuing families to distant foreshores. Terrapins perched on logs, moving faster than startled dogs at the sound of approaching footsteps, and blizzards subsided into midnight heat, inspiring bullfrogs to sing in shallow ponds alongside railway crossing bells, as freight trains slipped through the sleeping town.

Chanhassen, Minnesota

We saw Prince's all-girl groups and listened to him rehearse the New Power Generation in the room next to our studio.

I visited the Purple Vault, a room strewn with chiffon and petals. I saw the motorcycle from *Purple Rain* parked underground; I recorded bullfrogs behind the bowling alley, and I got hit on by farm girls looking to try something different once they heard an English accent down at Pauly's sports bar.

The BBC rolled in and filmed a documentary about funk, with the J. B.'s in the studio across the hall. The crew's British accents sounded too clipped and weird as I made tea for Maceo Parker in the kitchen. We talked together about his love of London and my love of funk, inwardly embarrassed to even mention it in the presence of such a legend. Waiting for sessions to start I jammed with the other members of Terri's band, confused by the numbers they kept calling out. They were so good they could've left me for dead, but took me in as one of their own, looked after me when they saw what was really going on, and encouraged me to play the way I *wanted*, praising my 'English, indie style'. They told me, 'Pay no attention, it's great,' when the word came back from LA, 'We don't want any of that English shit on this album.' I even felt good enough to funk with them; I relaxed, had fun, felt good. I fed off their praise until that guitarist from Prince's band sat in and the funk left me in its dust. I just shook my head and laughed. He was so good, even his smile had funk!

One night, we all piled into the Ford and headed down to Glam Slam to see Miles Davis. I'd seen him at Wembley, years before with Rick and the Turbosound crew. He'd blown me away, playing with his back to the audience. *Bitches Brew*, *Kind of Blue* were deep in my bones. Miles was in the house – it was too small a club to be anything but within touching distance; we'd be breathing the same breath, something I couldn't miss. The place was packed, the boss was sat on a white sofa up on the balcony, directly in front of the stage, quiet, watching, soaking it all up.

When the Man took the stage I levitated. I don't have the words to recall the feeling. The things I witnessed that night I carry with me still. The only thing Miles said to the audience all night (and he remained *facing* us all through the show), spoken in that inimitable rasp, into the bell of his trumpet mic, was, 'Prince! Prince! Prince!'

The king of brevity, all twinkle-eyed, smiled, raised a hand and left. Word was, the last time he'd passed through town he'd jammed out at the studio with the boss, and right now the Purple engineers were preparing for another session with them both, to which we were invited! Then the rumour was Miles was too tired, couldn't make it.

Our bubble burst. We drove silent back out to the prairies, fantasising about what could've been and what legendary recordings were concealed in that Purple Vault.

Glam Slam, Minneapolis

Miles Davis – 'Jo-Jo'

After another bender, I'd returned to my hotel room to sit alone and ponder my future.

It might've been the ferocious storm raging outside, or the quantity of alcohol in my veins, but I had a dream in which I was playing guitar to a packed stadium, behind a famous blonde female singer whose face I couldn't see.

Going back over it the next morning, I concluded that the most famous blonde female singer of the day was Madonna, and that I would soon be summoned to New York to meet her as my new employer. The phone rang as I lay in bed chewing over how to face another day. It was the hotel manager: 'Hey, Karl, there's a guy on the phone from London, England. Says he knows you. Do you want me to put him through, or tell him I couldn't find you?'

This was the call my dream had prophesied, so I took it.

'Hey, Karl, Geoff Dougmore. How you doing? How long you going to be out there?'

'Hey, Geoff, it's strange you ask, 'cause the session is nearly done. I'm heading home in a couple of days.'

'Great! Any chance you can stop off in New York on the way? I'm putting a band together for a tour, and there are some people I want you to meet.'

Bingo!

'Yeah! What's the gig?'

'Debbie Harry.'

Chanhassen, Minnesota

Blondie – 'Union City Blue'

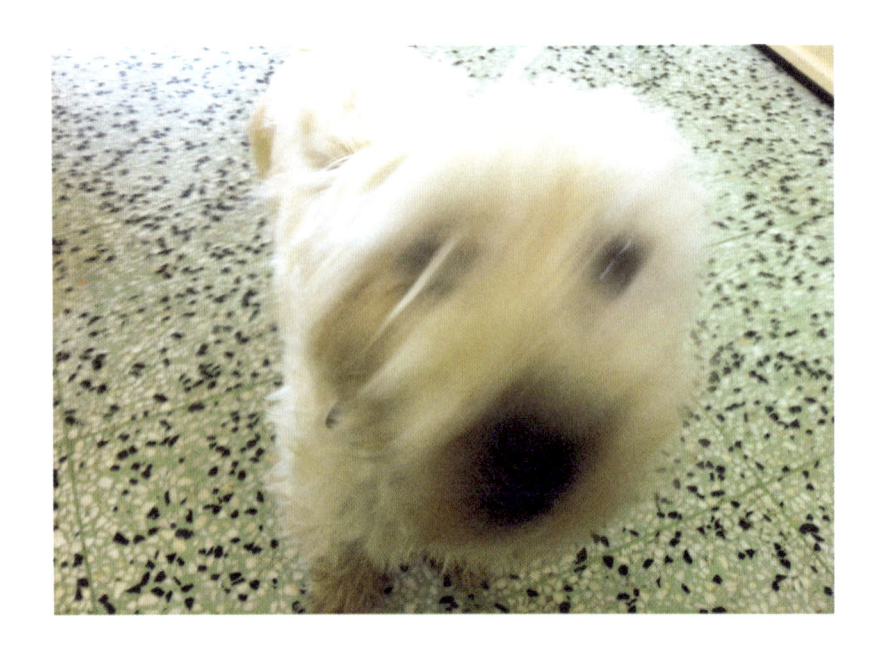

MEMORIES OF DUDLEY MOORE

Back at the hotel between shows I logged on and watched
old films of Peter Cook and Dudley Moore as Derek and Clive –
remembering how we laughed the night you fell through
the floor into the coalhole in Cardiff unloading amps.
As you rolled around in agony on the floor of an upstairs flat
we nursed you with brandy and the Lobster sketch,
getting drunk and sleepless,
laughing till the sun came up.

Derek and Clive – 'The Worst Job I Ever Had'

BRANCH DANCES AT SUNSET

I found you running at sunset, wires in your ears, smiling.
'It's so great to be running again!' you shouted, music pumping
as the light turned from gold to pink. I watched, sheltering in
the warmth of a streetlight.
'You don't have to wait,' you said,
but I was too happy to see you running to look away.

Rare Earth – 'Ma'

The blonde dream I had in Minnesota, then the phone call from England, changed my plans – my life – and put me on a flight to New York, where I 'auditioned' to play guitar in Debbie Harry's band. I was dumped, like Arnie in *The Terminator*, direct from six weeks in a gentle prairie town, straight into the heart of the fastest city on earth. Those six weeks would set the tone not only for the rest of the year but for the rest of my career.

I first met Chris Stein through the grille of an iron door, at a loading dock on an abandoned street in the warehouse district of the city. Larger in life, I instantly liked him. Cool stuff happened around Debbie and Chris, amazing things, and if you happened to be on their team amazing things would happen to you if you were paying attention. Two hours later a phone call was made: 'Yeah, he's here. Yeah, he looks OK, like Paul Weller. Dressed in black and white stripes. Come down and meet him, he's OK.'

Debbie breezed in smiling, lit up the room and took me shopping, as it became apparent that *everything* was part of the audition. I was trying not to lose my composure, through lack of sleep, the shock of the city and the strain of maintaining this façade of cool in the presence of such illustrious company. I was shaking like a clockwork monkey, vibrating, head on backwards, everything sped-up. I managed an hour at most, cruising clothes shops on 14th Street, and I knew I wouldn't be able to hold it together much longer, 'Er, I have to go.'

'Oh, you're leaving?'

'Yeah, it's been a long day. I have to lie down.'

'OK, are you right or left handed?'

'Pardon?'

'Do you play guitar right or left handed?'

'Oh. [pause to remember my name] ... right.'

'OK, give me your left hand.'

I obeyed, dazed, watching a film through pinhole eyes. The calloused tips of my fingers passed the test. I'd *qualified*.

'OK, see you in London.'

Manhattan

LATE AND LONG

Day starts early,
the time for writing diaries slips by like a supertanker shrouded in fog.
The sky is on fire,
dirty grey smudges of clouds drift low,
ripped open on the barbs of pylons, releasing showers of sunlight.
The luminous heads of purple grasses nod approval as rush hour's
children fearless, down tributaries to swim down the great black-top river
heading out to sea.

I turn the key and the engine moans.
My tyres follow the poetry of curves
through tunnels of May blossom and succulent greens.
No radio today, but with the window down and the speed low,
surfing a wave at the edge of summer.

Danny Kaye – 'Tubby the Tuba'

With no record deal or means of paying the rent, Alf left the band. He bought a small van and looked for work as a delivery man. One morning, as he left the engine running to go buy cigarettes, his van got nicked, leaving him with no money and minimal assets. The next I heard he was a night porter in a West Country hotel. That made me smile. Alf – ever the outsider, I visualised him dressed in black, walking the silent corridors of a sleeping hotel, clock ticking on the wall of his office, a cigarette smoking in an ashtray, cup of instant coffee steaming, and the Jesus and Mary Chain turned down low, with the shipping forecast tuned crude on a little transistor radio. He left music, but I don't believe for a second music ever left him.

He loaned us his '62-Precision and his ARP 2600 – the one whose keyboard hadn't been nicked when we'd had our storage cage robbed a few years back. The thieves took the small stuff, that ARP keyboard and a flight-cased 808 drum machine. The loss of that 808 made us buy a 909 with the insurance money. Although we didn't originally like it, by the early nineties it was the house music drum machine of choice, and we had one in mint condition.

Alf's '62-Precision had the sweetest tone – he'd played it that first time we met, and all through the Screen Gemz, even Freur. The Stray Cats had borrowed it for their encore the night we supported them at Dingwalls. After that night it was retired to the studio, too precious to risk theft. It featured on Freur recordings (the demo for 'The Theme from the Film of the Same Name', though Pino Palladino, who I'd made a promise to years before, actually recorded the bass on the album version). In the early nineties it left its most significant mark when Rick and I used it for the twin bass parts on 'Mother Earth'.

There are some instruments you hold in reserve as 'problem solvers', the ones you know will always get you out of trouble. Looking for that indefinable something? Can't put your finger on what's missing? These are the instruments that deliver the things all your other gear can't – and that's why you hold them back, so your ears won't tire of them. They remain aural candy, the circus come to head-town.

When, inevitably, Alf recalled the dream bass, we heard silence turn in on itself as it left Essex forever.

Romford – Essex

UNDER THE BRIDGE

On Argyle Street, Sydney, a cool spot beneath a stone bridge,
the rocks ooze liquids, the camera twitches in the hand as traffic
glides overhead.
Fingers dance impatiently, fumbling with a black and white camera app
embedded in a phone with a cracked face.
The app is stubborn, the fingers want it now, the eyes see things
they need to capture, the light won't wait. Two tourists follow close
behind photographing something out of sight, walking slow, pausing
every time you want to take a picture, making you feel self-conscious,
your skin begins to itch.
The man in his forties wears his hat backwards,
the woman smiles benignly, they walk as if in a trance, but always
close enough to interfere with you taking pictures. You don't
know them, but you have the impulse to say something blunt.
Just as you go to speak they pass and walk on ahead.
You breathe a sigh of relief, but not loud enough for them to hear,
and as you
finish capturing a face within the rock you turn and find them
standing exactly where you want to walk, making out they're
photographing something high above them, watching you from the
corner of an eye and smiling.

Lonnie Holley – *Just Before Music*

'I can't do this. I won't ever be able to do this. They've picked the wrong bloke!'

Standing alone in the kitchen of our tiny Romford flat, guitar in hand, *The Best of Blondie* in the ghetto blaster, I panicked.

I don't recall how many tracks the band had to have down before Chris and Debbie's arrival, but it was way beyond anything that I'd ever had to learn in one go. I kept thinking back to that last meeting in Pete's front room, drunk, refusing to do any more covers. The rebel in my head was feeding me fear, standing in the way of me holding onto this fantastic gig. Convinced I was bound to fail I hesitated before pressing 'play', sure that I was about to expose myself as a faker. I *wanted* the gig, *needed* the money. The wolf at the door was my best ally in times of conflicted emotions, straightened the head out, had never let me down. Never underestimate a wolf!

Everyone in the band was a phenomenal musician, each with years of experience touring at the highest level. I was by far the odd one out – the runt. It was Paisley Park all over again, the horror of waking from a nightmare to discover reality was worse.

Geoff Dugmore was at that time one of the most popular session drummers on the planet. He was fresh from playing on hits by Tina Turner, Stevie Nicks and Rod Stewart. Carrie Booth on keyboards was vibrant, colourful, confident, an intimidating and powerful woman. She was a redhead I wasn't about to cross, though she was only ever kind to me, watched my back and knew when I needed support. She knew the road for real, not like me, who had nothing more than a 'taste', a romantic snapshot of an idea of what it really took to tour. Then there was Steve Barnacle on bass – an outwardly ebullient man, black leather waistcoat, black wide-brimmed hat, who always greeted me with a smile and a laugh, yet I knew he was focused, loyal and dedicated to his role in ways which I hadn't a clue how to be. I was a sham, a faker, a petty con-artist in comparison to Steve, and I felt sure he could see it, caught him glance at me sometimes, waiting for the 'click' in my head, that inevitable crumble and chucking in of the towel. He helped me when I couldn't hear the right notes, played them back to me when I was 'ear-blind', made me look better than I was, like with that tricky run on Zeppelin's 'Black Dog' that Debbie wanted us to do.

It was a great band. Friends, laughter, we had fun, travelled the UK and then Europe playing our own shows before playing festivals. Years later Underworld would play the same festivals and I'd recall this tour as a series of snapshots: the main stages, dressing rooms, loading docks, and the nirvana of European festival catering.

That summer we were part of what felt like a 'package', touring with the same bands, performing at the same festivals in the same order: Sisters of Mercy, Debbie and Chris, Iggy Pop, Billy Idol. Bands and crews intermingled backstage and met again late at night in hotel bars. People became friends, swapped numbers, stories and equipment tips.

Every night, I stood behind one of the most iconic frontwomen of all time. I was playing some of the greatest pop songs of my generation, with clear knowledge of exactly what the singer required from her band. And I was happy to deliver it every night. It was cool and great and I felt momentarily larger than myself, up there in such fabulous company. Debbie and Chris treated everybody decently, like human beings. They *cared*, a lesson I tried never to forget. Ultimately, I would let them both down, but that came later.

The best moments from that tour? Standing on the side of the stage every night, watching Jim turn into Iggy. He'd stride on cocky – stripped to the waist, dangerous, radiant, carefree, lobbing mic stands and guitars randomly over his shoulder – always abandoned to the character of the onstage man (something I soaked up and reused years later when Underworld returned to being a band again). To be lost in the sound, in the head of someone who doesn't play by the rules and is getting paid for it – that was what I wanted. I watched every night in awe, face hurting from grinning.

Here I was, standing on the side of Iggy's stage (the man whose concert videos I would one day play before every Underworld tour to remind me not to fake it). 'Even if you hurt yourself, it doesn't matter: don't stop, never stop, get completely lost in the music, and go beyond yourself.' The blueprint for how I might bring something worthwhile to a future band with Rick was forming in my head, stuff was being revealed to me for a reason. I hoovered it up and stashed it for later. Every night was a standout experience for me, playing tunes that had helped shape pop music in the late seventies and early eighties, watching Debbie radiate charm to woo every audience that came before her, so they were eager to do whatever she wanted them to do – tens of thousands of smiling, happy faces, just grateful to snatch a glimpse of that towering relentless presence and bliss-out to the sound of her inimitable voice.

On a night off in Athens, we shared a minibus with a bunch of American jazzers, rumoured to be the ex-Miles Davis band. We were all making the pilgrimage to a downtown football stadium to see the Godfather of Funk himself, James Brown, live, in the flesh. The stage was set up on the turf over the centre circle, the half-stadium in front was packed. We drifted onto the pitch behind the stage, from where we could watch the Master directing Maceo and the rest of the J. B.'s with signals plucked straight from the book of legend.

Shedding that cape and sliding back across the stage with an agility I wanted, his body sinuous as a snake, showered in sweat, he was 100 per cent dedicated to the course, conducting the flow of the groove with flicks and flinches, body rocking, a human dynamo transmitting electricity from a planet at the heart of the universe of pure soul funk. The geezer standing next to me clapped a hand on my shoulder, but I didn't move a muscle for fear of missing even a second of the Master's groove, the tiniest inflection, soaking it all up for a future time when I might need it. 'Maaan, that's JAMES BROWN up there! JAMES BROWN! The MAN! This is sooo COOL!'

When I glanced to see who it was I looked straight into the face of Carlos Santana,

CARLOS fucking SANTANA! Straight off the silver screen of the Stourport fleapit where I lost my soul to the groove of his cherry red SG, the polyrhythmic beats of his rhythm section and the trancing cyclical chants of his singers. One of the legends of Woodstock, standing right here, talking to me! It was his band, the jazzers, ex-Miles players who had ridden down with us to the show. They were spirits who played on a plain higher than anything I would ever come close to, people who could *really play* – no, I mean really *play*. Nothing that this bullshit Midlands chancer would ever be able to do, and here I was standing on the same patch of turf, both of us thrilled to be fans in the presence of the Godfather. I smiled back, feigning cool, 'Yeah, amazing!'

To my right, and beaming back at me, was Ian Anderson from Jethro Tull – a man whose voice I'd hijacked as a kid, whose early singles I bought because they sounded fresh and like nothing else on the radio. His were songs that took unpredictable twists and subverted the blues into something new and exciting. Carlos, Ian and me sharing a groove in the same stadium where the crowd had rioted the night before during Iggy's gig, burning his bus as police fired teargas into the arena. Iggy had just kept on playing.

I was nothing. A dot hanging out with giants.

The most emotional of all the shows with Debbie and Chris was playing the old Wembley stadium at the Summer XS, an extravagant sold out event put together by the then world conquering Australian pop group INXS (who Rick and I had supported as Freur at Amsterdam's Paradiso club in 1982).

The staff of CBS records, who had dropped us in the eighties, were shocked to find me backstage. They kept asking, 'So, remind me, what are you doing back here?' ... 'Wow! Really?'

Having come from a family where every male for generations had been a great footballer, and some had even gone on to play for professional league teams, I was the black sheep. Crap at footy, I was a musician, an 'artist' – and a hockey player! There was no way my dad was ever going to experience the pride of seeing me play on the pitch at Wembley, so this gig was a once in a lifetime chance, an opportunity to redress the *shame* I'd brought to the Hyde male bloodline. At least I would be able to say I'd played *something* at our country's 'football cathedral'. I hoped this might go some way to re-paying him for his support and faith, all the cars he bought just so he could transport my equipment to gigs, all the hours he worked to find the money to support my *hobby*, and the years he worried if I'd ever make enough to support myself, watching me fail again and again.

You'd have to ask Dad what it meant to him, but for me it was a completion, the closing of a circle. I could feel my needy grip on rock loosen, and could even imagine myself walking away from guitars altogether. Life had delivered me exactly what I needed – to be able to begin to let go of the past and move on. I'd ticked all the boxes, played with one of the best frontwomen in the world, performed era-defining pop songs in a fantastic band, and all in front of my dad at Wembley stadium. It took *all* of this to satiate my crippling reluctance to let go of the familiar. Wembley put my Little-boy-Rock to bed, and finally enabled me to imagine making a different kind of music with Rick.

Athens–London

Santana – 'Soul Sacrifice' Live at Woodstock, 1969; Iggy Pop – 'Candy'; James Brown – 'The Payback'

INTO THE LIGHT

The Edgelanders smiled, one to another, the happiness at their reunion unfurled around them like Christo-wrapped islands, waiting together at the hole in the sky. Bleary eyes and kisses, sleeping rough up the walls of planes with stale tongues and salty skin.

Godflesh – 'Like Rats'

The tour finished. We partied and parted at a posh London hotel. Then I returned to Romford, ready to sell all my guitars.

I didn't know if I had a place or a future in Rick's rapidly forming new vision for Underworld. I didn't know if I could bring *anything* in myself to his project. I'd witnessed mad and beautiful things, I believed could make a difference – set us apart – especially if (unlikely) we ever played live again. It was a flight of fantasy, but so was everything else that had happened since the band had split in LA.

Rick had returned to Romford to salvage what he could from our recording studio while taking on the miserable responsibility of paying off our debts by selling surplus equipment. We had no label, no press department and no way of getting our music out via the conventional routes, but these were unconventional times. Acid house, vast illegal raves and records made in bedrooms were offering an exciting and viable alternative to the traditional music industry.

Wanting to make music with a DJ, Rick asked his brother-in-law Martin for advice on who he should approach. Of the two suggested, it was the nineteen-year-old Darren Emerson who was invited into the studio. Darren was local, he pretty much lived in the same street. He brought with him first-hand experience of DJ culture, and a youthful attitude. He had no qualms about calling Underworld's previous incarnation 'shit'.

Rick and Darren quickly moved on without me. They were writing and recording; searching for a sound and starting to find it. I was on the outside looking in – my choice not theirs. I'd been away, on and off and on again, for a long time. There was no reason for them to wait for me. I found Darren intimidating. He had all the confidence of a frontman. As far as I saw it, he could easily make me redundant.

When Darren played me 12s from his set, barely any of them featured many words or vocals – especially by *men*. Fingers Inc. were played a lot as reference. I just didn't get it: too stripped, too sparse, but the voice on the records caught my ear – Robert Owens, whose lyrics were way out of my league. His was a planet I'd never been to. Weirdly, I would soon visit in person when I got invited by him to play guitar on a new track. I watched the way he worked, laid out on a couch at the back of the control room, listening. Then, at the moment only he knew was right, he would spring to life announcing, 'OK, I'm ready. Set up a mic!' He'd lay the vocal down in one. Another penny dropped for me when I witnessed Robert in action. My old toolbox had been emptied. Now it was being replenished, filled with new toys in readiness for whatever it was this new direction of Rick's demanded.

The phone rang. It was Geoff Dugmore: 'Debbie and Chris want you and me in New York.'

We'd been recalled – the brilliant, rock-steady Geoff Dugmore and the faker guitarist from Essex were heading west for a ten-day recording session. Ten days as residents at the fabulously ragged old Gramercy Park Hotel, Manhattan: the piano bar with its knackered lounge singers and dazed waiters who worked the breakfast tables like lifers with no hope of parole; nylon carpets in the bedrooms that sparked when you walked across them in your socks; TVs that only had terrestrial channels – a world without cable untouched by progress since the seventies. There were full time residents there too, old as the peeling paper on the walls of the upper floors, who endured our jokes. Ghosts who had shared their elevators with generation after generation of forgotten musicians. This was New York like I'd never seen it. I'd never loved it or 'got it' before. I'd always stayed uptown, midtown, tourist-town, everywhere but 'downtown'. That was real New York, somewhere you could drift through without taking a taxi, where you could wander the streets, drawn to the perfumed night.

Sunrise, breakfast, walk down to 8th Street, past the shop selling rubber rats, where the crackheads whored at night, past stoners and hunters who'd come in search of sweet meats. We were recording at Electric Lady Studios – nothing grand, and just the way I was coming to prefer it. Press the buzzer; say *her* name, door opens. Doors always opened when you said her name. Everything was in Technicolor, the contrast up full. All I had to do was stand on street corners and write it – the words would fall into my notebook. It all 'came to me', words just appeared on the pages, stained my paper, filled my pockets, got under my nails. I couldn't stop the torrent, the scraps of lines I'd salvaged from the prairies were absorbed into the deluge of toxic exotica that cat-walked for me day and night. I couldn't sleep, daren't sleep for fear of missing something more succulent and dirty than the last fragment wriggling in my net. New York, through the eyes and ears of Lou Reed, Sam Shepard, the Beats, the boys at the Cedar Tavern, was easy pickings, the fattest piece in the jigsaw.

Leaving every session after dark I'd walk back to the hotel, sniffing the air, accepting all flyers – *free street poetry*. Graffiti, the personals in the back of the *Village Voice*, parking-lot tariff boards, stray conversations … all were diamond worlds straight out of *The French Connection*. Crude, ready cut-up, no need to paste, just make sure you keep a pen in your hand at all times and learn to write fast! Drunk most nights after work, I tagged along to clubs down in the Meatpacking District, opened my eyes wide, couldn't look away. The rhythms of a city singing to anyone who had ears to hear, and it was all 'free'.

New York, the lover I never had, was now my sweetest muse, parent to a child locked away from the world all its life, reborn, liberated, let loose in the heart of the magnificent Apple core as it oozed dark stuff for me like mother's milk. I had the missing thing I never knew I needed. I was primed to be the future singer of Underworld – if there was ever to be one.

It turned out that we'd flown in prematurely, the session was eventually abandoned, but we found ourselves rehearsing in Chris's basement: Leigh Foxx on bass, Geoff on drums, Chris and me on guitars, Debbie and a girl I'd never met before (or since) on electric fiddle, getting ready for one last gig at the mythical (if broken and austere) CBGB. Joey Ramone showed up dressed in black, hair down into his nightshades, sunk low into a ragged backstage armchair, gripped the arms, fingers splayed like pink tarantulas. He talked with enthusiasm: 'Yeah, we should definitely all do a world tour together. it would be great!'

I was an asshole at that gig: played too loud, Debbie turned my amp down in frustration, cut me *the look*. I was even dressed wrong, not black like she'd asked, but a bright orange T with the word 'WORLD' on the front (like the band in Essex that I wanted to be in).

I knew my future was back in Romford, and wanted to shout about it, but I should've waited and paid respect, done my job for the good people who had taken me in, who had employed me and had always had my back. All I had to do was wear black and set my volume right, but I was full of bullshit ego.

Two weeks' scraping poetry off the streets of New York and my relationship with the city irrevocably changed. As our plane rose and banked out of JFK, I looked back towards Manhattan, and it looked more beautiful from up there than I'd ever seen it before. You'd never believe all that dark stuff was oozing out of its cracks. Everything gets cleaned up when you're that high, feeling like an astronaut who gets religion looking down on a fragile planet from out in space. 'It's a beautiful thing and you're a beautiful thing and everybody's a beautiful thing,' I wrote as the pilot announced, 'We're climbing to a height of 30,000 feet.'

New York

The Cure – 'Friday I'm In Love'; The Future Sound Of London – 'Papua New Guinea'

Now Rick had given me a tape that we'd done together, the three of us – Rick, Darren and me. I'd taken it to Paisley Park, but put off listening to it, partly because I knew that if I played it too soon I'd get bored and my ears would go snow-blind. I was also afraid that it might not be as good as I remembered and I had a lot of hope riding on it, so I stashed it out of fear. I wanted to distance myself from what was going on back in Romford for a while to see what happened, see how I felt.

The first time I played it was in the control room at Paisley Park. The only people in the studio were the young tape-ops working after hours. They got excited and their response gave me the confidence to play it to the others. Everyone else? Nonplussed. Nobody really got it. People had problems getting their head around tracks with unorthodox structures; the songs on the tape didn't sound like 'hits'. You have to remember that at this time Minneapolis was about the sound of Jimmy Jam, Terry Lewis and Prince – nineties funk with a specific dynamism. I guess the very British sound on our tape was a reaction against that but to everyone but the young kids I played it to it just sounded wilfully weird.

What we were doing was evolving out of an attitude that discouraged anything 'showy', 'showbiz' or 'glamorous', anything that said classic 'frontman'. It was partl influenced by bands like the Roses and the Mondays, bands with relentless attitude that weren't flash. They were anti-glamour; deliberately not seeking to appeal to the American rock establishment.

It's difficult to put my finger on any one thing that finally hooked me on this new direction in Underworld's music. Maybe it was Rick, returning our first ever profit from a record. He'd been out selling the 'Mother Earth'/'Hump' 12-inch to London DJ shops out the back of our Ford Sierra ('the Brown'). That was a big one. We'd never made a single penny of profit from selling records before. There was no future at that point in selling records via the old music industry route.

Then there was the feeling I kept getting whenever I played with other musicians, be it at Paisley Park, Ocean Way or Electric Lady Studios: the familiar smell of traditionalism. Something in me went, 'You're doing it again, Karl. It's exciting because you're getting to play your guitar, but you're just doing the same thing all over again, and there's something new happening back in England. You've tried "this" for years, and it keeps bringing you back to the same place.'

I was out in America working on projects based on traditional song structures, sticking to a path that had never got me anywhere. I could see that my place within all these set-ups was always going to be as a subservient session musician at best, whereas I was being offered a place in something that had no precedent, nor the pressure of an A&R department bearing down on it. The old system had never produced results. Rick and Darren had got momentum back in Romford, and that momentum offered more hope than sticking with the old tried and tested. It was clear there and then that my faith was better placed in two guys recording in a back bedroom of a terraced house in Essex than in any project based out of a major record label.

At the same time, I was living in a hotel in Lower Manhattan seeing New York with fresh eyes and ears. Alive and vibrant and shouting to me, the city spoon-fed me fabulous imagery that I couldn't absorb fast enough. I was getting nervous that back in Romford there was this young kid who was making friends with my mate and he was part of a scene that didn't want guitarists, didn't want singers, and was growing fast. Rick was offering me an opportunity to be a part of that scene, but I was running away to somewhere else, unable to take up his offer.

I decided I'd better use my time in New York wisely then get home fast. It wasn't Darren's fault, but my inherent insecurity made me feel I had better tread carefully around him. I convinced myself that if he didn't like me, or what I did, then one word from him and I would be out. I needed to get back to Essex and start earning my place with these two guys, because they were getting on too well without me. When I eventually started recording with them properly, tracks like 'Mmm, Skyscraper ... I Love You' and 'Dark & Long' began to appear. These 'songs' were without precedent, they were creating shapes that didn't belong in the pop charts. Musical trends weren't informing us any more; these tracks offered a completely new vision.

The studio itself had become Rick's primary instrument in ways that he had never been allowed to make it so before. He was mixing on the fly, and it was inspiring. He was playing as he mixed, and what he played affected the melodies I sang, which in turn affected what he played, and so we went on, taking the music on a journey that had no preconceived conclusion. We'd never worked like this before – it was liberating. I was no longer singing to something that was fixed. We were twisting in and out of each other, influencing the way the other responded.

Each one of those songs was a journey. We started them with no idea how they would end. Rick pressed 'record', the beat kicked in, and something about the process clicked for me. I liked it, I *really* liked it. There was a mantra that we stuck to: 'You'd never ask Miles Davis to do a 7-inch edit.' He wasn't chasing after the radio. Why would we cut these songs down to an arbitrary length?

Miles was someone I had always upheld as a composer who kept exploring, unafraid to reinvent his music or risk losing his audience; an artist who never stayed still or repeated himself just because it had worked in the past. Now all of that was happening right here with a bloke from South Wales and a young kid from Essex. I was part of something that was no longer living in the past nor trying to imitate what was 'avin' it in the charts, and it felt *right*.

When I came home from America I walked into a world that had a lot of art school about it. That 'I-don't-know-what-this-is-but-it's-good' feeling was a refreshingly different state of mind to be around. This wasn't 'clever' and it wasn't 'traditional'. There was this young kid bringing his experience of what worked for him on the dancefloor, and Rick was absorbing that, translating it into something that sounded different from anything the other DJs were playing. It was music that had its own voice, and when I heard it I started to believe.

My buddy was offering me a chance to be a part of his band *again*. The alternatives, by comparison, were dull. Having spent all that time in the States, I felt British to the core. The most exciting music for me was being made right there in the UK. At that precise moment in time Essex seemed the coolest place in the world.

LA–Minneapolis–New York–Romford

Gil Scott-Heron – '"B" Movie'

BACK FROM MIDNIGHT TAPAS

Walking back from midnight tapas,
two homeless guys sleep in the lobby of an ATM outlet,
safe on the other side of the security glass.
From the street all you see are legs and feet.
They've made an artwork on the floor out of red and blue cans,
arranged in the shape of a cartoon heart, and underneath,
with the leftovers, written the word 'LOVE'.
Outside on the pavement a hunk of meat, with arms like calves' thighs,
pauses to repeatedly kick his dog in the shadow of a bus shelter,
wearing a Brazilian football shirt like a badge of honour.

Primus – 'Tommy the Cat'

LAUGHTER IN THE RAIN

Body coming back online,
surviving another French air traffic controllers' strike,
twelve-hour flight, midnight tapas,
baked in the sun with an attack of something bad in the stomach
fixed by flat Coca-Cola.

Jan Dukes de Grey – 'Sorcerers'

IN THE NOISE OF LEARNING TO LET GO AGAIN

Crucial systems collapse due to absence of porridge-honey shock!
A cacophony of mothers talk too loud, too long and too overexcited
about dust.
I'm driven numb.
Post school-run moms snatch time back from years,
exchange exploding stories, fevered exhilaration,
mini-whodunits, Hitchcock thrillers, the micro-details of A-to-B.
Voices that if I woke up next to them would drive me back to drink.
A brutal pedal-to-the-metal enthusiasm all the way to punchline.

I've got a substitute for maple syrup, an un-wiped plastic spoon,
the first soothing hit of black tea nectar.

Tiny wind-up kids skitter about the floor, taunting danger,
mouths dipped in chocolate, animal fingers root for infection,
carried in on soles, fresh from streets,
the thinly spread pastes of dog-doos and ammonia-splashed loos.

A jungle of broadcasters gather without transmitters,
on day release for good behaviour, out from solitary,
divided and conquered too long, their whispering-muscles long gone.

Brainticket – 'Brainticket'

FLAT WHITE

They met in a coffeehouse on Berwick Street,
the village boy and the boy from Oz. Both a little older
than when they used to own these streets, when everything
they did was regarded with wonder and heralded as blessed.
They chuckled, one to the other, 'Still here, then?',
laugh lines pointing like arrows to the light in their eyes.

The coffee was too strong too early, but its aroma hit the spot
as they planned the road ahead. People came and went, new faces,
new lords and ladies of Soho, as confident and full of it
as they had once been.

The coffee boy behind the bar played his mix CD,
he was that kind of retro in his style,
with a tight and tiny beard, de-rigueur for the day.
The music jarred, but no one noticed, only the village boy
and the boy from Oz.

Supertramp broke out of the speakers,
the rasp of a distorted harmonica
transforming unexpectedly into violent green spikes
that grew out of the speakers and into the tiny shop.

The boy from Oz didn't see, or if he did he didn't let on,
as the village boy flinched to avoid the aggression of
the erupting sculptures threatening to impale him.

Just as he was about to shout, 'Oi! Turn it off, you wanker!'
it stopped and the spikes receded,
replaced by the thick hiss off a chromium coffee boiler
as steam curled down from the ceiling like phantom surf
and they were wrapped once again in soporific aromas.

Moondog – *Moondog*

WHAT IS SOUND?

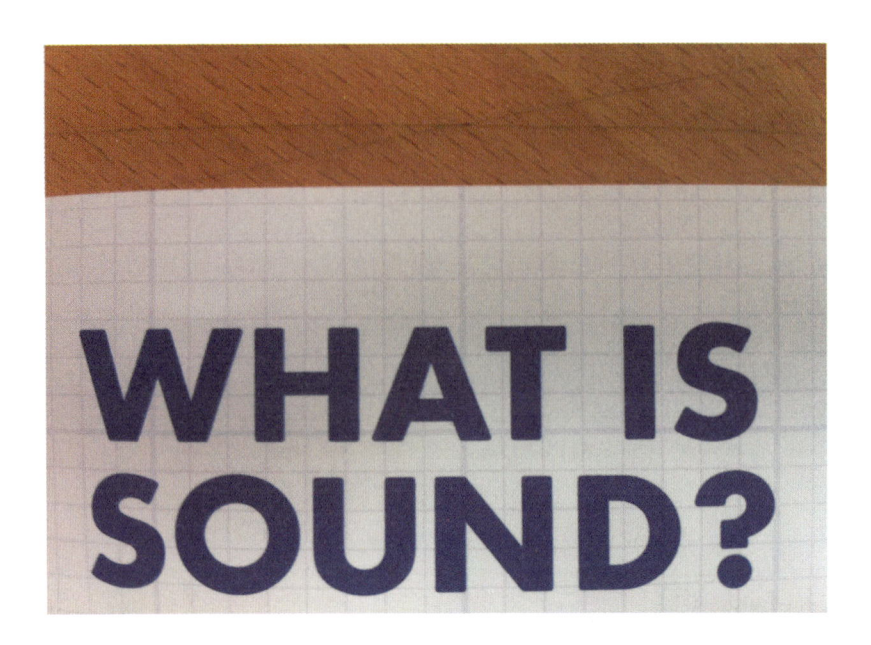

WALKING AT 45 DEGREES

At 4.30 a.m. this morning, ragged from an excess of Technicolor dreams, I ran, growling, into the wind, rescuing the flags of Essex straining to escape pegs and lines, flying free across sodden fields of mud to impale themselves on the amputated limbs of hawthorn hedges. Heads buried deep beneath duvets, we groan, surf the rim of sleep, agitated divers hunting elusive dark as windows fling themselves wide, welcoming the storm's forced entry, grinning,
spitting broken grooves like shattered teeth.

Taraf de Haïdouks – *Band of Gypsies*

SPEEDING THROUGH SPACE

On a ball of dirt and water – breathing oxygen.

Tito Puente – *Top Percussion/Dance Mania*

WAKE UP CALL

Saw the sunrise, gold, pink, a secret Essex landscape, close and wrapped around us. Laptop in the kitchen with birdsong, writing to invisible faces on the other side of the world. Some nights, sleep sees you coming and takes off in the other direction, we kissed before it left. The phone rings, I wake up on the sofa, check the name and smile. Three crows pose on the grass outside, thick black swipes of ink strutting in white-hot sunlight.

The Four Brothers – 'Makorokoto'

A FEW THANK YOUS

Stepped out into a floodlit alley from a brutal room,
exposed pipe and air-conditioning duct, the heat of eyes
on seated bodies. No one sees what goes on behind the wizard's curtain.

William Byrd – *The Three Masses*

1991. All change.

We were summoned to a meeting called by our long-time collaborator John Warwicker at the offices of his soon to be defunct graphic design company, Vivid ID. Nine of us were gathered by a master who had an eye for the subtleties of life – enough mastery to combine unlikely people with the aim of producing extraordinary things. Though we hadn't all met previously, we were unified by a common malcontent with the eighties and all its attendant miseries. Some of us were old enough to have been bitten, some young enough to still have ideals. There was a disaffected frustration that John saw in all of us, allied to a passion for making things outside of the box. As some of us watched our businesses crumbling, while others were looking for direction, he intuitively knew it was time to bring us together for an experiment.

There were kids fresh out of St Martin's School of Art – confident, full of attitude and flying, doing fine; cool record-sleeve creators; graffiti jammers; street-wear designers; musicians; a music manager. They were all artists from the 'other side of the tracks' – people whose chosen paths I'd been educated to look upon with disdain (artists who worked for 'money'). Then I saw their work and heard them speak, and all my prejudices crumbled.

It had been twelve years since I'd last exhibited in a gallery. Twelve years since I'd enjoyed the company of other visual artists gathered round refectory tables, exchanging solutions to each other's problems. Twelve years of self-exile from the art world. These guys may well have taken the Queen's shilling, but as I looked around the room something in their faces told me not to judge them, to remain open. After all, John had brought us together for a reason.

Graham Wood, Simon Taylor, Greg Rood, Colin Vearncombe, Steve Baker, Dirk van Dooren, John, Rick and myself ... we went round the room, talking about our experiences and skills – just a bunch of people getting to know each other, dropping their guard, opening channels. Tomato, as we found out we were called one day (when it made us smile, we knew it was right), gave me the community I'd been craving since leaving art school. These were people who *understood* things I hadn't been able to articulate for twelve years, people who were passionate about their art, who were obsessed more with 'process' than with end results. They made stuff because they *wanted to*, they didn't wait to be commissioned, and they all had drawers full of fabulous unseen things, stashed, ready to be pulled out when a job required unhinged magic. It reminded me of the Purple Vault at Paisley Park. They were more fine art than any fine artist I'd ever known, *and they made money doing it*. I wanted to share their journey, this generous, open, free exchange of ideas.

This was a cross-disciplined feedback the like of which I hadn't experienced since my time in the Space Workshop in Cardiff, soaking up the trickle-down from the originals at Black Mountain College. Tomato was a gift. It was where I wanted to be – making art again – surrounded by artists who loved making marks and made such out-there images that it raised my game, challenged me to be as good and, when the time came, provided an opportunity to return to exhibiting in galleries. Tomato was a spiritual home – a place to sit and soak up vibes or roll up the sleeves and engage.

London

Seal – 'Crazy'

MONSTER PUPPET MACHINES

A parade of metal monster puppets walked through the audience
Dangling off cranes at altitude.
Spain.
Oxygen 'just appeared' out of thin air up on stage when I needed it.
Didn't think I'd make it last night,
but the kick drum is still my dealer.

Francisco López – *Buildings (New York)*

WE FLOAT ALONE

We float alone in a sea of white linen, me and the notebook,
cruising breakfast like flightless birds, one choosing fruit,
the other - words. In walks a delicate boy with coiffured hair,
horn-rimmed, beautiful, sleeves rolled up crisp, inch perfect.
The notebook plots his course across the room as I skewer melon.
Morning sunlight sings through plate-glass walls, we watch it casting
shadows deep and black between unnatural architectural trees arranged
like chess pieces, kings and queens watching our five-star sanctuary
from the luxury of perfect lawns, awaiting the fingers of giants.
In walks Torpedo woman. I don't see her face but I hear her coming,
talking loud to the delicate boy as she crosses the room at speed,
oblivious to our reverential floating, oblivious to everything,
focused hungry on the prize of her solitary beautiful boy.
The notebook opens to receive, the pen dances across the page,
sinuous curves and curls embrace, laying ink as joyous as the dance
of feet to kick-drum grooves. Her mouth hurts my ears, but I don't
glance, imagining a face, her tones abrasive, every thought falls
out between her violent lips - relentless. The delicate whispers of
the boy, she broadcasts everything he says directly to the pen and
page and I won't glance for fear of letting her know this dance is
choreographed alone for her.

A lover? - no, though I entertained the thought and shuddered. How these two come to this time and place, such incongruous union could never be so misconstrued as lovers.

A business arrangement? A manager? An agent? Yes! An agent hotly courting one so fresh and up and coming, flew in just for the occasion and almost blows it with sycophancy (but does he notice, does he care?) now it's clear he wants her just as much as she wants him - they were made for one another.

Bukka White – 'Parchman Farm Blues'

There were bands in the charts who were hijacking club beats, stitching them to pop songs before slapping some old-shit guitar over the top. Hearing that kind of music turned my stomach. Why would anyone want to steal a beat to fake being contemporary and then smear it all over with that rock-guitar noodling? That just made me embarrassed to be a guitarist. I thought, 'If that's what guitar playing does to this incredible scene then I've got to do the scene a favour and stop playing guitar immediately.' The way guitar was being played on these clubbed-up pop tunes was just aimless noise to me.

I decided to sell all my guitars. Fortunately, I worked with two people who had a different way of looking at the problem. Darren was into the Balearic sound, loved a guitar, and was a lifelong Beatles fan. He used to say, 'Play some of that funky stuff. I like it when you do that.' Rick was always thinking ahead, finding new ways to subvert cherished sounds from the past – ever the one to find solutions to impossible problems.

I was the only one who thought the guitars had to go, but the two of them outvoted me ... thankfully.

Kyme Road, Romford, Essex

RETURN TO JAPAN

Take the M25 clockwise, turn right at Heathrow,
drink coffee, eat something sweet to counteract
the bitter taste, drink water to neutralise the
sweetness, shop for throat lozenges, mints,
AA batteries, buy a magazine.
Jump through the sky hole, sleep if you can,
drink water, get up, walk around, watch a film
that's saccharine and over-egged,
suspend your disbelief and love it anyway, watch it
get dark, watch it get light, feel cooked on the
inside and lightly fried, touchdown, step out into
humid heat, a familiar aroma unlike anywhere else
and a colour palette to match, see shapes dance in
your head to a calligraphic rhythm unfettered by
your understanding, let the figures dance, cartoon
characters everywhere and gentle images, clean and with

a pride that gets under your skin until you believe
it could be like this back home as you drive in
air-conditioned chill, the sweat running cold down
your back, watching rice fields slip past on the
other side of the glass, believing it's just as
cold out there, until you pull into a service station
on request and fry, window-shopping, amazed by what's
on sale, buy stuff to show friends at home
because you know they won't believe what they can't
touch, fall asleep, your head rolling on crisp white
lace dreaming dreams of cellphones of the future, you
wake to discover they are real and all around us as we
climb through mountain forests, wild monkey signs line
the road and eventually arrive and step out into clean
cool air, feeling human again, grinning to discover
yourself returned to the world.

Chicago – 'Wishing You Were Here'

IN THE ABSENCE OF INTERNET

I haven't got any internet connection.
It happens with increasing regularity out in the fields where wires are subject to heat and cold and vegetation, and telephone exchanges are either so far away or old-style slow or, in our case, all of the above and more.

During this lull in direct communication, I thought I'd prepare something inspired by that kitten and ball of wool they used to put on telly when the broadcast broke down, or the picture of a girl writing on a blackboard with some weirded-out padded creature in the background. This is my weirded-out creature.

Iggy Pop – *The Idiot*

Our friends and mentors from Turbosound asked if Rick and I would like to test our music through their new system – on the main stage at Glastonbury. There was no chance of us actually getting 'on' the stage – like we'd tried years before, when we had parked in the rain and mud behind the Pyramid, sheltering in Rick's nan's caravan, our gear stashed in his brother-in-law's van, primed for any no-show, hoping to blag a vacant slot (you could do random stuff like that back then). This was different: a weird (therefore appealing) offer from the Turbo crew for the two of us to set up and play from the main mixing desk out front, *behind* the audience. And so, during what someone deemed to be a lull in the afternoon, Andy Kershaw, the resident changeover DJ, was turned off and Rick and I were turned on (sorry, Andy).

There were no monitors – everything ran through headphones to compensate for a massive delay coming off the front of house system, our friend John Newsham (of Turbosound) at the controls. At first, the crowd looked confused when I introduced us, looking around to see who was talking. But one by one they started turning, until the whole audience at the main stage was facing in the opposite direction.

A one-off, four-song set, two mics, a vocoder, drum machine, guitar and something (a computer?) playing back other parts. It was sunny, the audience responded warmly, clapped and cheered, while those at the back (right at the front of the main stage) remained confused.

I tried not to be a 'frontman', turned off the desire to 'perform', found a gentler space to play from, listening and locking onto everything Rick was doing instead of leading from the front. I liked how it felt not trying to be a superstar. The music Rick had created was effortless, generated energy and lifted us. It didn't matter that our set was so short – in fact that made it even better. Restraint instead of pomp returned the best feeling I'd ever had playing live. Rick was working hard, taking all the strain off me, creating spaces for a voice that had to play a supporting role this time.

The only song I remember us playing that day was 'Mother Earth'; the sound of Alf's vintage P-Bass returned to Glastonbury nine years after Freur had played there in a muddy tent. It was a total thrill being in this weird no-band thing with Rick. I was hooked.

In the sun, Glastonbury

AT FUJI ROCK, 2013

I'd had a premonition I would meet Wilko Johnson, then I found myself sat down next to him on the plane. His guitar playing is like great slabs of techno, he's the godfather of sampled guitar, and a gentle man. Flew out of London with a sandpapered throat, had to laugh at its timing.
Bodies know how to mess with heads. Popping Beechams capsules to fend off flu, locked into a twelve-hour air-conditioned metal tube then squeezed out into a hot and humid world, a gingerbread man walking in diver's boots.
Slept on the back seat of the bus, coats over our heads.
Ate noodles in a service station, ice cream and glutinous balls, red bean paste cake and peach iced tea.
Slept another two hours on the back seat and woke in a valley where clouds stoop to kiss the heads of mountains,
and trees rinse their leaves in its blue caress.

Gil Scott-Heron – 'Small Talk at 125th and Lenox'

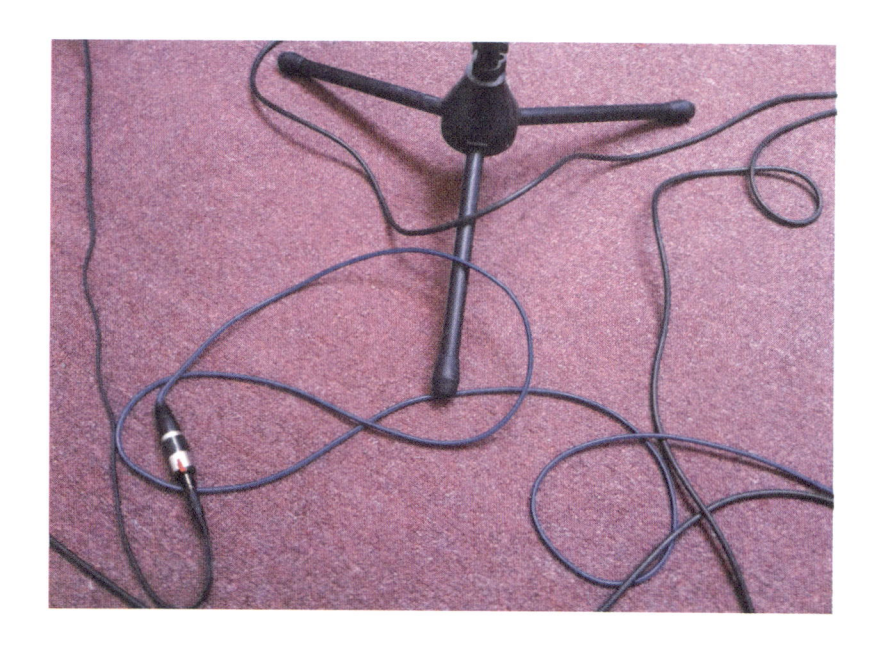

I WANTED TO BE AN ARTIST BUT I GOT A CAREER INSTEAD

I don't have to build sculptures, I find them lying around,
scattered across cities, alleys, tracks and fields, you
leave these cairns to mark your passing, dumped, ditched,
spattered, meticulously arranged, I follow where you leave.

It started as a distraction
from the boredom of waiting at bus stops as a child,
getting lost in minutiae, the details and stuff
between the cracks in concrete and blacktop.
Brutalist constructions, ritual spaces, the red and white cones
and poles of navvies laying and digging up roads.
Industrial packaging, cardboard, sticky tape,
the marks accrued by passing through postal systems.
Road markings, tar, chalk, white and yellow lines.

I have a piece of Cardiff in my studio,
a chunk of yellow line painted inadvertently across a scrap of
card left lying in the gutter when parking restrictions were laid.
It languishes between the Pioneer CDJs and the Technics deck.
Art, squeezed between the tracks of a silent groove.

Nico – 'My Funny Valentine'

WHAT WAS IT LIKE IN JAPAN?

Still hot 'n' sticky! Street-walking poetry,
scooping T-shirt prose off pavements.
Beetles in the trees rub and sing
like they're vibrating twisted pipework
tweaking their frequencies as they jam across busy streets.

All the provinces have come to town for the seasonal sales.
A mad house of voices howling into bull horns competing for attention,
waving cards printed with loud text messages.
Money off and everything else thrown in for free.

The only antidote is homemade ginger ice cream
in the favourite backstreet curry house
down the road from the favourite weird shop selling crazy everything.

Today I was presented with free gifts of Indian medical wall charts.

Trojan Dub Box Set

On stage. The calmest, most peaceful, centred place I go.

Weekends, mostly

LAST NIGHT IN SHIBUYA

The neon men in hard hats wave electric sticks at empty taxis
cruising for fares beneath Shibuya flyovers. We walk on
sweat-stained
pavements,
cool grey slabs with sour complexions that only decades of footfall grease could
fashion. This part of town could be Leicester Square, Times Square
on a Saturday night; any city centre where the lonely are drawn in
search of a solution.
Drunk boys teeter on tip-toe at the lip of the abyss,
couples squat on dirty pavements smoking through courtship.
White-shirted, black-trousered 'straight' non-offenders sleep off
the effects
of after-work bars on walls in car parks, as the homeless who sleep
through the cacophony of the day vacate cardboard beds to hunt in
the cool of night.

I don't want to close my eyes though I need sleep,
don't want to miss a thing for fear I'll wake up only to discover
it was nothing but phantoms.

Miles Davis – *Sketches of Spain*

CANNOT THIS WATER BE DRINK?

To see Essex through jet-lag glass is to be one's own ghost, a shadow of the thing you forgot you left at the back of the wardrobe years ago. Time zones slip, sleep fragments and breaks away from night to float through the day in random pieces. This skin I'm in is someone else's coat, disconnected from the soft stuff, the tissue inside. I'm observing the world through pin holes wondering what these mouths are speaking. What is this noise these languages are saying?

The Heads – 'Barcoded'

CONCRETE FOUND AND WET THINGS RED

The fog thins, the body shakes, aches, stumbles.
Something big, lumbering and clumsy fumbles around
in a twilight room, the drag of heavy footfall
on wooden boards, head bowed, confused and muttering.

Captain Beefheart and the Magic Band – 'Tropical Hot Dog Night'

Once again, our friends at Turbosound invited us to be part of a new project – one they also wanted to take to their spiritual home, Glastonbury. Inspired by years of watching bands from the mixing desk, perhaps out of frustration at controlling the sound but never *making* it, the vision they had stretched all the way back to the night they'd seen the light at Parliament's *Mothership Connection* gig. They'd taken us to our first rave, turned us onto a new superstar-less genre, where the kick drum was the frontman, the audience the band, and no one needed a hero. These guys had helped build the first of the famous Pyramid stages, and were now assembling an event that would become the stuff of legend: 'the Experimental Soundfield'.

Even though Michael Eavis was understandably cautious about letting sound systems loose in his festival, he generously gave us our own field across the tracks at the foot of the hill, far from the main stage, *exactly* where we were all at, spiritually. Out there on the edge of that huge site I discovered a festival I'd heard about but had never shown much interest in. The original voice of Glastonbury, perhaps – it had all seemed too earthy for my blinkered cravings for a fast-track pop career. This other Glastonbury had nothing to do with 'success', so had been of no interest. This was where outsiders 'belonged'. It had taken me a long time to accept that I was one.

Rick's nan's caravan was towed down from Essex for the last time, parked up in the hedge where the grass was permanently wet and smelled of piss. The boys from Hornchurch parked their vans on the opposite side: combat fatigues and scavenged wood for the long cold nights ahead, crates of Stella, smiles, tins raised – happy dancing men.

A two-storey scaffold tower was erected in the middle of the field, courtesy of John McHugh (sadly no longer with us). Four smaller towers formed a circle further out into the field to hold the PA, but unlike other systems the speakers faced in, creating a ring of sound to wrap around the audience – everybody would get it sweet and clear, with plenty of bass wherever they went.

Outside of the PA, a huge semi-circular cyclorama was erected to carry projections transmitted from under the roof of the second tier of the central tower by the old-school projectors and oil wheels of Jon Brodel's Shiva Photonics light show. On the lower floor a mixing desk was placed in full view of the crowd, next to DJ decks, a couple of mics and Pink Floyd's quadraphonic mixer – to send our sounds in whatever combination of directions felt good.

In one corner of the lower tower nestled a compact electronic drum kit for our friend Trevor Morais (who'd slipped out of the session business five years previously to build a palatial recording studio in southern Spain). He was desperate to play again – was in need of a place to lay his groove – and we were happy to have him on board. It was good to return the generosity of his favours: nights spent jawing on the stoop of his studio up in Amersham when Underworld MKI cut that first album.

On the decks: Darren Emerson, Danny G and his mate Anton. Rick was on electronics, vocoder, keys and mixer; John Newsham was on the mix with Rick, and me on guitar, harmonica and voice. No lights, no 'look at me', no back or front of stage. All of us were the band; there was no distinction between crew, live musician or DJs. I remember at our first meeting, catching the DJs' eyes when the word 'musician' was used in the context of being somehow different to them. It was the last time anyone used the term 'musician' to divide us.

From Friday to Sunday people found us by word of mouth. It felt right, no hype, not even our name on flyers. I had no idea what my place in this ensemble was, only that I mustn't be a 'frontman'. I was to remain part of the band, blend in, play my part, support the others where I could and shut up if I had nothing good to give. We played Underworld tunes - 'The Hump', 'Big Mouth', 'Can You Feel Me?' - while the DJs dropped 12s and we jammed live along with them. They looked uncertain at first - we were transgressing, messing with their best plates. This was new territory for all of us - we were making it up in front of a crowd that was happy to come on the journey with us. There were no claims from us, thus no preconceptions from them.

That first night, we played until we ran out of ideas. It was OK to admit that too - you could leave the stage, wander off, come back when you had something to say, be a part of the crowd if you wanted, hear things from their perspective. I was being reprogrammed, and it felt good. The Friday night finished early compared to other parties. I drifted back into the field from a break to hear quadraphonic birdsong under rippling lights gently playing over happy bodies lying in the grass watching the stars. It remains one of the most truly magic moments in my life: Rick on the mixer, working in that unique way he has of creating exquisite spaces with sound alone. The experience of the Friday night, along with the feedback we'd received, made us realise the crowd were hungry to dance through the night, and there was nowhere else on site for them to do so. Saturday at the festival and a lot of people wanted to party, but that aspect of Glastonbury was still some way off. Day two started around noon - gentle grooves, mixing up beats. Trevor, on drums, dropped in when he was feeling it. I'd play some rhythm guitar, keeping it light; Rick introduced electronics - a taste of what would come later. Late the night before there had been a renegade sound system pumping Hardcore from the outside of the metal fence that barricaded our field from the outside world. They'd been shut down and moved on, but we'd felt their tracks cut across our vibe, and it spoiled the night a little. They'd been sent packing, so Saturday night was all ours. With a collective of DJs on board, we began building towards a full-on party.

At some point, bursting from holding in the adrenaline, I spontaneously climbed up the tower while singing. The crowd liked it, then I realised what I'd done, glanced at the rest of the 'band', expecting frowns, but got smiles and a thumbs-up: 'You should do that a bit more,' they said. A little confused, I stashed that one for later, realising that perhaps I could 'go Iggy', after all, but only if it brought something positive to the party. I got a glimpse of how a next generation Underworld could be. If this was the blueprint, it felt good.

The night built and the audience swelled and surrounded us. No one had heard a system like this nor experienced visuals so far-out since the sixties. We played, left and returned as we felt, no longer tied to having to be on stage. Each of us wandered through the crowd to feel how it felt out at the furthest edges. The Hornchurch posse danced, drinking their beers around junk-wood fires. Musicians from other bands wandered over and asked to jam. I remember feeling protective the first time that happened, but an infectious spirit of openness and generosity put paid to that.

Then, sometime late in the night, one of our crew said that the DJs from the system that had been shut down were asking if they could play with us. Right there, a chunk was edited out of time, my heart started pounding. Darren Emerson was seducing the crowd; everyone had their hands in the air, the whole place was smiling. I calmed down. The guys from the other system were smiling too when they dropped their 12s onto the decks, promising none of that dark stuff they'd been pumping the night before. They promised tunes that would slip right into our set and make us feel well sweet and chilled, nothing to shake our world.

But then I saw it unfold. It was so cool how they did it.

To start with everyone was super-friendly – then they turned, and we were being taken over, boarded by pirates, nothing we could do. They mutated into a completely different crew to the peace, love and trance family of the Experimental Soundfield. One second their record was on the deck, slotted right into Darren's groove, then everything turned nasty. Darren saw it coming before I did, that 12-inch spinning sweetly, everybody happy, nodding. People were saying, 'These guys are all right, we got 'em wrong.' Then a hand reached out of the dark, eyes wild and wide, grinning, fingers on the speed control, twisting, up, up, up, cranking the BPM, the beats climb from Trance to Hardcore, and we'd been shafted!

We recoiled, horrified. Darren shook his head: 'I told you so.' Our gear is in their hands, all our precious stuff, our dreams – our crowd. What was gonna happen to these beautiful people? A familiar cold fist in my stomach again. The tower was crawling with them, they were climbing all over it. We were not fighters, and there was no backup, no security, no rescue plan. Giant red spiders were in the rigging, we were alone at sea, miles from dry land and sinking. Wild razor grins came up close, pushed us out, took our places. There was no space for us now, there were too many of them – they were *ready for anything*.

And then … something weird and incredible happened. Something that changed my perception of audiences and restored my faith in humanity.

The crowd stopped dancing, faced the tower and began to boo. They could see and feel exactly what was happening. And they didn't like it. They weren't going to take it and there were a lot of them feeling aggrieved, looking to get hostile if things didn't go back the way they wanted. Wild glances were exchanged, shocked looks, pale expressions from the Hardcore crew. The DJ pulled his record off the decks and they were gone – arrived fast, but left *faster*.

The crowd let out a howl, punching the air as Darren took the decks back. He dropped the needle and they got back to the serious business of dancing. Cigarettes were lit, beers cracked, air expelled, relieved glances exchanged. We'd not only come this close to losing our gear, there had been a very real danger of a lot of people getting hurt. The audience had saved us. *Never underestimate your audience. Collectively they have the power to do extraordinary things.*

Eighteen hours later, sun up, we were sat around the fire, mugs of tea, silent, rinsed out, cleansed, nothing left to say – had said it all over *eighteen hours*, eighteen hours! The longest gig we'd ever played. Smiling to one another, happy and fulfilled, the audience drifted off, waving and shouting gratified 'thank yous'. The Hornchurch posse were in raptures. I was empty and feeling good, a rare silent space between my ears. It felt so good to be sat on a log, with a growing sense of excitement that somewhere in this abstract, improvised, unfettered event was the seed of a new band, a blueprint, a direction for what we could become if we wanted.

It hadn't been my vision or my idea and, for once, I hadn't tried to interfere or control things. I'd trusted a little more in Rick and the good people around us, gone with the flow, and it had turned out great. I'd arrived at a place outside of anything I could imagine, and it felt good and right and exciting. As ever, I'd hold onto that clarity of thought for a couple of days, bulk it up with words and concepts, normalise it with Hyde-isms, fight it and try to tie it down.

Rick's hands would be on the wheel from now on – something I remain eternally grateful for.

Glastonbury, 1992

Orbital – 'Chime'

I'm guessing Darren must have set up our first gig as Underworld at Ministry of Sound. We played from the DJ booth. Our set segued out of Darren's DJ set; possibly he even cut it short so that we could play for thirty or forty minutes at the end. I'd been to the Ministry many times with Rick and Darren. You'd see DJs building the vibe up to a fantastic peak, everyone lost in the deep of a heavy sound, barely able to see their hands in front of their faces, with whatever minimal lighting there was (every time I hear a new Underworld track I place it right there in the dark of the big room at the Ministry).

Then, at some point, the music would stop and lights would be turned on over a little stage at the opposite end of the room to the DJ booth (the opposing end - a metaphor?) and somebody would wander on and do a 'PA'. That would invariably mean someone singing over the top of a backing track, with a couple of dancers to tart it up - someone flogging the sequel to a song that had scraped into the back end of the charts.

It would completely kill the vibe. Everyone would be standing around wondering what the hell was going on - 'Why are we being subjected to this?' You could feel the vibe die right there in the room, and all that work the DJs had put in would be completely dissipated by an echo from a past time. It was like watching music hall, like Flanagan and Allen had gate-crashed a rave. It was radio-wave breakthrough from that other place, that old A&R world, which had put two and two together and come up with some outmoded logic miles wide of the mark. The DJ who followed this travesty would be dumped with the task of dragging the night back to where it was before the 'PA' had flattened it.

We'd been thinking, 'Wouldn't it be cool if a band could play live in a dance club without killing the vibe?' To play in a way that was like one DJ taking over from another, so that a band's first track was an in-the-moment response to the last track played by the DJ, and that the band could respond live to the crowd in the same way that DJs could. There'd be no setlist; the running order dictated purely by the mood of the crowd, making it up as you went along. No two nights would ever be the same. What a fantastic band that would be!

The night we played the first Underworld MKII gig, we turned up with a tiny amount of gear (I might even have brought a guitar) and we set it up in the DJ booth next to the decks. We couldn't afford (or trust) a monitor engineer so we mixed our own monitors, which we listened to on headphones so as not to interfere with the out front sound. Knowing from past experience that letting someone else mix us out front was never going to work, Rick took control of the sound of the band himself while playing from right there in the booth (from that point on, the mixer became his primary instrument on stage). With almost no space to stand, and with no desire to make people stop and look at us, we started playing from behind our piled-up gear - at first nobody even knew we were there; none of the crowd realised it was a live band coming out of the sound system as Rick cross-faded us into the end of Darren's set, and we set off on a journey, a blur of music, evolving and improvising as we went along. Yet nobody stopped dancing for the whole of our set: that was the measure of our success. Overnight we'd developed into this group that could be accepted into a scene – more like a tidal wave – that was about to take over the world. We were a live band and yet we weren't in opposition to DJ culture, and no one had to make allowances for us or even clear a space for us. We could operate like a DJ, turning up with our music, responding to the moment. We could reinterpret every track on the spot, with an approach that was often compared to improvised jazz. It was the most thrilling live performance we'd ever done, and was almost totally anonymous.

After the gig, Darren disappeared and left me and Rick holed up in the club's back room with a couple of chairs and a naked light bulb between the walls. We tried to catch an hour's sleep as we were pummelled and tenderised by the club's sub-bass, waiting for the Ministry to close at 8 a.m. so we could load our gear into the van Rick had borrowed from his brother-in-law. Struggling to stay awake at the wheel, squinting into the glare of a rising sun, he drove us home up the A13. What seemed most significant to me that morning was that we were driving in the opposite direction to everyone else.

The second gig soon followed, perched on a tiny balcony in the Soundshaft at the back of Heaven. As we started to play, a lone voice in the crowd was heard sneering, 'Oh no, not a fucking guitar!' The dancefloor filled and remained that way until we stopped playing. Nobody ever commented again. Another milestone had been reached.

Elephant and Castle, London

HAPPY RAINY DAY, ESSEX

To breathe again!

La Düsseldorf – 'La Düsseldorf'

THE MAN WHO WALKS ON WATER

Skinny girls in tiny sprayed-on dresses
serve us rich food late into the night
down by the sea.
Some of them are tattooed,
moving fast between the tables,
laughing always laughing,
dancing, dancing, choreography.
Active, never passive, smiling,
swift and fleet of foot untouchable like humming birds,
they know the drill.
The tables full of carefree couples,
tables tucked away for lovers
and the tables full of dazed and optimistic men.
We all turn round to watch the sun
and smile our tired eyes, see the world turn silhouette,
a cut-out,
then the floating man slips past us walking on the water

Supersilent — 12

LAST NIGHT IN IBIZA

'You're crazy!' said the blonde with the razor fringe as I slipped
away last night.
I took it as a compliment,
body buzzing though two hours craving sleep as we hit the stage
at 3.30 a.m.
But the kick drum always gets me in the end.
Hands raised in the air,
smiles and screams and whistles – all the girls and all the boys
look beautiful.
Sweat-soaked as we drove through empty streets, wrapped in towels,
let the energy percolate in silence as we sit on the hotel roof,
waiting for the sun, with cameras and quiet eyes.
The moon was a thin slice of lemon as we laughed,
high in the after-groove.
The party was still rockin' as we reached breakfast.
No one had been to bed, you could see it in their gurns.
Luminous eyes, glasses clinked like wind chimes,
the speed of conversation a clear indication
that the kick drum had done good business
dealing sweet preparations.

Nic Jones – 'Clyde Water'

Steve Hall from Junior Boy's Own overheard 'Mmm, Skyscraper ... I Love You' in an office while someone else was rejecting it and offered to put it out. While most people we played it to looked at us with total confusion, Steve got it (thankfully he still does).

Under the wing of an understanding label who'd grown up in the scene we were making fledgling steps into, our music was starting to get played in clubs - tracks we'd made and early remixes we'd done for other bands. Darren played places like the Milk Bar on Sutton Row (RIP) a lot - it was a good room to road-test new music or to suck up a little inspiration (it was there that Rick heard Darren mix together two copies of a Red Zone remix of a record by Thompson Twins - them again! - that inspired the drum fills in 'Skyscraper'). I'm guessing that early on I'd have heard 'The Hump' in a club, and people would have danced and, although it wouldn't have been the greatest track played that night, it would have kept people on the floor. A record that Rick had made in his bedroom in Essex was getting people up and moving on crowded floors in fashionable spots in the West End.

One hugely significant moment early on - one point where we realised things were working, the path we were on was straight and true - arrived as a complete shock to me. We'd headed down to the Soundshaft (RIP too) to hear Sven Väth DJing. Midway through a set that was peaks and peaks and peaks, he played what we all considered the album version of 'Skyscraper'. This was after Rick and Darren had painstakingly constructed club mixes that were specifically designed to work on dancefloors.

The album version was bold and extreme and had been built with some other space in mind - not here, not yet anyway. In my head, I saw several years of transition, where people would buy our records on 12-inch, then maybe one day, they'd flip the vinyl and put the album version on. Some of them would then hopefully go on to explore further.

Sven turned all of that on its head. The record began, the floor filled - properly filled. I turned to Rick and mouthed, 'Wow. I didn't expect that.' In my head, this was time folding. The years I was projecting that it would take until people discovered what we were doing away from the dancefloor had happened overnight - from that turntable, with Sven dropping that 12.

From then on, whatever came out of Rick's studio was for the dancefloor.

Charing Cross, London

Rarely backwards in coming forwards, I always had a mouth on me.

A typical frontman: ego-driven and insecure.

I had to fill any hole before it sucked me in. I needed constant praise and attention, and even then it was never enough. I thought it was the end of the world if I didn't get my own way. I'd convince myself I was being ignored, snubbed and disrespected, that I was losing control. At which point I'd descend into raging gloom. I'd build towers, swagger to the top and fall off.

Though I instinctively knew how to generate weird stuff, I couldn't sustain it. I never knew what to do with it when I had it in my hand. Driven by fear, I would revert to imitation. But put me in a box and I'd climb out, bring back what I'd found on the outside and hand it to you. Make you smile, make you laugh. Leave me on my own and I'd find a box to climb into, and sit there expecting praise for what I'd just done.

Maybe I was always meant to be working 'for' someone, 'inside' a system that I could subvert. Although I was never good without boundaries or direction, I could never willingly hand over control. I had to be in the front seat, or I'd turn sullen.

For most of my flailing career I insisted on driving, even though I crashed the car every time.

I came to believe that Rick saw all of this. At times he got away from it, left the band, put some distance between him, me and my corrosive mediocrity (I took up a lot of space). Then, for reasons best known to my buddy, he took me back (luckiest days of my life) when I asked to join his band, not once, but twice.

The music we wrote the first time had a unique sound because he was directing it, producing it and it didn't play by any rules. It transmitted an unrepentant joy of exploration. By increments I infected it with my fears and insecurities – my 'normals'. I drove it onto the rocks, and yet he never kicked me out, wouldn't desert me. Did he see something in me I never saw myself? It must have been gut-wrenching and frustrating, though he never gave up and always included me in his plans, let me back in to slip back up front and take all the applause. When we were eventually dropped that last time in the eighties, was it both a curse and a blessing to him? Without the constraints of a band or a deal, and without me around, he was more free than he'd been in ten years to do what he wanted. And *what he wanted* turned out to be the best thing I've ever been a part of.

Did I bring something to the party? Yes, but it came wrapped in a ton of grief – an erratic alcoholic who left his partner to do most of the work while accepting the praise. I got myself into so many scrapes it became the norm, excusing self-obsession by calling it 'trawling the streets for lyrics'. The scrapes got worse, more embarrassing as I became increasingly unreliable. I'd show up at the studio to lay down a vocal or guitar lick, a little synth line, a noise, then plot up at the back of the room for the rest of the day, firing off comments and 'directions'. I was living some kind of fucked-up dream so far up inside myself I didn't have a clue what day of the week it was let alone who I owed my career to.

Rick had produced everything we had ever released since that first deal with CBS, and had received not a jot of recognition – neither respect nor thanks. The frontman is traditionally seen as being the power *and* the throne: the writer, director and creator of *everything* – a visionary towing the band along in his wake. Because the studio was Rick's instrument, the place behind closed doors where his genius took its first breath, no one saw what he did.

And I never made sure he got the credit he was due. The hours Rick put into our music every day of every week until it made him so ill it put him in hospital more than once ... yet he kept working, experimenting, cutting loose, exploring – to give us a sound that set us apart and turned millions of people on. None of it was acknowledged or written about.

Leave my hands on the wheel and the car was guaranteed to crash. Give the wheel to Rick, that car would be flying in no time! Yet still I struggled and fought and could neither see nor accept my skills nor my limitations. Rick *could* and tried to nurture the good in me and discourage the bad. Once the group was freed from the constraints of my blinkered vision, people began to like our music, and most of that was down to Rick. I stood in front of the band on the band's first iconic *Melody Maker* cover, giving it the large one as he stood at the back. In interviews I said 'we' when it was 'he', and accepted all the praise and mythologising that my brother deserved all to himself. Was it greed that made me do that? Lust for another power trip? Or a lifetime of ego-driven insecurity that had left me so brutally self-centred that I could never get enough, while Rick was back in the studio planting the seeds of the next phase in our extraordinary journey?

Looking back, I don't think it was any of those things. I just had my glasses on backwards. We followed his vision and got famous. I had money for the first time. A nice house, nice car, holidays, clothes and stuff I'd resigned myself to never having since I'd laid in the long grass as a kid watching sleek silver airliners cruise overhead carrying luxury passengers to dreamland. Yet here we were, thanks largely to the music Rick was creating. His productions and the sheer head-down hard graft he put into everything – from making records to programming the band for performing live on stage – propelled us forward and never let us stagnate.

OK, I brought stuff to the party – stuff that helped set us apart from other bands in our genre – but without Rick's support, without him building a place for me in his dream, and without him endlessly searching for new ways to utilise what I dragged in off the streets and dumped on him, I wouldn't have had a space to do what I do. On my own I didn't have a clue what it was I did, what my skills were, my strengths, nor what direction to go in. Everything became overwhelming. I would lose perspective – *it's why I drank*.

With Rick, things became clear, calm. I saw the box and how to break out of it, how to bend the rules, how to step up. With Rick, I felt good about myself. I'd look at what I had in my bag of bits and work out how to bring it to his party, how to join in and start to give more freely of myself, like he'd done for all the years we'd been together. Never giving up on me, though I know it hurt him to be around me.

There was a day in Romford, nineteen years ago, when he turned to me in the studio he built (I used to say 'we') and asked, 'Do you think you have a drink problem?'

I was offended. Outraged. Couldn't believe that someone who I thought knew me couldn't see that alcohol was my *best* friend, my *solution* to a life that, without it, was too much. I left the studio that day spitting venom at the insensitivity of his question. Then, the same day, when my girlfriend asked the same thing – busted.

Damn! I'd been with them both since Cardiff, how could they not understand? And yet ... together they'd planted a seed.

Gratitude doesn't come close to describing how I feel – that we're still alive, still together, and Rick and I are still getting off on making music with one another. We've transcended pain to arrive at a place where working together with my brother Rick is the highlight of my week. Every morning I wake up, count my fingers and look out the window. Whatever the weather I chuckle, 'Thank you.'

Then I stick on Radio 5 and shower off the night. The luckiest, jammiest Brummie alive.

Romford, Essex

AC/DC – 'Hell Ain't a Bad Place to Be'

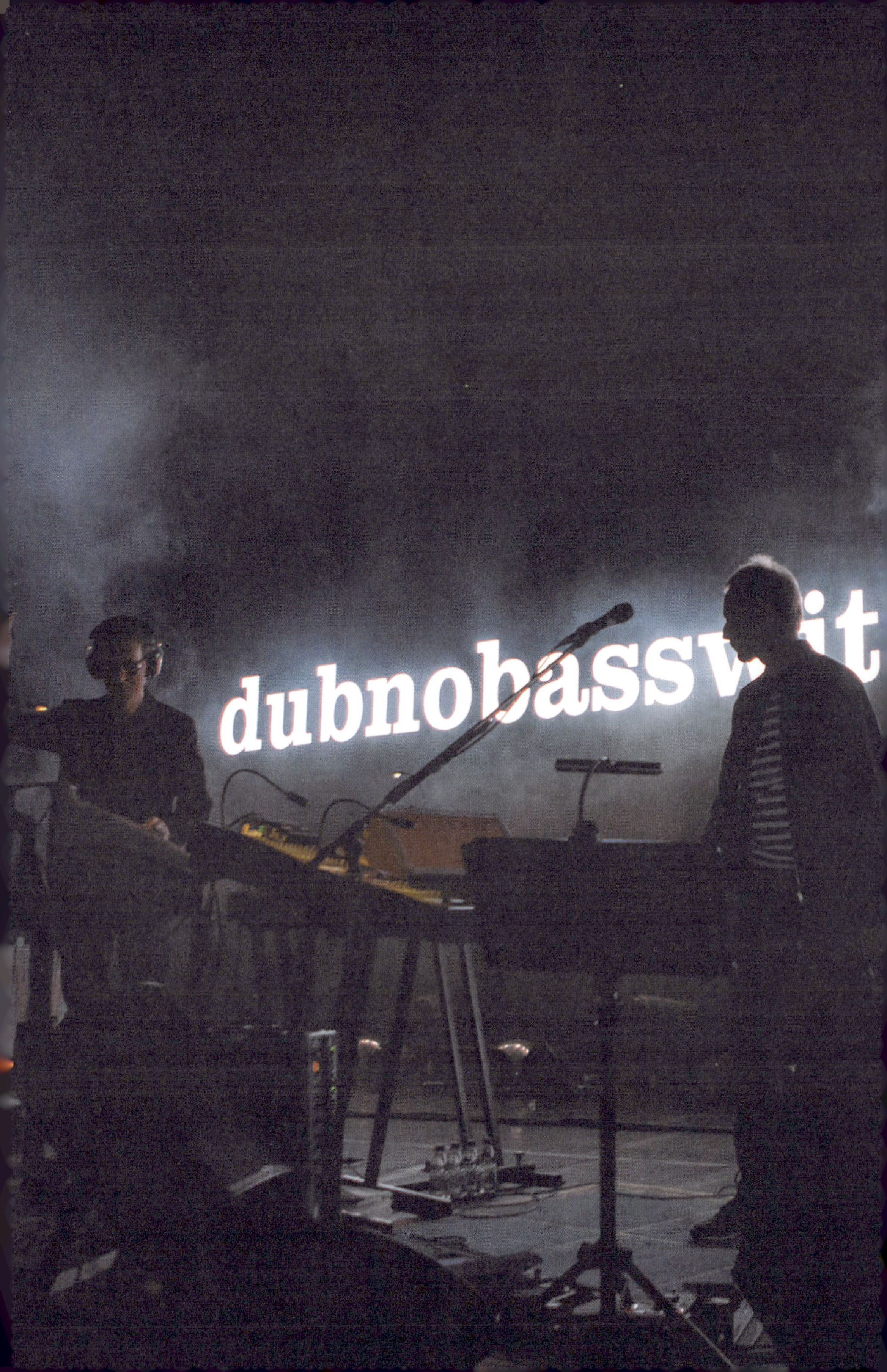
dubnobassw

THE DUBNOBASS ... TOUR, 2014-15

I hated the idea.

    Really didn't want to do it.

    Couldn't bear the idea of looking back.

    I didn't want to play or join in or remember the hurt and the wreckage, didn't want to relive that dark journey or take responsibility for past actions.

    I just wanted to let it sleep in its grave and keep moving on.

    Rick's vision for the show involved us performing every track exactly as it was on the album, right down to the breaths and inflections of every one of my vocal takes. In my head I was looking for a compromise. A way out. Trading on the past was shameful, it made bile rise in me.

    But I knew to trust him.

    One hour of mapping out the nuances of vocals recorded twenty years previously and I was hooked, engaged in the *process*. By the first day of rehearsal, we were smiling, relaxing into our work and developing a friendship that I don't believe had existed in all the years we'd been together. Rick directed and I tried to follow a little more each day, leaving my ego at the door to go with a flow that had never let us down. I forgot all my prejudices as the joy of working with my mate increased. It became an exploration, re-connecting me with an attitude and a headspace from a time when we were buzzing, fresh on the successes delivered to us through Rick's direction and the (now long-term) support of Steve Hall from Junior Boy's Own records.

    What we were thinking? Who we were hanging out with? What we were doing back then? What inspired us? What had turned us on? What had we rejected, reacted to, and turned against? Memories were reignited and I was back in that '94 headspace.

    Soho. Romford. Tomato. The Drum Club. Megadog. Graham Wood in a baby-doll nightie marching through a nightclub banging a drum, followed by his loyal girlfriend dressed as a giant teddy bear. Magazines we created on a whim, pasted to streetlights. Faxing our art to random numbers, because we could. Poetry jams in the back room of the Ministry of Sound. Goldie jamming artworks with Simon Taylor. Goldie blocking Soho in his Merc to stop and shoot the breeze. Vic and Bob and *The Fast Show* riffing scripts in the bar of the George on D'Arblay Street. Bill Bailey's shocked expression the night I handed him a tenner to get a round in at the Ship on Wardour Street and staggered off into the night to write (and live), 'Lager, Lager, Lager'.

    Plugging back into the electricity of the time, rediscovering that so much of what we'd left behind was still alive and beggin' for it. This time I'd come to the party sober.

    Today, I feel blessed to be working with a man who, after thirty-six years together, I can call my best friend. A man who's given me direction and a home for my *peculiar* idiosyncrasies. Looking back at the photographs, the reviews and YouTube clips of the *Dubnobass* ... tour I start to grin, still unable to comprehend how it became the first *best tour of my life*.

Essex

LAST REHERSAL IN ESSEX BEFORE

There's a weird light illuminating Essex.
It feels good, something different,
on the verge of casting thick black shadows but not.
A smudged charcoal sky, blue but not, grey but not.
Solitary clouds creep low to the horizon, trying not to be noticed.
Essex looks ready to be filmed, body feels ready to rehearse,
still coughing, but slight, low to the horizon,
trying not to be noticed.

BRISTOL COLSTON HALL

'Ah yeah, they've all played 'ere one time or another,' says
security, rattling a big bunch of keys.
Outside the Arnolfini gallery the morning shadows are freezing.
The sunlit bits feel good for the soul.
Woman in red walking fast with a boyfriend
looking distant, *'What hope is there of us having a decent fucking
relationship if you're not going to do something!?'*
He walks by her side, fists in pockets, staring straight ahead.
The rats have been at the bin-bags again.

HAMMERSMITH ODEON

The sun is shining in the alleys behind the Odeon.
Stumble through the stage-door, grab a clean towel, shower, float to catering.
Newsprint scattered over tables.
Catch up with the crew, the drivers, runners, riggers, heads down, humming.
The serious business of fry-ups.
Spill tea on the sports pages, ketchup, hot ginger, toast and blueberry juice.
Sit out on the fire escape in the sun and breathe.

They're flying tonnes of boxes in the house, rigging lights and running cables.
The tattooed arms of the house crew move in a clockwork motion, dressed in black with heavy boots, wool pulled down around their ears. 'All right, Karl?' they nod in passing,
carrying heavy trusses like children's toys.
The backbone of the show, disappeared long before doors, returned after everyone's left, to break down, load the trucks and slip back into the night, unsung.

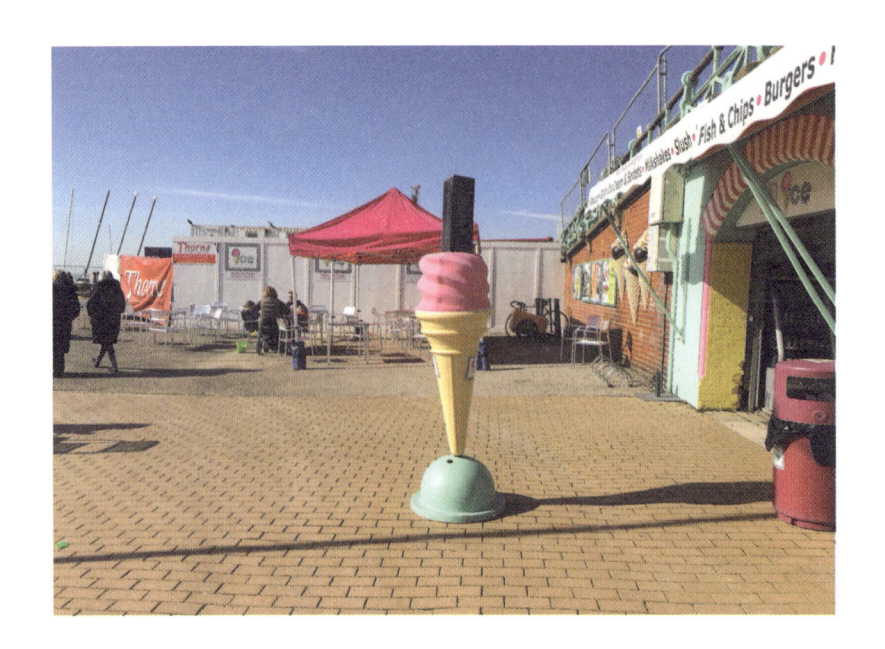

BRIGHTON DOME

Seaside strolling, sun and wind, showered, fed and phoned home.
Guitar browsing, spiced apple tea and ginger cake,
another copy of Jerry Lee Lewis's autobiography, after the last one I gave away,
not read a book so beautifully written since Mailer's The Fight.
Browsed second-hand vinyl, bought Neil Young's A Letter Home
and Studio One, Jump Up, mix it up on the bus, set me up good
for tonight's groove on the southern shore.

RETURN TO PLANET ESSEX

Woken up in Essex 2.30 a.m.
Bags and me left the bus for a taxi home.
That familiar bed feeling weird after nights on the road.
The bunk is my cocoon.

Woke in time to see the sun kiss everything,
Spring bursting out of the ground.
I walked around, took unfamiliar routes around town
In a day-off state-of-mind.

Click, flick the switch, turn off the phone.
I'm here, but until tomorrow, nobody's home.

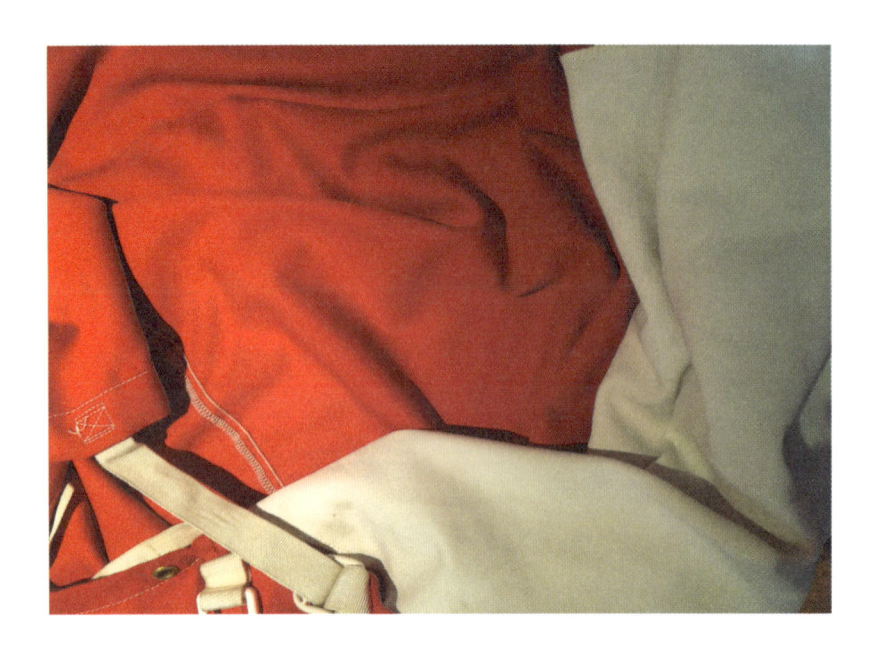

NORTH OF ESSEX

Where are you, weighed in at eighteen tonnes, out with the world?
Smiling with him before the city wakes, is 'he' the one?
Living life as a ghost roller, slumped over your morning laptop coffee,
staring into the electric hole, to give a name to it,
enjoy it, waking with you is strange.

GLASGOW ROYAL CONCERT HALL

Woke up in a Glasgow bus station, a stickman on the blacktop
between the buses. People go about their business and I'm invisible.
High up above the streets, crane drivers sleep off heavy nights,
wake them when you want them, catching zeds in their glass cocoons.
Chemically rearranged, still dreaming of bouncing Barrowlands.
I lie down between sleeping buses to let the city's song drift
over me.
You're back and I'm glad.
Rejoined the tour from another beating.
No one sees the pixels dance or pushes me like you.

MANCHESTER ALBERT HALL

Woke up at 7 a.m. to Manchester in the rain. Showered in a building site amongst rough bricks and decay,
breakfasted on street cracks and alley poetry, photographing debris.
Found the pop-up cafe of Hunt and Darton at Piccadilly station, toast and jam and potted tea, the stuff they bring to the cities they land in makes me laugh like a kid, lifts the soul of a lonely boy assailed by spring holding all its chemical triggers at bay.

GATESHEAD SAGE

Me and the gulls breathe clean before the world wakes, the hiss
of traffic crossing bridges, white wing, black wheel, the Nice.
Lone walkers skirt walls, hunched, pockets full of fists,
approach me suspicious, black wool pulled low to the eye.
Heavy stone construction on the other side,
Newcastle memories cling to staunch architecture, the pride of times.

River Tyne, liquid chocolate, stilled by the incoming tide, quiet
as bath water,
heavy as the industry that built this city, confident it will outlast
us all.
Reassuring animal friend slips through the valley.
Cold morning, everybody wrapped up tight.
Two lads in geezer-T's, unshaven, fingers dipped into bags of salties,
feed on the move.
Images of back-end G-strings in black and white across their chests,
stare down a chill wind, let you know exactly what they're thinking.
Men chase women laughing, collapsing into tickled heaps on
pavements screaming, happy, red-faced, sunglasses concealed in bottle
hair.

'Oh Jesus!'

Down on Wesley Square, along the reinvented waterfront.

ESSEX BEFORE PARIS

Woke on the bus, parked between random wheels, 7 a.m., pulling bags
to another taxi rank, cold drivers watch, agitated by our anarchy,
texting alone over cigarettes outside branded buses, uniforms,
unshaven, grunt as I chirp, 'Good morning!' out of habit,
spat back out into the world, alone again, compass pointing home.

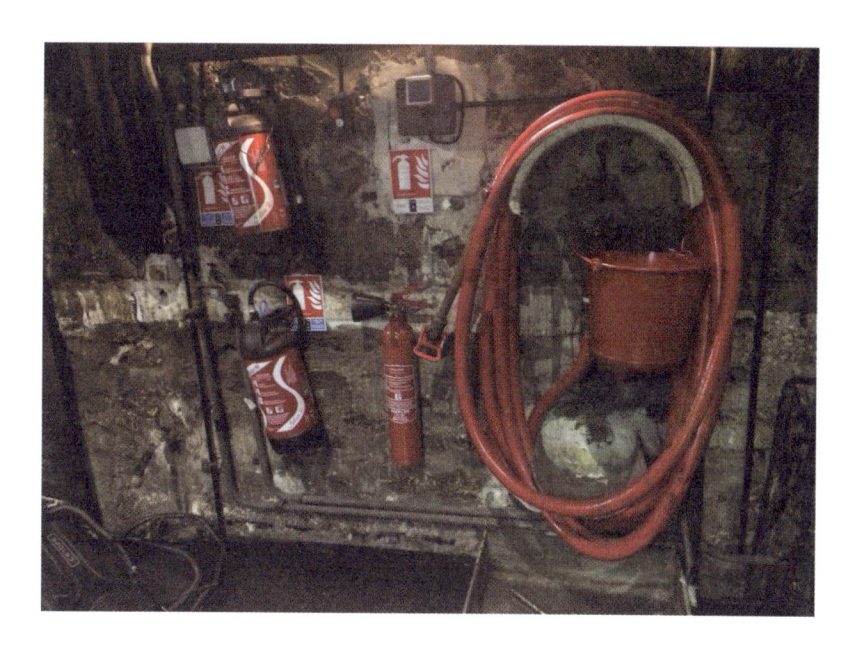

CASINO DE PARIS

Breakfast on the bus in Parisian rush-hour log-jam wake-up shock.
The scooter crowd weave cool between crawling killer metal.
Slim late night 1970s BBC 2 film-star women threaten the city
with their cultured beauty,
fierce as ice-breakers.
Cut through crowds,
poised and fabulous in muted shades
on the outside of our tinted glass.
We fire up our stumbling bodies with teas, mashed wheat,
nuts and rice milk.

Playing Derek and Clive to remind us we're alive. Good morning.

ANCIENNE BELGIQUE - BRUSSELS

My angel has many professions, builder, petrol-pump attendant, postman.
Today he's a bus driver.
'Would you like a bit of toast?' he asks, bright-eyed and full of life even after hours behind the wheel.
I stumble around, toothbrush in mouth, raise a hand declining.

Everyone's asleep, parked up a Brussels street.
He talks about his sons with pride, the truck driver and the medical insurance salesman, about his love for them, about being a parent, a partner, a man. This is stuff I need to hear, sitting across the table, nodding, scooping mashed wheat and rice milk as he hands me a mug of camomile and honey.

I'm unsure if the damage I did to my throat last night will allow me to sing so I shut up and listen, feeding on his medicine, growing stronger, cleaner.
Riding next to him, up front in his cab,
Beethoven piano concertos underscoring the stone faces of
a Belgian rush hour.

SECOND NIGHT AT THE ANCIENNE BELGIQUE

Awake in a sea of crisp white linen, sipping water in the dark to the music of drunks smashing glass and howling in the narrow cobbled streets below my window. The woman at the breakfast desk smiles and pouts, asks for my room number. I wonder how many times she's hit on every day, whether there's someone home somewhere hoping she's OK. It rains, we drag our bags to the bus, laughing, buy more records at the Collector and Caroline, rare seventies vinyl, and CDs by Sleater-Kinney, whose posters haunt our tour.

DAY OFF IN LUXEMBOURG

Awake on a moving bus at 4 a.m.,
broken sleep through prolonged road vibrations.
I'm a human milkshake.

Woke up in a lorry park on the edge of town,
throat still a mess, waiting for a hotel room.
Power off, grey light, ribbed in Top Rank rope lights
like a gentlemen's club, alone at a rubber-topped table.

There's an oil lamp in front of me, dancing voluptuous erotics,
evoking 1960s swinging London,
the entire contents of my adolescent longings in one little table
lamp.

Mashed wheat and rice milk, tea-less.
Scrub teeth, wash face with bottled water.
The power turned back on brings kettle resurrection,
delivers black-tea joy, clouds part, shadows sharpen.
The call expected hours away comes early, offers sanctuary.
A hotel room, four walls and a shower, amazing hot-water spiritual
revival dance amongst clean white towels.

Radio 4 on the laptop, kettle's second brew,
body coming back on line, divine.

DEN ATELIER, LUXEMBOURG

The shock of an 'almost' breakfast at the hotel hits me hard.
Egg-mess so yellow you need sunglasses to eat it,
suck it through a straw.
Squinty little sausage things.
Crisped and flattened potato things.
Baked beans with carrot slices.
Over-sugared fruit juices.
Tiny boxes of processed cereals.
Soya milk the colour of pus.
Lukewarm water for loose tea in squat, stained, chip-spouted pots.
The room is haunted by the ghosts of sheepish breakfast staff
avoiding eye contact with baffled guests.

PARADISO #1

'Avoid street dealers, white heroin sold as cocaine,
three tourists died last November,' says the message
on the electronic billboard alongside the road over
the canal as we drive into town.

Black car, white car,
Silver grey bicycles ride in packs of giant rolling metal,
The flowers of spring, Loveland,
High-rise homes with windows big enough to let in light,
inspire a nation to look up to the sky.

PARADISO #2

I hear a woman's chocolate giggle, in the room across the corridor,
muffled by the fire-door as I leave to comb the streets for poetry in the rain,
go dancing between the cracks again.
They've been at it, up all night, cocktailed to infinity,
in the dark recesses of the hotel bar.
Girls in tight torn jeans, exotic, magnetic, to the boys in heavy jackets
with close-cropped hair.

I remember this hotel.
1991,
when I was too drunk to stagger, feet up on a gothic stone balustrade,
High,
Above the street,
Toes in the night sky,
An animal mind cut loose and hungry for more than could be found,
Burning from the inside out.

PALLADIUM KÖLN

Empty streets on the edge of town,
Old industrial architecture reborn, rebranded, dancing with the ghosts of industry.

Trucks reverse to kiss the lips of loading docks, disgorging heavy metal,
Blacktop inset with rails, torn strips of hazard tape flap in gentle breezes
like pony club rosettes tied to galvanised crowd-control barriers stacked against factory walls.
Red brick, precision engineered, catching the first rays of
the sun.

Heavy bread, real scrambled egg, crisp strips of salty bacon,
glistening in steaming trays, juices, fruits and tiny cakes.
The angels of catering greet us, smile in languages,
delivering us from chocolate temptation in T-shirts, jeans and last night's hair,
more fabulous than catwalk models, build cairns from salt, pepper, ketchup and tulips
to remind us others have passed this way before.

THE LAST OF THE DUBNO ... BUNK SCULPTURES

Back in Mother Essex, I miss the tour already.
The team around us, the venues, the house crews, caterers,
the traffic cones and debris,
the signature sounds and charismatic odours of the cities
we visited, the buses that were our homes,
the fresh towels, the shower stalls we scrubbed in every morning behind stage
and the trucks that were loaded-unloaded-reloaded every day,
carrying heavy loads as delicately as hen's eggs.

I miss mapping unfamiliar streets, scraping words,
snapping site-specific works
off pavements, notebook and camera, capturing the cracks,
the marks,
the beautiful dirt you leave for me to find.
The energy that's gone into this run of shows was enormous,
made good people ill and yet
produced results that have brought happiness to thousands
and left me with a clear thought.

Of all tours that I have ever been on this one was the first.

THIS IS ESSEX

The picture in my memory is different to the one I see waking amongst the fields of Essex. Without thousands giving freely their good energy and
support I turn to the kettle for encouragement and a glimmer of empathy.
In the silent kitchen, we empty suitcases, set washing machines in motion,
put away the trappings of a travelling life and the instruments of international wandering. Passports slip back beneath their stones like rock-pool crabs, and flight cases return to unlit warehouse corners, legends
stencilled on their sides concealed as the last truck pulls away.

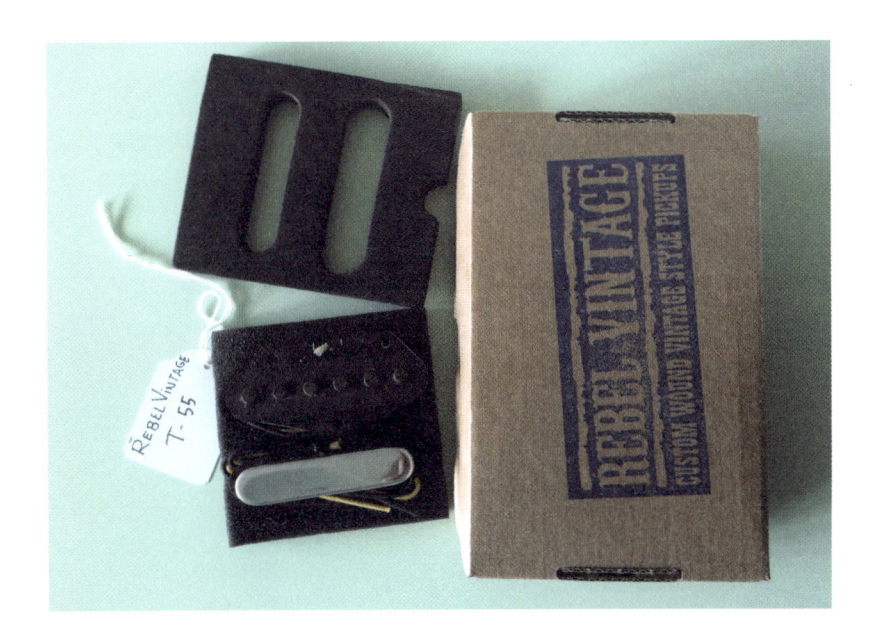

ESSEX FLAGS

Washing drying in the wind, the sweat-soaked stripes of nights beneath the lights, filtering the breath of smoke machines and random whiffs of 'erb blown in between cheeky grins, celebrates its spotless sweetness, born again as 'nice', returned to civilian life as garments good enough to visit Mom.

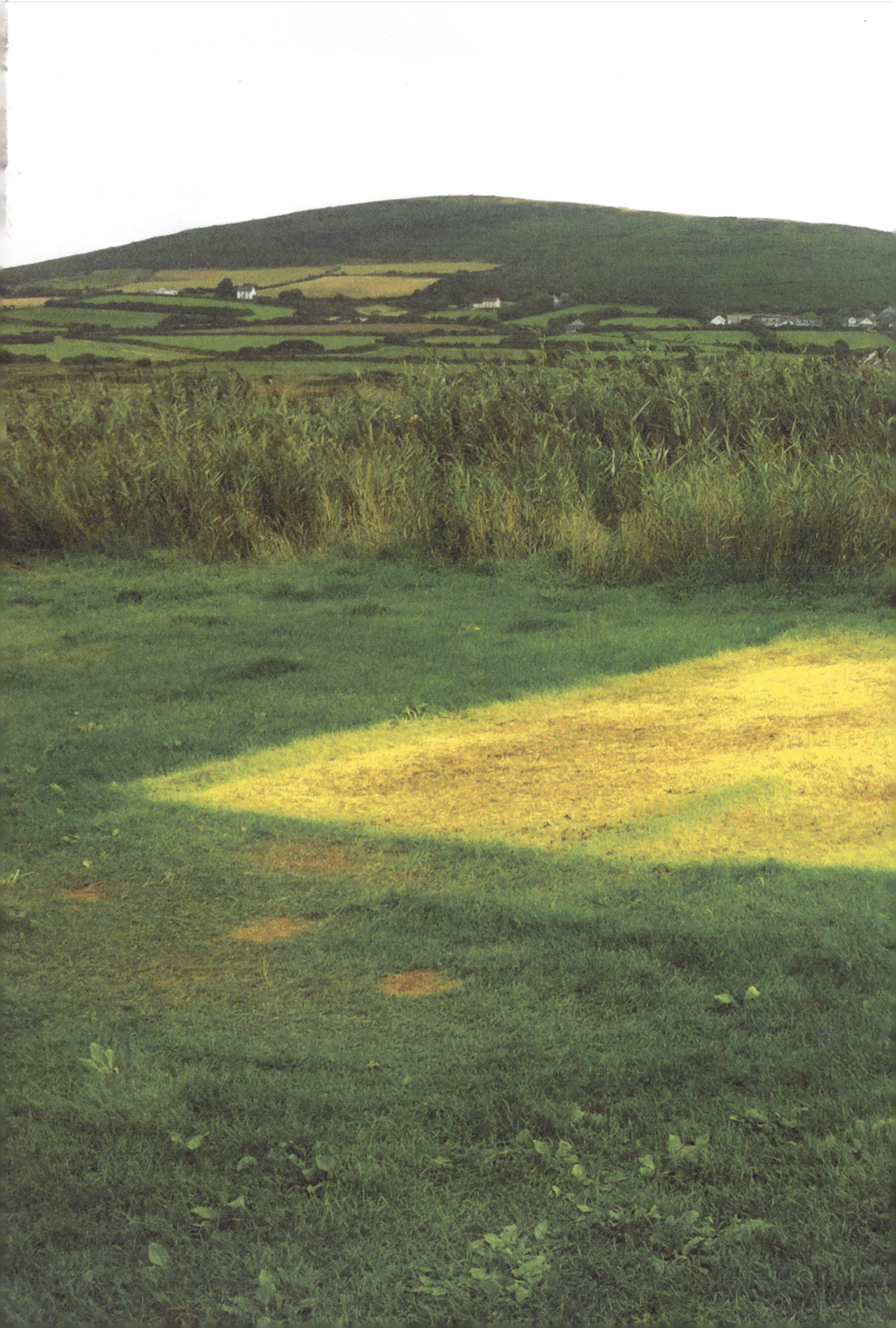

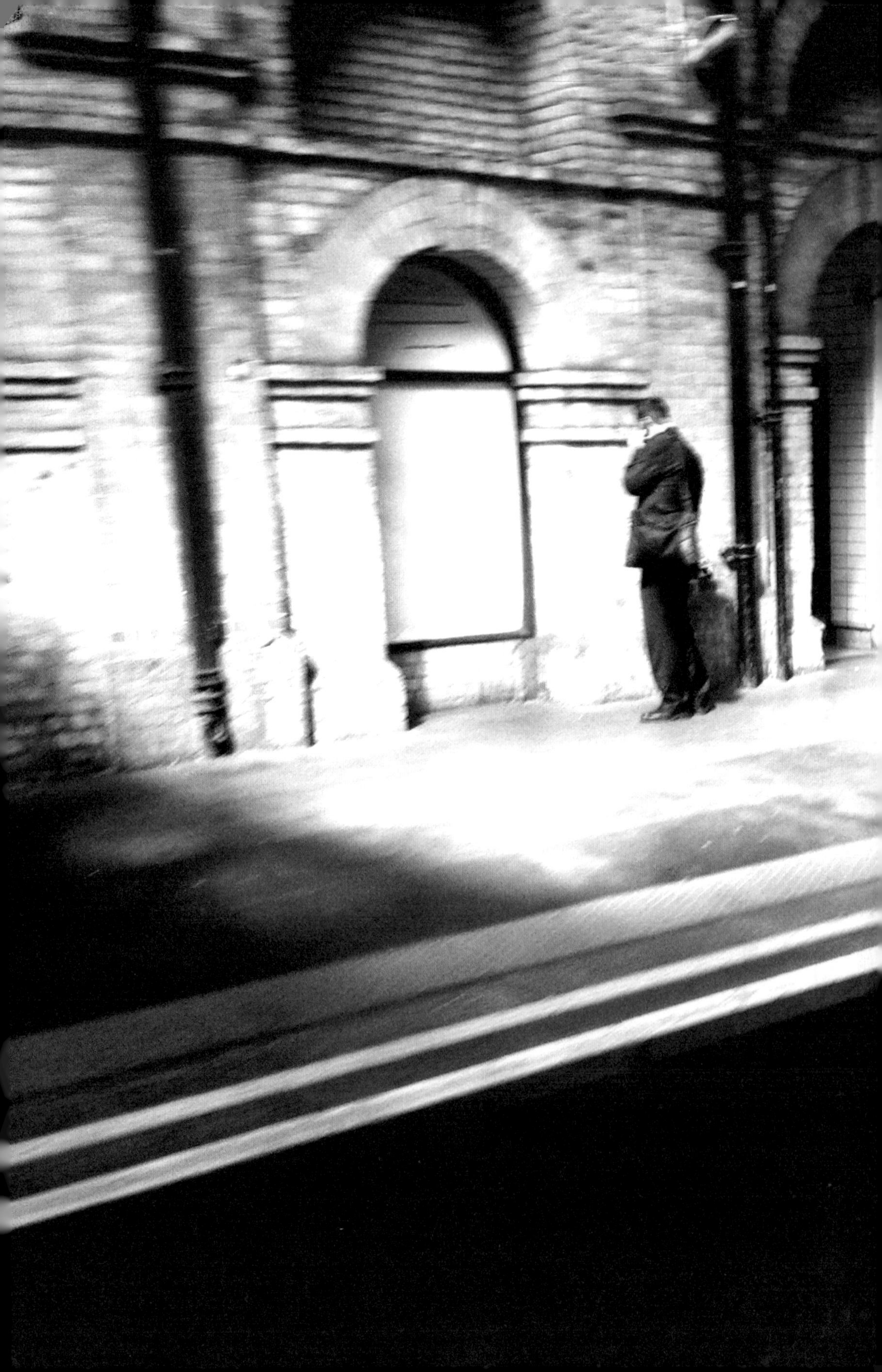